Rethinking Clinical Audit

In recent years audit has impinged on the working life of professionals in nearly all public- and private-sector services. This has particularly been the case for clinical audit and the NHS. The huge investment in this initiative, however, has failed to produce anything like the changes that were hoped for by its advocates. Why has this happened? What has been the experience of those health professionals who have been asked to embrace clinical audit as part of their working practice?

The contributors to this book examine the psychological dynamics, both individual and institutional, which can promote or obstruct the potential benefits of clinical audit. Focusing on psychotherapy services within the NHS it provides a unique perspective on the audit experience in the public sector and draws conclusions that are relevant to clinicians and managers across the range of the healthcare services.

Rachael Davenhill is a Consultant Clinical Psychologist in psychotherapy at the Tavistock Clinic, London, and former Chair of the Audit Committee, Tavistock and Portman NHS Trust.
Matthew Patrick is a Consultant Psychotherapist at the Tavistock Clinic and lecturer in developmental psychopathology at University College London. He was formerly lead Audit Clinician for the Tavistock and Portman NHS Trust. Both are also psychoanalysts in private practice.

Contributors: Geoffrey Baruch, John Cape, Bridget Dolan, Pasco Fearon, Michael Feldman, Andrew Gerber, Kevin Healy, Ruth Loebl, Graeme McGrath, Frank Margison, Kingsley Norton, Glenys Parry, Michael Power, Kate Pugh, Mary Target.

Rethinking Clinical Audit

The Case of Psychotherapy Services in the NHS

Edited by
Rachael Davenhill and
Matthew Patrick

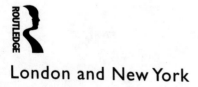

London and New York

First published 1998
by Routledge
11 New Fetter Lane, London EC4P 4EE

Simultaneously published in the USA and Canada
by Routledge
29 West 35th Street, New York, NY 10001

© 1998 selection and editorial matter Rachael Davenhill and
Matthew Patrick; individual chapters © 1998 the authors

Typeset in Times by Routledge
Printed and bound in Great Britain by Creative Print and Design
(Wales), Ebbw Vale

British Library Cataloguing in Publication Data
A catalogue record for this book is available from the British
Library

Library of Congress Cataloging in Publication Data
Rethinking clinical audit: psychotherapy services in the
NHS/edited by Rachael Davenhill & Matthew Patrick.
p.   cm.
Includes bibliographical references and index.
1. Psychotherapy–Great Britain–Quality control. 2. Medical
audit–Great Britain. 3. National Health Service (Great Britain)
4. National Health Service (Great Britain) I. Davenhill, Rachael,
1958–. II. Patrick, Matthew, 1960–.
[DNLM: 1. Medical Audit–organization & administration–Great
Britain. 2. Mental Health Services–standards–Great Britain.
3. Psychotherapy–standards–Great Britain. WM 30 R438 1998]
RC465.8. G7R48   1998
362.2'0941–dc21
DNLM/DLC
for Library of Congress   97–47788
                                                     CIP

ISBN 0–415–16207–6 (hbk)
ISBN 0–415–16208–4 (pbk)

To John and Karen with thanks
for their support and patience

Contents

Illustrations

Figure

Tables

Contributors

Geoffrey Baruch, PhD, is a Senior Lecturer in the Department of Psychology, University College London and Director of the Brandon Centre for Counselling and Psychotherapy for Young People in Kentish Town, London. He is a psychoanalyst qualified to treat adults, adolescents and children.

John Cape is Head of Psychology and Psychotherapy Services, Camden and Islington Community Health Services NHS Trust. He convenes the national counselling and psychological therapies clinical guidelines steering group, and is chair of the Management board of the British Psychological Society Centre for Clinical Outcomes Research and Effectiveness.

Bridget Dolan has written over 50 research papers on aspects of personality disorders, eating disorders and psychotherapy research and is co-author/editor of four academic books. She spent eight years specializing in personality disorder at Henderson Hospital before leaving to practise as a Barrister in 1997.

Pasco Fearon, BA, studied Experimental Psychology at the University of Cambridge. He is currently undertaking a PhD at the Department of Psychology, University College London, sponsored by the Medical Research Council. He teaches statistics at UCL and the Anna Freud Centre, London.

Michael Feldman was a Consultant Psychotherapist at the Maudsley Hospital Psychotherapy Unit, until March 1998. He is concerned with the application of psychoanalytical theories to the understanding and management of disturbed out-patients and has been involved in trying to develop the principles of audit in a constructive way. He continues to work as a psycho-analyst and training analyst of the Institute of Psycho-Analysis.

Andrew Gerber, MSc, studied physics at Yale University. He completed an MSc in Psychoanalytic Developmental Psychology at the Anna Freud Centre and University College London. He is currently completing his PhD at University College London. He teaches statistics at the Anna Freud Centre, London.

Kevin Healy, MB, BCh, BAO, DCH, DObs, DPM, MRCPsych, is a Consultant Psychiatrist in Psychotherapy and Director of the Cassel Hospital. He is interested in both evidence-based practice and practice-based evidence within inpatient, day-patient, outpatient and outreach psychotherapeutic services.

Ruth Loebl formerly Audit Project Manager, Gaskell House Psychotherapy Centre, Manchester Royal Infirmary, currently Technical Consultant to Royal National Institute for the Blind's Employment and Study Network, Liverpool.

Graeme McGrath Consultant Psychotherapist and Clinical Manager Specialist Services, Gaskell House Psychotherapy Centre, Manchester Royal Infirmary.

Frank Margison Consultant Psychotherapist and Clinical Director in Psychiatry at Gaskell House Psychotherapy Centre, Manchester Royal Infirmary.

Kingsley Norton has been Clinical Director at Henderson Hospital since 1989, and is Honorary Senior Lecturer in the Department of General Psychiatry St. George's Hospital Medical School. Dr Norton is also a trained Jungian Analyst with the Society of Analytical Psychology (London) and Sub Dean of the Royal College of Psychiatrists. He is the author of peer reviewed papers on psychosomatic medicine; eating disorders; personality disorder; therapeutic community treatment and inpatient psychotherapy and two books on the management and counselling of difficult patients.

Glenys Parry is Director of R&D for Community Health Sheffield NHS Trust, Professor Associate in Health Care Psychology at the University of Sheffield and Visiting Professor at University College London. She led the NHS Executive review of strategic policy on NHS psychotherapy services in England. She is a clinical psychologist and cognitive analytic psychotherapist. She has published in the fields of life events stress, social support, psychotherapy research, policy and practice.

Michael Power is Professor of Accounting at the London School of Economics and Political Science. He obtained a PhD at Cambridge before qualifying as a chartered accountant with Deloitte Haskins & Sells. He is the author of *The Audit Explosion* (Demos, 1994) and *The Audit Society: Rituals of Verification* (Oxford University Press, 1997), and his research interests concern regulation, auditing and risk management.

Kate Pugh trained in the Psychotherapy Unit, Maudsley Hospital where she now works as a Locum Consultant Psychotherapist. She liaises with medical and psychiatric teams and meets regularly with a group of local GP counsellors as well as supervising psychotherapy in the Unit. She has currently taken on responsibility for audit in the Unit from Dr Michael Feldman on his retirement.

Mary Target, BA, MSc, PhD, is a clinical psychologist and psychoanalyst whose research is mostly in the areas of child-psychotherapy outcome and measures of personality functioning in adults and children. She is employed as a Senior Lecturer at University College London, where she organizes an MSc course in Theoretical Psychoanalytic Studies.

Introduction

Rachael Davenhill and Matthew Patrick

Clinical audit is a phenomenon of the late twentieth century. In many ways it represents a wish and, at times, quite omnipotent hope for a rational, understandable, logical standardization of process and outcome, offering predictability and constant continued improvement within the human services. Clinical audit became a statutory and funded requirement for National Health Service (NHS) professionals in the late 1980s and early 1990s. There are, however, many texts that offer guidance on the practice of clinical audit. In this book we have tried to approach the subject from a somewhat different stance. Our aim has been to build on a tradition of applying psychoanalytic approaches and concepts to deepening our understanding of personal, social and institutional functioning (e.g. Menzies-Lyth 1988). This book will attempt to explore some of the components of both ambivalence and enthusiasm with which clinical audit may be received by clinicians, taking as a working example the provision of psychoanalytic psychotherapy within the NHS.

We would suggest that clinical audit, at its best, is fundamental in supporting good clinical practice. Parry highlights audit along with research, service evaluation, quality assurance and total quality management as conceptual tools which can be used in combination to improve psychotherapy services:

> They all serve the principle of service practitioners or service planners reflecting on practice to learn from experience, embodied in the concepts of the reflective practitioner (Schon, 1983), the learning organisation (Garrett, 1987) and the self-evaluating organisation (Wildavsky, 1972).
>
> (Parry 1992: 3)

Parry's definition of audit involves 'reflective practice within a self-evaluating psychotherapy service and a systemic approach which can take account of the perspectives of patients, purchasers, service managers, referrers and practitioners' (Parry 1992). In looking at this definition, it would seem likely that those clinical services which have a reputation for good, effective provision of treatment are most likely to be those which already have an implicit understanding of the basic components of audit. These components include the capacity to reflect, to look in detail at one area systematically, to maintain an open mind, and to give meaning to data which in itself holds no life and has to be understood within the complexities of human relationships.

The success or failure of audit very much depends on how it is used and understood by the individual clinician, the multidisciplinary team, and the clinical service in relationship to its external environment. Successful audit can facilitate dialogue and communication around areas of joint interest. Unsuccessful audit is experienced by clinicians as a constant criticism imposed from without and containing the 'never-feel-good' factor. Guinan writes vividly of the experience many clinicians have of clinical audit and total quality management as containing 'the implication that nothing is ever going to be good enough' (Guinan 1995). Within the NHS there is now a formal requirement built in to the purchaser–provider relationship for audit to take place, and where there are tensions within this relationship the danger is that audit will operate at an extremely concrete level driven purely by contracting pressures. There exists a real possibility that purchaser–provider relationships will be so configured as to create a situation where one party is inevitably felt to be scrutinizing another. Indeed, the pressures on purchasers of health care, both financial, ideological and otherwise, may be such that they feel forced to manage by relocating all anxiety in their providers. This often takes the form of demands for ever increasing volumes of information, with the implicit threat of loss of contracts should such demands be unmet. Psychoanalysis can contribute an understanding of the evolution, structure and functioning of the persecutory states of mind that characterize such relationships. As our contributors illustrate, such states of mind operate at a fundamental level against freedom of thought, the capacity for self-reflection, and the ability to learn from experience in developing high-quality services. Psychoanalytic insights also offer models for the ways in which individual and institutional anxieties may be understood and managed, affording the possibility for more creative ways of working across boundaries.

In this book the contributors explore some of these issues in the context of the development of clinical audit within NHS psychoanalytic psychotherapy services. Many draw on their expertise as senior practitioners and researchers in this field. Although we take psychoanalytic psychotherapy services as our particular 'case example', the themes which emerge cut across particular theoretical 'positions' and can be recognizable as elements, in essence, of the human condition: interest, curiosity, ambivalence, conflict, and so on. What is specific to the field of psychoanalytic psychotherapy is that the majority of qualified practitioners offering treatment have undergone their own personal psychotherapy as a valuable and necessary component of training. This experience enables the individual to know and reflect at first hand on the personal experience of being a patient, and to understand the dynamic of a therapeutic scrutiny that, while necessary, can be full of repetition and difficulty as well as rewards. From experience, there will be a hard-won understanding that when push comes to shove and real change is necessary there is inevitably conflict.

The audit process is no different. Certainly, all audits of the audit process indicate that the impasse in audit usually arises at the point of implementing and seeing through real change in an enduring way as a result of detailed audit work. When this is kept in mind, it can helpfully reduce the potential for unrealistic expectations of individual clinicians, the clinical team or the audit process in itself as a 'solve-all' for the broader service and the external demands upon it.

In Chapter 1 Glenys Parry looks at the central question of what clinical audit is and at the ways in which it can be helpful to psychotherapists. She examines the policy contexts within which clinical audit has been developed, taking into account international and socio-political factors. She goes on to examine the concept of service effectiveness and quality assurance, as distinct from efficacy of intervention. She also examines the difference between research and audit in psychotherapy; the advantages and pitfalls of research-based guidelines; and the value of using a range of research methods, both qualitative and quantitative, as a helpful tool in defining potential areas for audit. Finally she brings together a model of how to achieve evidence based practice in the psychotherapies, avoiding the worst problems of a narrow, doctrinaire approach to research, audit and service evaluation.

Chapters 2, 3 and 4 look from slightly different perspectives at the processes involved in audit and the necessary ambivalences contained within this process of scrutiny. In Chapter 2 Mike Power discusses the philosophical and economic dimensions of audit within public sector services. In Chapter 3 Kevin Healy examines some of the psychological issues raised when a new task such as audit is introduced into an existing clinical service. Making use of psychoanalytic theory, he explores the conflict inherent in the audit process and how very quickly it can be perceived as – and, if misused, can become – an authoritarian 'superego'-like activity. In Chapter 4 Michael Feldman and Kate Pugh highlight the nature of the states of mind that may come to dominate individuals and institutions, referring to Melanie Klein's concept of the paranoid–schizoid position. They then offer a model for the implementation of audit originating from the Japanese concept of *Kaizen* in working practices, which focuses on process rather than purely emphasizing outcome, linking this with Klein's concept of the depressive position. All of these authors explore the dilemma of functioning effectively within public-sector services at a time of great change, brought about by consciously implemented government policies throughout the 1980s and early 1990s which placed the public-sector human services in a financially competitive relationship to one another. Kevin Healy comments on the way in which the structure of the marketplace, when coupled with the anxiety engendered by change, can lead to displacement of responsibility and a fragmentation of services that, together, should be providing clinical containment for patients. In a later chapter (Chapter 6) Bridget Dolan and Kingsley Norton also discuss the way in which financial responsibility for patient care may lead to a narrow view of the remit of a purchasing authority's responsibility, when the cost of a patient at a national level through use of multiple services may be lost.

In Chapter 5 Frank Margison *et al.* give a description of a detailed working model of audit within an NHS psychotherapy unit in the north-west of England, which pays particular attention to the introduction and usefulness of computerized systems. Margison *et al.* also address the importance of attention to the process of implementing such systems if they are ultimately to be owned by clinicians. They argue that clinician involvement in the development of audit structures is critical to their ultimate success.

In Chapter 6 Bridget Dolan and Kingsley Norton offer a further account of the usefulness of audit, when they describe the processes leading to extensive and impressive audit work carried out at Henderson Hospital, an inpatient psychotherapy unit in south-west England. They write frankly and persuasively on the crucial importance of audit at both local and regional level as a determining factor in enabling the hospital to survive through a time of great turbulence and change. The chapter describes an audit of referrer satisfaction and user satisfaction which highlighted the importance of improving communication between the service and patients, and the service and referrers, regarding information sent out and key points of transition in the patient pathway through assessment, admission and discharge. However, the Henderson's *tour de force* of audit work is reported in Dolan and Norton's succinct description of a cost of service usage and a cost-offset audit, both of which had a profound impact on the process of deciding whether the hospital should remain open.

In Chapter 7 Mary Target reports an impressive example of a retrospective audit of 800 treatment cases from the 1950s onwards, illustrating how audit can complement and contribute to further research work in the area. Geoffrey Baruch *et al.*'s chapter (Chapter 8) then gives a detailed description of an ongoing contemporary audit of outcome based in a community psychoanalytic psychotherapy service for young people. This latter work illustrates Target's points well, in that, while Baruch *et al.*'s study has no control group, it is located at the interface between clinical audit and research.

In the final chapter John Cape examines audit in the context of the shifting emphasis nationally towards clinical effectiveness and evidence based practice. In particular, he focuses on the potential and problems of the application of clinical practice guidelines to psychotherapy. He gives various examples of psychotherapy clinical guidelines that have been or might be developed for different audiences, for example guidelines designed primarily for general practitioners (GPs) and other referrers for psychotherapy. He also discusses guidelines developed for psychotherapists and other specialist psychological practitioners to assist in decisions about treatment for specific conditions. Although the focus is on clinical guidelines, the issues discussed are common to other methods of promoting clinical effectiveness and evidence based practice in public-sector services.

Our hope is that by the end of this book the reader will understand more fully the processes involved in clinical audit in a way helpful to containing the complexity of the task.

References

Davenhill, R. (1996) 'Audit', in E. V. Welldon and C. VanVelsen, *A Practical Guide to Forensic Psychotherapy*, Jessica Kingsley Publishers.

Guinan, P. (1995) 'Through the looking glass', *Psychologist* 8, October.

Menzies-Lyth, I. (1988) *Containing Anxiety in Institutions: Selected Essays*, London: Free Association Books.

Parry, G. (1992) 'Improving psychotherapy services: applications of research, audit and evaluation', *British Journal of Clinical Psychology* 31: 3–19.

Chapter 1

Psychotherapy services, healthcare policy and clinical audit

Glenys Parry

The policy context

The policy context for clinical audit in psychotherapy is rich and varied. To understand it we need to review briefly the historical and current role of psychotherapy in health services, the influence of macroeconomic factors and recent policy developments on evidence-based health care and clinical effectiveness.

The major advances in psychotherapeutic treatments over the last forty years have been fostered by the National Health Service (NHS) and, in turn, are reflected in NHS services. However, psychological therapies predate the NHS. Earliest psychological treatments were largely psychoanalytic and, before the Second World War, were available to only a relative few, mainly in London. With the birth of the NHS in 1946, these treatments were made available to NHS patients in London through the Tavistock Clinic, which began to treat NHS patients in 1948. Psychoanalytic treatments continued to be developed in the UK and child psychoanalytic therapy was offered to children through the creation of NHS-funded child psychotherapist posts. The emergence of behaviourism as a theoretical force in the 1940s also had a profound influence on psychological treatments, as during the 1950s and 1960s theories of learning derived from animal experimentation were applied to humans, bringing experimental methods to human psychological processes. By the 1960s behavioural treatments were available in many mental health services throughout Britain. Then the so-called 'cognitive revolution' in academic psychology during the 1960s was followed by a new emphasis on cognitive processes in therapy. The application of specific cognitive techniques to depression and anxiety now extends to other neurotic disorders, personality disorders, psychosis, functional syndromes and physical illness. During the early 1970s the gulf between psychoanalysis and behaviourism was filled with an explosion of 'new' therapies, based variously on 'humanistic', 'experiential', 'constructivist' and 'existential' approaches. These were largely developed outside the NHS, in the self-styled 'human potential movement', although they have had an important influence within NHS services. Client-centred counselling, in particular, continues to be practised within the NHS, mainly within primary care. As cognitive behavioural therapies became more widely practised during the 1970s and 1980s, the field of psychoanalytic therapy continued to develop in parallel, with briefer, focal psychodynamic treatments, psychoanalytic groups, therapeutic communities and systemic family therapies becoming available within the NHS.

With an ever greater number of therapies being applied to a wider range of problems during the 1980s, many NHS professionals used a range of clinical techniques quite pragmatically, rather than training within a particular school. Recently, interest in pan-theoretical and integrationist therapies has burgeoned, for example through cognitive analytic therapy. In addition to psychological therapies developed and practised by specialists, the influence of these approaches has been widely felt within generic mental health professional practice, for example psychiatry and mental health nursing. Psychological therapies commonly conducted within mental health services by these professions include cognitive behavioural approaches, eclectic approaches, counselling and psychosocial interventions. These services have developed alongside a more general appreciation of the psychological aspects of physical health, and increasing public and media awareness of 'talking therapies'.

Despite the proliferation of therapeutic work within mental health services, until recently there was no formal Department of Health policy recognition that psychological therapies are widely practised within the NHS, and, although specialist services remain small and relatively poorly resourced, the overall provision of psychological therapies in the broader sense represents a significant public funding investment. Pressure on NHS funding in successive years has been experienced by NHS staff as threatening the basis of their services, and, indeed, funding to some services has been cut. These cost pressures need to be understood in a broader fiscal context.

Internationally, the costs of health care have increased and will continue to do so, as available health technologies proliferate and public expectations of better health services rise. Public demand for health interventions as they become available has outstripped health investment from direct taxation. Although the UK spends relatively little on health care – as a proportion of gross domestic product (GDP) – compared with other European countries or the US, the rate of growth of costs in the health sector is comparable, with similar results. Those responsible for third-party payment in health care – whether payment by government revenue, health insurance or employers – in the UK and elsewhere are concerned with (some might say preoccupied by) cost containment. The issue of which interventions for which conditions should be funded from public revenue through direct taxation is not likely to diminish, and will continue to influence the psychotherapies.

There has been a parallel concern to base health policy and management decisions on evidence of clinical effectiveness and to promote better standards of healthcare interventions (Muir Gray 1997). This concern arose first within hospital medicine, when wide variations in practice and outcomes were observed between physicians, leading to doubts about the reliability of procedures for medical decision-making. The resulting movement in evidence based medicine (EBM) aimed to help doctors make rational clinical decisions on the best available evidence and has now developed into a considerable industry, with a proliferation of books, journals, World Wide Web (WWW) pages, CD-ROMs and Internet discussion groups dedicated to pursuing this aim (Sackett et al. 1997). EBM has also generated considerable debate, with critics of EBM attacking the movement as arrogant, platitudinous, biased in its claims, and committing two cardinal sins against clinical medicine, 'the barely concealed view that scientific data are an adequate basis for clinical decision making and the conviction that there can be absolute authority to identify and recommend the "best external evidence" ' (Miles et al. 1997).

Evidence based health care takes the logic of EBM into broader multidisciplinary practice, into community health care, general practice and purchasing decisions. It evaluates the effectiveness of healthcare interventions through a rigorous programme of health services research, conducted to high scientific standards, then disseminates the results of research in intelligible and useful forms to the organizations and individuals who need to know. The point is to use the results of research to change clinical practice and the provision of health care.

'Managed care' initiatives, particularly in the USA, have attempted to address both cost and effectiveness concerns through the greater use of clinical practice guidelines and reimbursement decisions to change clinician behaviour (Schwartz and Brennan 1997). These initiatives are controversial: concern has been expressed by some clinicians that they damage the relationship between clinician and patient and can paradoxically lower standards of care, whereas others have accommodated to them and have changed their clinical practices in response (Austad and Berman 1991). The debate suggests that some moves to contain costs leave many clinicians suspicious of demands for evidence based practice, and it generates adversarial processes between funders, clinicians and researchers.

Within the UK, the NHS has so far avoided the approach of making funding dependent on compliance with care protocols. However, there is an explicit commitment to drive policy and make commissioning decisions on the basis of research evidence of what is clinically and cost-effective. This includes assessing evidence of need for a service or an intervention (basically defined in terms of people's capacity to benefit) and the measurable health gain for a given investment of revenue, sometimes expressed in terms of cost/utility ratios, or £/quality-adjusted life-year (QALY). This is a prospect which often provokes strong feelings. Some people argue that, ethically, some generic measures of health benefit in relation to cost are essential in an equitable and transparent allocation of limited resources. Others, equally appalled at the prospect, are also equally convinced that there are no such easy utilitarian solutions to complex issues of power and value in the use of resources.

There has been growing investment within the NHS in health service research and development (R&D), with greater emphasis on specifying research priorities on the basis of health service needs and then commissioning research to meet these, with relatively less funding for 'curiosity-driven' research. NHS research is supported in several ways: central commissioning (including a health technology assessment programme), local commissioning through Regional Offices, indirect support through the health services research initiatives of the Medical Research Council, and direct funding of Trusts' research support costs (Culyer 1994).

The Department of Health review of strategic policy in NHS psychotherapy services

The policy drive towards a knowledge-based healthcare system has, as yet, hardly influenced the provision of psychotherapies. However, the policy framework for such developments has recently been established. In 1996 the Department of Health published its first formal statement on good practice in psychotherapy services, having undertaken a review of these services in the NHS in England (Department of Health 1996). This strategic policy review included consultation within the NHS, with professional associations and with organizations representing consumers. It found that the unitary term 'psychotherapy' is often unhelpful and misleading, being used to mean entirely different things in different contexts. There is a need to specify which type of NHS provision is referred to, and a simple framework was proposed describing three types of psychotherapy delivery: type A refers to psychological treatments integral to wider mental healthcare programmes; type B refers to eclectic psychological therapies and counselling; and type C is formal psychotherapy based on a single theoretical approach.

The key policy messages from this review can be summarized briefly. Psychological treatments are an important part of mainstream mental health care, one of two main classes of treatment. If well conducted and appropriate for the presenting problem, there is evidence that they can be clinically effective. Within the NHS, demand for these therapies outstrips supply, and there are long waiting lists. However, the review also found evidence of poorly targeted, inappropriate interventions, ineffective organization, and poorly coordinated services, leading to wasted resources.

The current policy framework sets out five aims for NHS psychotherapy services. There should be *comprehensive provision* to meet needs of people for all three types of therapy services. Services should be *coordinated*, for example better links between primary and secondary care and brokerage assessment for treatment of choice to avoid sequential assessment. Services should be *user-friendly and accessible*, taking into account the preferences and social circumstances of service users and providing good information to patients. Psychotherapy should be *safe*, minimizing the risk of harm to patients through therapist incompetence or inappropriate treatment. Finally, psychotherapy services should be clinically and cost-*effective*, based on best research and clinical evidence of what is likely to be most helpful.

There are several implications of this for NHS Trusts and psychological therapists working in the NHS. The policy direction is towards a more systematic approach between different services within a Health District, e.g. psychology services, psychodynamic therapy, cognitive behavioural therapy, primary-care counselling, with agreed joint guidelines on criteria for referral and cross-referral, shared core assessment and audit processes, including agreement on which outcomes measures should be routinely used.

Placing psychotherapies on the mainstream mental health policy agenda, if indeed achievable, is more likely to have long-term than short-term effects. The desired consequences would include increased legitimacy for psychotherapy provision within the NHS and an improved mandate for practice, training, audit and research. It is too soon to judge whether this will happen or, if it does, whether it will have a beneficial effect on revenue flows for these activities, but early signs are encouraging, at least within research and clinical effectiveness.

Psychological and psychotherapeutic topics are at last emerging within a number of government- and charity-funded initiatives. A Cochrane Collaboration in neuroses has been established to build a systematically reviewed database of controlled trials, using rigorous search criteria and including psychotherapy research. The NHS Executive Health Technology Assessment Programme has funded research into the efficacy of counselling and is likely to fund further psychotherapy-related work. The Wessex Regional Development Evaluation Committee appraises systematic cost-effectiveness reviews on behalf of health authorities, and has recently examined therapeutic communities for personality disorder and cognitive behavioural therapy for chronic fatigue syndrome. A psychotherapy research initiative has been launched by the Mental Health Foundation, funding research into a common core battery of outcome measures for psychotherapy and work on therapeutic competence in transference interpretation. The Department of Health has recently funded the British Psychological Society Centre for Outcomes Research Evaluation to develop national clinical practice guidelines for treatment-of-choice decisions in psycho-therapy and counselling. The implementation of the Culyer Report (Culyer 1994) in providing research support funding to NHS Trusts also offers opportunities for psychotherapy developments.

The Department of Health review does not recommend a list of 'validated therapies' to service commissioners and, indeed, recom-mends caution in basing funding decisions solely on the existing base of research evidence in this field. It notes that there is a notable absence of outcome research on some widely practised therapies and also that the weaknesses of psychotherapy research in relation to external validity are severe. Furthermore, research compares treatments within diagnostic groups, whereas other factors will govern the clinical choice of therapy, such as the patient's capacity to form a therapeutic alliance or to tolerate anxiety, or the level of social support available to them. Outcome measurement in this research continues to be problematic, for example in relation to levels of functioning or quality of life, and, although well-designed group comparisons can yield results which are generally true, the specific applicability of these findings to the individual case remains a matter for clinical judgement. A review of research findings on the efficacy of psychotherapy was commissioned as part of this work and published separately (Roth and Fonagy 1996).

Instead of 'prescriptive' commissioning, an alternative way of fostering evidence based psychotherapies was recommended in the review and is also summarized by Roth *et al.* (1996). Clinical audit plays a significant role here, but forms part of a wider strategy. This strategy recommends single-case studies and case-series evaluation of innovative practice prior to formal research. Research findings are then incorporated into clinical practice guidelines and other influences on psychotherapists' clinical decision-making. Research and clinical consensus, sometimes formalized in guidelines, can be used as the basis for setting audit standards and benchmarking outcomes. These activities should also influence education and training in the psychotherapies.

The recommended approach depends on psychotherapists being able to achieve a level of consensus on standardized practices and to specify them more clearly. It can be argued that the current absence of consensus in this field damages the credibility of psychotherapy as an evidence based, replicable form of treatment in mental health. The task of achieving consensus may not be as impracticable as is sometimes thought; for example, when psychotherapists move from arguing abstractions to formulating single cases, significant levels of agreement can be obtained (Persons *et al.* 1991). Psychotherapeutic formulation in routine clinical practice has also been shown to have considerable validity in terms of formal research instruments (Bennett and Parry 1997).

Standardized practice, clinical practice guidelines, therapy protocols, etc. should not be used prescriptively. Psychotherapists are wary of the concept of clinical protocols and guidelines, seeing them as a threat to clinical freedom, but clinical guidelines can be used to benchmark best practice and as an aid to clinical judgement. They should be informed by service-evaluation evidence, formal research findings and clinical consensus. Research evidence is incorporated into standard clinical practice through these protocols, but it is the prerogative of the clinician to make a judgement in the individual case, on the basis of assessment and case formulation, to do something different. However, the guideline acts as an aide-mémoire to the therapist in formalizing normal expected practice, so that deviations from this practice are made thoughtfully and are justified by clinical evidence. The psychotherapist must always remain free to generate idiosyncratic ideas; all valuable approaches to therapy are born from theoretical and clinical innovation.

New approaches are then tested through single-case studies, case-series evaluation and $n = 1$ research, and if they continue to show promise they reach a stage of development where it is appropriate to invest in formal research. This stage includes randomized controlled trials (RCTs) (where possible), followed by field trials. The role of qualitative research, as the only way of answering some types of questions, should also be acknowledged. This form of research is sometimes misunderstood: it is not about eschewing measurement or simply letting people talk for themselves; nor is it an easy option of small scale, non-generalizable research. It does emphasize meaning, the negotiation and social construction of meanings. The strengths of the qualitative method for health care generally are in such areas as patient perceptions, understanding health behaviours or exploring taken-for-granted practice in health care. It can also enhance and complement quantitative research, for example in explaining unexpected findings. In psychotherapy research, for example, intensive process analysis complements outcome research, by examining the meaning of key events in contextual detail (Rice and Greenberg 1984; Safran *et al.* 1990). This method is a vital antidote to the assumption within outcome research that psychotherapy is analogous to a drug and can be studied in a similar way. Stiles and Shapiro (1994) argue that the drug metaphor underlying psychotherapy breaks down at several points; for example, therapists monitor patients' responses to interventions and constantly make adjustments to what they deliver.

Standard practice which can be described in clinical practice guidelines also has the great advantage of focusing and clarifying the audit effort, since the guideline states 'the right thing to do', whereas the audit asks 'has the right thing been done?' and 'has it been done right?' If audit is targeted on those processes derived from research-

and consensus-based protocols, a clear link can be established between research and audit (Firth-Cozens and Ennis 1995). Audit based on research evidence, in turn, will reveal gaps in knowledge, leading to developments in theory and new hypotheses for formal psychotherapy research.

As clinical and service audit examines the reasons for failures to deliver to an agreed standard of practice, it often reveals gaps in the skills and competence of psychotherapists which are preventing them delivering as effective a service as they would like. For example, a common problem for psychotherapists from all schools is how to master the specific techniques of the approach while maintaining a good working alliance with the patient. There is evidence of the negative impact of practising technique in the absence of the alliance, an effect demonstrated in relation to both cognitive and psychodynamic therapy. Thus Castonguay et al. (1996) found that increased use of cognitive technique was associated with poorer outcomes, though this effect was abolished if the alliance was controlled for. This finding echoes that of Henry et al. (1997), who found that in increasing their technical competence trainee psychodynamic therapists neglected to attend to the alliance, to the detriment of outcomes. These dilemmas of therapists in training are often revealed in auditing levels of therapeutic alliance using a standard instrument. This sort of finding from audit highlights quality of psychotherapy training, new education and curriculum needs, and integrated attention to questions of professional skills updating.

Clinical audit in psychotherapy services

Clinical audit has a role to play in achieving each of the five aims set out in the Department of Health review (1996). The purpose of clinical audit is to improve services to patients by a formal process of setting standards, gathering data to find out how the service is performing in relation to them and changing practice as a result. It is led by practitioners, reviewing aspects of clinical care systematically and critically. Ideally, it is a short-cycle affair, where an aspect of clinical practice can be identified, monitored and reflected upon relatively quickly, to allow changes to be implemented and the effects of these changes to be examined. Since the late 1980s the requirement that NHS clinical staff audit their work has been clearly established. Formal contracts between Health Authorities and Trusts specify audit goals, and ring-fenced funding has been made available.

Many clinical audits focus on elements within the process of delivering care, for example on attempting to reduce the length of time that patients have to wait before being assessed or before starting therapy, or monitoring and reducing the proportion of patients who drop out of therapy prematurely. Standards for user satisfaction can be set and an audit conducted on sources of dissatisfaction in order to resolve these. A range of process audit topics are described by Fonagy and Higgitt (1989), and a review of clinical audit methods in this field is covered by the Department of Health review (1996: ss. 4.5–4.6).

It is also possible to use audit methods in relation to clinical outcome. An example within the mental health field is given by Firth-Cozens (1993), who describes an outcome audit in a psychiatric day hospital. Staff agreed a criterion for clinical improvement (in this case in terms of one standard deviation from the intake mean on a standard measure of psychiatric symptoms). This helped the staff of the day hospital to examine more critically the characteristics of those patients who were not improving, finding that they were the older women and those who had been sexually abused. These findings allowed the staff to introduce more appropriate services for these two groups, to provide different training for some staff and to plan a more coherent approach across the district to the needs of these patients. Thus the audit loop was closed, and ideally the audit would be continued in order to establish that improvements in effectiveness were actually achieved.

Clinical audit in the psychotherapies has to be distinguished from psychotherapy research or, indeed, service evaluation. These three activities are often confused and, indeed, have much in common in that are all committed to gathering evidence, often using similar methods. Their purposes differ, however. The purpose of psychotherapy research is to generate new knowledge which is generalizable, not just of local interest. It tests hypotheses or addresses research questions using systematic research methods, whether quantitative or qualitative. It follows a protocol for the research design, which is peer-reviewed and ethically approved, and the results are published in refereed journals. Service evaluation has yet other purposes: to monitor service effectiveness, justify the use of resources and inform decision-making. It tends to be planned on a larger and longer scale than audit, for example in examining the impact of a new service or a redesigned service-delivery system. It describes service processes and outcomes and checks whether service objectives are being met according to external criteria. It may be undertaken by evaluative researchers, who may not themselves be clinical practitioners (Parry 1996).

The apparent simplicity and clarity of the audit process masks some complex difficulties, and in reality psychotherapy services have found it difficult to achieve productive and useful clinical audits on a routine basis, for a number of reasons. NHS staff who deliver psychotherapies are typically very busy, have long waiting lists and are attempting to juggle competing demands, with little administrative support, training or funding for audit work. Furthermore, different types of psychotherapy have their traditional ways of maintaining standards of work, which do not derive from audit methods, but are nonetheless valued by practitioners. For example, in psychoanalytic therapy there are widely accepted norms, standards and criteria for good practice which are explicitly taught during training, and emphasized and monitored through the process of clinical supervision. There is a lack of formal evidence on the relative effectiveness of traditional methods compared with clinical audit programmes. Finally, the large and complex range of topics which potentially could be audited has also proved daunting, with the danger of audit projects being overambitious, getting bogged down in long-term data collection with insufficient or long-delayed feedback, so that the audit cycle is not completed. The question of whether, in practice, audit methods are an effective way for psychotherapists to change their practice remains open.

Does evidence change clinical practice?

A major difficulty for any health service policy based on promoting evidence based practice is that clinical practitioners tend not to change their practice on the basis of research evidence.

In general, just sending out information about research evidence on clinically effective practice does not work. The information has first to be received, then read, then discussed; then an explicit commitment to action must be obtained, then that action needs to be monitored and, finally, followed up. A recent survey of NHS Trusts and Health Authorities attempted to find out the extent to which the many central initiatives on promoting research and development, evidence based health care and clinical effectiveness have taken root and been implemented within the NHS (Ham and Walshe 1997). The results suggest that at each of these stages fewer and fewer Trusts manage to stay the course, with the results of, for example, Effective Health Care Bulletins, published by the Centre for Reviews and Dissemination at the University of York, being received by a large number of Trusts, discussed in rather fewer, leading to clinical management actions in yet fewer, and monitored or followed up in a minority.

If the traditional method of disseminating research findings (simply to publish the evidence and let people absorb it) has failed to influence mainstream medical practice sufficiently there is even less chance of it succeeding with psychotherapy provision. Many psychotherapists feel alienated from both the biomedical research tradition, including the RCT, and the positivist-empirical approach of academic psychology, which has influenced much psychotherapy research. Negative attitudes to research are one reason for the lack of impact. The Department of Health review (1996) acknowledges that in many cases there are coherent reasons for these negative attitudes. Many psychologists and psychotherapists are wary of reifying complex human problems such as anxiety, depression or anorexia into 'disorders', believing that diagnostic nomenclatures are unacceptably simplistic descriptions of psychological conditions. From this point of view, diagnostic categories are, at best, limited approximations to the understanding of psychological distress and, at times, misleading and unhelpful. Critics would argue that, for example, 'anxiety' is not a coherent disorder, but signals underlying problems with about the same degree of precision as 'abdominal pain' does a medical condition. It can also be argued that outcome research has been dominated by diagnostic categorization, so that those seeking a research justification skew their work accordingly, so that, for example, depression becomes that which is measured by DSM-IV (the *Diagnostic and Statistical Manual of Mental Disorders*, 4 edn). On the whole, scholarly and research efforts within psychoanalytic therapies have eschewed this approach. A range of psychoanalytic research uses empirical, naturalistic single-case studies which, whilst providing a prima facie case for the relevance of psychoanalytic psychotherapy for a range of problems, do not meet the criteria for inclusion in a research review of experimental studies. Much of this research has deliberately not involved RCTs (especially in relation to longer-term psychoanalytic therapies). The difficulties of designing such trials are fully acknowledged by Roth and Fonagy (1996).

Apart from negative attitudes, there are many other reasons for the weak impact of research on psychotherapy practice. These include poor-quality research (whether quantitative or qualitative, process or outcome research); psychotherapy research which has no relevance to practice, or is of little interest to therapists; difficulty for the average clinical practitioner in reviewing results of many studies, with no easy access to relevant results, insufficient training and skill in knowing how to read or appraise research; and, finally, shortage of time in most busy clinical jobs to keep up with journals and research publications.

In seeking to improve the influence of research and audit on psychotherapy provision it is worth examining what is currently known about successful ways of changing professional healthcare practice towards clinically effective interventions. The Cochrane Collaboration on Effective Professional Practice (CCEPP) systematically reviews the evidence for the effectiveness of interventions to change professional attitudes and behaviour (Oxman *et al.* 1995; this is also available on the WWW and on CD-ROM). The reviewers found that clinical audit and feedback had a moderate effect on professional behaviour in the studies reported, but we can assume that the most widely used methods of audit are likely to have weaker effects than this, because many audits gather data but give insufficient feedback. Educational outreach is a method of influencing practice where clinicians receive a personal visit by the 'evidence based healthcare representative', analogous to a 'drugs rep' in general practice. This seems to be a promising approach, rather more effective in influencing practitioners than clinical audit alone, but the characteristics of effective educational visits are not well understood. There is also some evidence for the value of working with opinion leaders – people who are nominated by their colleagues as educationally influential – although the reviewers found mixed effects and some difficulties in implementation. Computer support for clinician decision-making has some value, for example in giving reminders for decisions on drug dosages, but, on the other hand, the evidence is relatively weak for computer-aided diagnosis. The review concludes that there are no 'magic bullets' in implementing research findings and that a range of different approaches are required to incorporate research evidence into routine clinical practice. All these techniques will need to be specially adapted to psychotherapy services if we are to see significant change.

In summary, there appear to be three priorities emerging from current policy. The first is to improve the evidence base in psychotherapy through upgraded investment in research, including developing research methods suited to investigating process and outcome in all commonly practised forms of psychotherapy, psycho-analytic work included. In addition to research within therapeutic schools, there needs to be a continuing focus on the underlying principles of all effective therapies, in terms of processes of change which transcend theoretical 'schools' – such as patient readiness and aptitude for change, and therapist competence.

The second priority is to develop consensus across psychotherapies on a range of topics: common outcome measures, approaches to audit, best evidence on the indications for a specific approach, knowledge of factors influencing optimal treatment length, methods of predictive assessment, and so on. The development of clinical practice guidelines is one structured way – but only one way – of achieving this.

The third priority is to increase the accessibility of research to practitioners through a variety of mechanisms – such as 'practitioner-friendly' reviews of evidence in popular journals; better teaching on a range of research methods and findings within psychotherapy training courses (indeed minimum standards for competence in basic research awareness could, in time, be a condition of accreditation); educational initiatives in useful techniques in psychotherapy audit; professional or research centres offering access to information services (such as the Internet, CD-ROM databases, systematic reviews); and, finally, 'benchmarking' clubs of psychotherapy practitioners interested in comparing outcomes. As gradual but discernible change occurs the number of psychotherapists who are clinically skilled, research-aware and interested in clinical audit as a tool for self-reflection will increase.

References

Austad, C. S. and Berman, W. H. (1991) 'Managed health care and the evolution of psychotherapy', in C. S. Austad and W. H. Berman (eds) *Psychotherapy in Managed Health Care*, Washington, DC: American Psychological Association.

Bennett, D. and Parry, G. (1997) 'The accuracy of reformulation in cognitive analytic therapy: a validation study', *Psychotherapy Research*.

Castonguay, L. G., Goldfried, M. R., Wiser, S., Raue, P. J. and Hayes, A. M. (1996) 'Predicting the effect of cognitive therapy for depression: a study of unique and common factors', *Journal of Consulting and Clinical Psychology* 64: 497–504.

Culyer, A. (1994) *Supporting Research & Development in the NHS*, London: HMSO.

Department of Health (1996) *A Review of Strategic Policy on NHS Psychotherapy Services in England*, NHS Executive.

Firth-Cozens, J. A. (1993) *Audit in Mental Health Services*, Hove: Lawrence Erlbaum.

Firth-Cozens, J. A. and Ennis, W. (1995) 'Marriage guidance: why research programmes need clinical audit', *Health Service Journal* : 24–5.

Fonagy, P. and Higgitt, A. (1989) 'Evaluating the performance of departments of psychotherapy', *Psychoanalytic Psychotherapy* 4: 121–53.

Ham, C. and Walshe, K. (1997) *Acting on the Evidence: Progress in the NHS*, NHS Confederation.

Henry, W. P., Strupp, H. H., Butler, S. F., Schacht, T. E. and Binder, J. L. (1997) 'Effects of training in time limited dynamic psychotherapy: changes in therapist behavior', *Journal of Consulting and Clinical Psychology* 61: 434–40.

Miles, A., Bentley, P., Polychronis, A. and Grey, J. (1997) 'Evidence-based medicine: why all the fuss? This is why', *Journal of Evaluation in Clinical Practice* 3: 83–6.

Muir Gray, J. A. (1997) *Evidence Based Healthcare. How to Make Health Policy and Management Decisions*, New York: Churchill Livingstone.

Oxman, A. D., Thomson, M.A., Davis, D. A. and Haynes, R.B. (1995) 'No magic bullets: a systematic review of 102 trials of interventions to improve professional practice', *Canadian Medical Association Journal*, *153*, 1423–31.

Parry, G. (1996) 'Service evaluation and audit methods', in G. Parry and F. N. Watts (eds) *Behavioural and Mental Health Research: A Handbook of Skills and Methods*, Hove: Lawrence Erlbaum.

Persons, J. B., Curtis, J. T. and Silberschatz, G. (1991) 'Psychodynamic and cognitive-behavioral formulations of a single case', *Psychotherapy* 28: 608–17.

Rice, L. N. and Greenberg, L. S. (1984) *Patterns of Change: Intensive Analysis of Psychotherapy Process*, New York: Guilford Press.

Roth, A. D. and Fonagy, P. (eds) (1996) *What Works for Whom? A Critical Review of Psychotherapy Research*, New York: Guilford Press.

Roth, A. D., Fonagy, P. and Parry, G. (1996) 'Psychotherapy research, funding and evidence based practice', in A. D. Roth and P. Fonagy (eds) *What Works for Whom? A Critical Review of Psychotherapy Research*, New York: Guilford.

Sackett, D., Richardson, W. S., Rosenberg, W. M. C. and Haynes, R. B. (1997) *Evidence-based Medicine: How to Teach and Practice EBM*, Edinburgh: Churchill Livingstone.

Safran, J. D., Crocker, P., McMain, S. and Murray, P. (1990) 'Therapeutic alliance rupture as a therapy event for empirical investigation', *Psychotherapy* 27: 154–65.

Schwartz, K. and Brennan, T. A. (1997) 'Integrated health care, capitated payment, and quality: the role of regulation', *Annals of Internal Medicine* 124: 442–8.

Stiles, W. B. and Shapiro, D. A. (1994) 'Disabuse of the drug metaphor: psychotherapy process outcome correlations', *Journal of Consulting and Clinical Psychology* 62: 942–8.

Chapter 2

The audit fixation

Some issues for psychotherapy

Michael Power

Introduction

It is undoubtedly a sign of the times that an accountant with financial auditing experience might have something to say about the field of psychotherapy. Accountants may require therapy and psychotherapists probably need good tax advice, but the fields themselves have, until relatively recently, had little to do with each other. However, this has changed with the advent of administrative transformations in public finance and the growing role of audit in many different sectors unaccustomed to such a practice. Not just health-related services but also the criminal justice system, social work and all levels of education have been and are being transformed by the implementation of audit practices.

Of course, not all audits are the same and the financial audit process is undoubtedly different from the emergent 'audit' practices within the field of psychotherapy. But there are systematic similarities and overlapping issues. In this chapter I wish to explore some of these similarities and develop their implications for psychotherapists. Being a non-specialist contributor to a specialist volume allows one a certain freedom to stand outside the field in question and locate it in a broader context of organizational and administrative transformations; psychotherapists are far from being alone in their experiences of, and reactions to, the audit process. I hope I shall also be forgiven for playing with the language and concepts of the field itself. The title of this chapter suggests that audit is a 'fixation', something with which our society is currently obsessed. This introduces a certain critical tone into the discussion which is necessary to balance an incautious enthusiasm for what auditing can do. In the end it would be implausible to be against auditing per se; rather, I wish to draw attention to some of the systematic dangers and difficulties which are often overlooked.

The argument is structured as follows: in the next section the diverse causes of this fixation with auditing are elaborated in order to emphasize that the administrative changes being experienced within psychotherapy are common to many fields of practice. Second, I review the evidence from medical auditing and develop some implications for psychotherapy. Finally, I offer a few general observations which may be relevant to psychotherapy practitioners.

The new managerialism in public-sector administration and the demand for audit

The management changes within psychotherapy practice have their roots in a more general transformation of public-sector management style. The demand for audit is a demand for a new kind of knowledge of publicly funded practices, one which enables them to be more transparent to users of these services, more conscious of their resource implications and more oriented to the improvement of what they produce. The need for this new knowledge has emerged from a number of different pressures for reform:

- *Fiscal crisis*. The assumptions sustaining the provision of welfare and related services are facing real financial limits, notwith-standing arguments about what those limits really are. In response, many states have invested heavily in reforming public-sector management practices with financial disciplines, such as accounting, at their centre (Hood 1991). Audits, both for probity and programme effectiveness, have emerged as prominent instruments of change within the 'new public management' (NPM).
- *Political commitment*. Closely related to the theme of fiscal crisis is the fact that many neo-liberal states in the last decade or so have been committed to a reduction of state service provision as a matter of principle. Executive agencies have been created, industries have been privatized, internal markets have been stimulated and deregulatory initiatives have been accompanied by the emergence of the state as regulator of last resort. All of these changes have taken place with little consultation or testing. Perhaps the most significant structural innovation in the field of health care has been the creation of quasi-markets for medical services. The administrative goal is to stimulate effective use of limited

resources by creating an element of competition between suppliers of medical services relative to purchasing 'customers'. This separation of purchasing and providing institutions reflects administrative ideals of autonomization and disagreggation. Complex contracting arrangements are intended to enable purchasers to exercise control over the nature and quality of the medical services which they buy. Medical auditing in the UK is evolving around this contracting process as a form of quality assurance for medical services.

- *Public accountability.* It has also come to be widely accepted that the accountability and transparency of public- and private-sector operations require constant attention and enhancement. In part, this is an extension of neo-liberal political commitment to a small government state: taxpayers have a right to know how their money is being spent, and citizens – in their varied roles as students, patients, commuters and so on – can demand certain minimum standards of performance from public services. In part, it is also a matter of constitutional significance in which supreme state audit bodies, such as the National Audit Office, have begun to play a more prominent role in mediating representative and executive organs of government (Harden 1993). In the UK, the Audit Commission has played the role of overseeing the implementation of financial reforms, often criticizing the government for compromising its programmes for change (Day and Klein 1990; Henkel 1991). Private- and public-sector scandals have also stimulated regulatory experiments with the aim of improving organizational governance and accountability.

- *The limits of regulation.* For many years legal and administrative scholars have recognized and analysed the operational difficulties of so-called traditional styles of regulatory control in many different areas. It has come to be widely accepted that hierarchical command-and-control philosophies are giving way to experimentation with other mechanisms and systems. Binary notions of state versus self-regulation are no longer conceptually adequate to represent these changes. Notions of 'mutual regulation', 'self-organization' and 'responsive regulation' have come to the fore, and there are calls for regulation to be redesigned around the need to understand the incentive structures of regulatees and the desirability of promoting voluntary self-observation and control (Ayres and Braithwaite 1992). Audits are attractive instruments of control in the face of these demands because they embody the promise of effective regulation which operates close to the cognitive and economic resources of the auditee. More generally, the commitment to regulatory internalization has created new career opportunities, as practitioners in many different fields have changed sides from operations to audit.

- *Quality assurance.* Another important stimulus to the growth of auditing has been the rise of quality-assurance ideals and practices. From relatively humble industrial origins, quality assurance has become a standardized and generalized product in its own right. Standards such as BS (British Standard) 5750, now internationalized as ISO (International Standards Organization) 9000, provide a basic model of quality assurance which can be applied in diverse contexts: schools, universities, hospitals and psychotherapy institutions (Walsh 1995). In many respects, auditing in medical and related fields can be regarded as a particular variant of the quality-assurance model.

In general, quality assurance emphasizes the need for a structured management system which controls the quality of the practice in question. For any practice or productive process there are a number of key elements: objectives must be set; ways of measuring conformance to those objectives (performance standards) must be established; actual measurement of performance and feedback must take place in the form of comparison between desired and actual results. The idea is that the development of such a system leads to constant self-generated improvement in performance standards. Rather than performance being imposed from above, the intention is that it should evolve organically as part of a learning process from below. Enthusiasts argue that it is through such measures and commitments to cyclical monitoring and feedback that substantive improvements in a practice can take place. Finally an external audit process certifies the functioning of this system, and thereby provides assurance for outside purchasers and stakeholders.

Taken together, all these elements have fuelled the demand for different kinds of auditing and auditors – an 'audit explosion' (Power 1994). As a consequence, the distinctions between the public and the private sector and between state and self-regulation have become increasingly blurred. Models of auditing and auditing standards have been borrowed from the private sector, at the same time as state pressures for enhanced corporate governance have stimulated and unsettled the statutory financial audit. Auditing in all its guises has emerged as a popular tool of control because it satisfies different features of the regulatory mood of the times: value-for-money audits promise a basis for tightening up on public expenditure; financial services audits serve the state in its capacity of regulator of last resort; and quality audits make visible and stimulate a process of permanent ongoing improvement.

As might be expected, the impact of these reforms in the field of health care has been the subject of considerable debate. There remains widespread concern that the creation of markets and related managerial imperatives will undermine the ethos of health care on which the National Health Service (NHS) is based. General questions have been raised about the appropriateness of performance measures for services where immediate 'outputs' may bear a complex relation to longer-term 'outcomes' (Beeton 1988). Many medical practitioners have also resisted market-based changes which intrude on their professional autonomy (e.g. Broadbent *et al.* 1992), although, equally, a new hybrid manager-clinician has also begun to emerge (Ezzamel and Willmott 1993). Since the late 1980s these reactions and reservations have begun to focus on medical auditing as it has begun to assume a more prominent programmatic role within health care.

Auditing healthcare provision

Within medicine and related services there is a long-standing, if informal, tradition of case review and data gathering with the goal of improved diagnostic and management practice (Pollitt 1993a, 1993b). Formalized approaches to medical auditing originated in North America and, although British medical practitioners have tended to prefer more ad hoc approaches (Dent 1993: 257), transatlantic influences have percolated into practice. Since the mid-1980s, as particular elements of the NHS have been subjected to NPM-style reforms, medical auditing has begun to emerge as a discrete element of clinical practice. Between 1989 and 1994 approximately £220 million was allocated specifically for the development of medical auditing practice. This was officially and broadly defined as 'the systematic, critical analysis of the quality of medical care, including the procedures used for diagnosis and treatment, the use of resources, and the resulting outcome and quality of life for the patient' (Department of Health 1989: para. 1.1).[1] This definition is much broader than the verificatory emphasis to be found in financial auditing; it extends to the entire system for quality assurance for medical care and implicates a multidisciplinary approach involving doctors, nurses, management and other support staff. Furthermore, this vague and perhaps uncontentious definition conceals complex tensions.

The struggle to preserve professional autonomy

Professionalism can be defined, in part, as the self-control of quality judgements (Pollitt 1990: 435), and it is to be expected that practitioners will react to externally imposed changes by attempting to preserve this operational autonomy. The medical field illustrates a politics of audit and quality assurance whereby practitioners have tended to resist both managerial definitions of quality and also managerial participation in the definition process. The meaning of quality is a stake within hierarchical struggles between medical practitioners and emergent managers over the control of the evaluation process (Pollitt 1993a: 162). *Who* decides on the objectives and purpose of auditing in the medical field is crucial (Nolan and Scott 1993).

Initially the Royal Colleges promoted a conception of medical audit which was voluntary and local in emphasis, thus pre-empting a US-style formalized system of peer review (Pollitt 1993a: 163). In addition, the funds earmarked for audit were used for education and research purposes, indicating a determination not to distinguish between auditing and clinical learning processes more generally. Furthermore, there has been a willingness on the part of purchasers to delegate audit activity to medical practitioners themselves. In the absence of a developed tradition of using audit results, purchasers were initially content *that* an audit was done rather than with knowing *what* exactly was done. In short, the early days of medical auditing do not suggest that it was an instrument for radical cultural change in the medical field, and contract monitoring was crude. Many general practitioners (GPs) argued that medical audit was already operating successfully and did not require extension or formalization (Laughlin *et al.* 1994: 104). Others adopted a minimalist approach to auditing (Broadbent *et al.* 1992), which is nevertheless expensive in its attempts to absorb external pressures for change.[2]

The question is whether these strategies represent a successful defence of professional autonomy and control over definitions of auditable performance. Medical practitioners, in common with psychotherapists, teachers, social workers and others, have been concerned to preserve audit as a local learning process which facilitates professional development. In this respect, medical quality assurance has been conceived as a bottom-up, holistic process led by professional activity (Nolan and Scott 1993). However, educative self-auditing of this kind has proved to be a Trojan horse for the imposition of more far-reaching accountability and monitoring requirements.

The rise of the managerial imperative

Audit could never survive as an autonomous and focused clinical practice: 'soon after (medical) audit was established, the potential for audit to operate in a wider environment was recognised' (Exworthy 1995: 31). Packwood et al. (1994) show how public accountability ideals have been increasingly superimposed upon the fragmented base of existing audit routines and practices. Medical audit has also begun to emerge as a management priority, particularly as purchasers and providers learn new roles, as hybrid clinician-managers are created and as pressures for multidisciplinary representation increase. There are demands that management involvement remains sensitive to practitioner autonomy and that audit does not operate in a blaming culture. However, many practitioners remain suspicious of management involvement in audit and are concerned about the possible routinization of medical practice (Black and Thompson 1993: 850).

Audit has never operated as a purely verificatory practice, despite definitions which suggest this. Even within modern corporate financial auditing the identification and rectification of control weaknesses play a central role. In the context of public service provision, auditing practices have been intended, in part, to shift organizational power away from doctors and teachers by making them accountable to taxpayers, patients and parents, and by defining auditable performance. However, not all the effects of audit are necessarily intended, even by those who promote it as a vehicle for change, and there is increasing evidence of behavioural changes around measures of auditable performance. For example, the significant side-effects of the Research Assessment Exercises for UK universities are beginning to be understood, such as the systemic damage to transfer markets for academics. In addition, it is well known that value-for-money auditing tends to emphasize financial values of economy and efficiency in cases where notions of effective performance are difficult to define or are controversial.

This last point is particularly relevant for psychotherapy practitioners, who are being restructured as providers of services to purchasers (Health Authorities and GPs). The development of audit for psychotherapeutic services has tended to follow developments in the medical field more generally and much can be learned from these experiences. However, psychotherapy is distinctive because there is a more extreme history of internal controversy about effectiveness. Different schools of thought and practice exist, together with competing professional sensitivities about the nature of care and the meaning of outcomes. Because of this, the introduction of audit can be expected to heighten tensions in the field. Suspicions of external management encroachment may be amplified by practitioner tensions about the possibilities for measurable, and hence auditable, change. As in other fields, there are general worries about the incompatibility of short-term audit cycles and longer-term cycles of therapy. Moreover, whoever gains control of the audit process can legitimate his or her concept of therapy over rivals by building it into accreditation processes. In short, audit may exacerbate professional rivalries, supporting Dezalay's (1995) argument that regulatory initiatives, such as audit proposals, become stakes in professional competition.

The relationship between management and clinicians is constantly evolving around the audit process. Within medicine, audit has been successfully co-opted for local and ad hoc purposes but there are anxieties about its possible disciplinary role in the future (Black and Thompson 1993: 854–5). Pollitt (1993a,1993b) argues that internal and external audit arrangements should be explicitly decoupled from one another. This is echoed by Hopkins (1996: 422), who contrasts the potential for simple, low-key commitments to clinical improvement, involving all relevant staff, with the detailed needs of contract monitoring where measures of outcome are necessary. The hope is to distinguish clearly between audit as a part of medical self-reflection and audit as a tool of accountability. However, evidence from other contexts of audit suggests that there is pressure to combine these roles; once a form of clinical accounting for one purpose, e.g. monitoring or billing, becomes legitimized it tends to take over (Chua 1995).

How far local mechanisms of self-inspection are coupled to systems for external monitoring is therefore a key issue for psychotherapy practice. We are only just beginning to understand the consequences of 'making things auditable' (Power 1996) in many different fields. At worst, audit is expensive, heightens stress and distrust (Sitkin and Stickel 1996), erodes professional values and collegiality, creates disproportionate attention to formal process and systems and increases games of fiddling and 'creative compliance'. For example, Patient Charter requirements for specific waiting times in casualty departments can be 'massaged' if patients are seen initially by a nurse.

Auditing: an essentially contested practice

The problem for medical auditing is that, despite many attempts to define it in restricted clinical terms (Dent 1993: 263), it remains a vague and poorly integrated practice which is loosely coupled to other audit practices and different specialisms. Nolan and Scott (1993: 760) point to the continuing ambiguity of the Department of Health definition of medical audit, and Hopkins (1996) argues that the questions of who or what is being audited, for whom audit is intended and how topics for audit are selected remain confused. However, it should also be remembered that such ambiguity enables audit to be attractive to different groups and to satisfy multiple expectations (Exworthy 1995: 101).

Although operational procedures have developed and expanded the principles articulated by the Royal Colleges, the contracting function is evolving, and the normative and operational boundaries of medical auditing within this context are varied and often criticized. For example, it is argued that audit cycles remain incomplete, that it is impossible to attribute change to audit and that patients' (the customers?) perspectives play little role in the process (Black and Thompson 1993). From this point of view, medical audit is a fragile practice which can be 'readily ignored or omitted, its results argued away as idiosyncratic, its insights seen to be duplicated by other sources, its purposes conflicting, with no perceptions of any serious detriment to medical practice resulting from its absence' (Packwood *et al.* 1994: 310). Faced with this evidence of operational difficulties, enthusiasts demand more resources and status for audit (Thomson and Barton 1994), and greater attention to completing the audit loop (Hopkins 1996: 420).

The field of medical and related forms of audit is constantly evolving, and the scope of the practice is negotiated between overlapping medical and managerial concerns, in which purchasers are learning to be economic 'principals' who monitor contracts. Quality-assurance practices in the medical field which embody performance indicators are also taking shape. The medical profession, like all professions, tends to prefer evaluation oriented towards quality of process (Dent 1993: 262). As medical auditing becomes part of a quality-assurance system it concerns itself with the auditable object of managerial capability and measurable outputs rather than directly with care itself and more complex outcomes: 'the need to introduce audit in short order will make easily collected, quantifiable data very appealing' (Nolan and Scott 1993: 762). Furthermore, the systems emphasis of quality assurance is alien to many practitioners: 'the changing environment of CA [clinical audit] has meant that purchasers and provider managers are not necessarily concerned with quality of clinical care per se but increasingly with the systems established to ensure that quality is developed and maintained' (Exworthy 1995: 95).

In conclusion, audit in the context of clinical and psychotherapy services is moving inexorably away from its local, ad hoc, bottom-up origins towards a more standardized, national framework, a process which necessarily weakens professional autonomy: 'Top-down models generally apply a generic instrument administered by outside assessors, whereas bottom-up systems are generated and largely applied by practitioners themselves' (Nolan and Scott 1993: 762). As bottom-up educational schemes are transformed and formalized by top-down monitoring and accountability requirements, the audit process may heighten conflict and psychotherapy practitioners should be under no illusions about the difficulties of managing conflicting demands as their practice is 'made auditable'.

Conclusion: making psychotherapy auditable

Audits change practices in intended and unintended ways, but in the end it is an empirical issue as to whether audits damage local cultures of trust and heighten conflict or whether they stimulate learning and collective commitment to improvement. The problem is that there has been, until recently, very little systematic investigation of the consequences of auditing. Auditing, in the medical field and else-where, has been prompted as an article of faith, a key component of the NPM programme (Pollitt 1995). There is some evidence of auditee mentalities, meaning that a new subject of the audit process is emerging, but we still know very little about this. Regulators and politicians do not wish to be encumbered by systemic doubts about audit; they need to be reassured that it works or can be made to work better. Empirical inquiry creates discomfort and uncertainty.

The way societies call individuals and organizations to account can be enormously varied: formal and informal, financial and non-financial, detailed performance measures or broad aggregates. Audit, as opposed to forms of inspection and evaluation, is one style within a range of options (Chelimsky 1985; Power 1995; Broadfoot 1996). Audit is perhaps a symptom of the times, something in which hopes have been invested and which breathes life into the rallying cries of accountability and control. Organizations and practices must be made auditable, and the creation of a database of auditable facts is a crucial part of defining clinical performance. Within accounting, it is well known that financial accounts are selective measures which do as much to construct an organizational reality as to represent it (Miller 1994; Chua 1995). Within the medical field there has been much discussion about the records base which makes audit possible; not only do poor records lead inevitably to poor auditing, but an emphasis on records may divert attention from crucial aspects of clinical process, such as timeliness and clinician empathy with the patient (Hopkins 1996: 418). Moreover, records designed with one purpose in mind – such as diagnostic coding for billing – may be highly unsuitable for audit purposes oriented to learning, even though they satisfy some monitoring or account-ability role. Also, records created at point of discharge are unlikely to illuminate the complexities of the presentation process. In short, the way that a practice, such as psychotherapy, is made auditable depends, crucially, on the forms of record keeping which define the performance of its practitioners.

One might, without too much exaggeration, conceptualize audit in the language of therapy itself. Companies clear accounts through the audit process, thereby coming to terms with their commercial past. Of course, as many companies with hidden liabilities have found, one cannot deal with the past so easily, and the hygiene of a 'clean' audit report is often only superficial. However, borrowing from the anthropologist Mary Douglas, it is possible to suggest that audits are a form of ritual purification; they banish the devil of inef-ficiency and alleviate the anxieties of politicians who require assurances of the success of their programmes for change. But to suggest that audit is, or has become, a social ritual is not necessarily to criticize it. Anthropology reminds us of the important functional role of many rituals. The question is whether audit has become a political fixation which smothers the possibility of real learning, an article of faith because of need to produce symbols of comfort in an increasingly fragmented and uncontrolled society. The worst of the quality-assurance style of auditing is precisely this kind of 'counter-productive regulation' (Grabosky 1995) – abstract and heavily systems-based with costly but shallow and noncommittal statements of comfort by consultants who take little responsibility for their opinions.

Although this chapter has endeavoured to introduce some scepticism about auditing, it is not wholly dismissive, since this would mirror the faith of uncritical audit enthusiasts. Rather, there is a need for empirical knowledge of the costs and benefits of audit practice. The lesson for psychotherapy practitioners is that there is a need for caution and sensitivity in balancing demands for monitoring and financial clarity with clinical values. To maintain such a balance requires a wider set of competencies than audit itself: we need to understand what makes organizations work and feed this back into the clinical audit process. Indeed, there is a need to develop performance indicators for the audit process itself, not merely within it. Such indicators could enlist the views of the practitioner auditee, and would attempt to understand (and not just measure) the financial and non-financial impacts of internal and external audit processes.

Some degree of formalization of local practitioner self-reflection is undoubtedly a good thing; in a spirit of cooperation this provides, on a small scale, the conditions for learning and future knowledge production, which contribute to local structures of trust. It does not really matter what this process is called. Furthermore, teachers, doctors, social workers, researchers and psychotherapists will always be left with discretion. The policy decision is both how much discretion to permit and how to understand the effects of audit on that discretion. The danger is that audit can never be an absolute value: effectiveness is as much a function of how we leave individuals alone to get on with their work as it is about how to monitor them.

To summarize: there is now much talk of audit and its potential as an instrument of control in a wide variety of areas. Perhaps there is even enough of this enthusiasm for audit to say that modern Britain is an 'audit society' (Power 1997). The word 'audit' has come to be synonymous with a certain kind of institutional legitimacy, and audit practices seem to be assuming an increasingly significant social role. This tendency provokes at least two questions: do audits actually provide the forms of control that they promise?; and how does auditing affect the environment of the auditee? An affirmative answer to the first question is often presumed, and we have very limited knowledge that could inform an answer to the second. In short, the audit society is a society that is experimenting on itself.

As far as psychotherapy is concerned, audit – in one or more of its varied forms – is here for the foreseeable future. It will be important for psychotherapy practitioners to have a robust collective and consensual clinical discourse which can present an acceptable face to the outside world and avoid the imposition of silly performance measures. It is also important to understand the audit process, for all its dangers, as an opportunity for self-improvement. Nevertheless, in years to come historians may judge that this audit explosion, and the forms of management enthusiasm which have accompanied it, was in fact just so much froth relative to the reality of reductions in public expenditure.

Notes

1 I shall use the term medical audit in a broad sense. However, there is a distinction to be drawn between clinical auditing – relating to the entire cycle of care, including nursing and outpatient arrangements – and medical auditing, which has a narrower diagnostic focus (see Exworthy 1995). The present discussion does not rely on these distinctions. However, Hopkins has argued that the distinction between medical and clinical audit, though understandable, has contributed to a fragmentation of the field (Hopkins 1996: 415).
2 Similar absorptive, decoupling strategies are visible in schools' responses to the Local Management of Schools (LMS) initiative, which was initiated in the wake of the 1988 Education Reform Act (see Broadbent *et al.* 1993).

References

Ayres, I. and Braithwaite, J. (1992) *Responsive Regulation: Transcending the Deregulation Debate*, New York: Oxford University Press.

Beeton, D. (ed.) (1988), *Performance Measurement: Getting the Concepts Right*, London: Public Finance Foundation.

Black, N. and Thompson, E. (1993) 'Obstacles to medical audit', *Social Science and Medicine* 36(7): 849–56.

Bowerman, M. (1995) 'Auditing performance indicators: the role of the Audit Commission in the Citizen's Charter initiative', *Financial Accountability and Management* 11(2): 173–85.

Broadbent, J., Laughlin, R. and Shearn, D. (1992), 'Recent financial and administrative changes in general practice: an unhealthy intrusion into medical autonomy', *Financial Accountability and Management* 8 (2): 129–48.

Broadbent, J., Laughlin, R., Shearn, D. and Dandy, N. (1993) 'Implementing Local Management of Schools: a theoretical and empirical analysis', *Research Papers in Education* 8(2): 149–76.

Broadfoot, P. M. (1996) *Education, Assessment and Society* Milton Keynes: Open University Press.

Chelimsky, E. (1985) 'Comparing and contrasting auditing and evaluation: some notes on their relationship', *Evaluation Review* 9(4): 483–503.

Chua, W. F. (1995) 'Experts, networks and inscriptions in the fabrication of accounting images: a story of the representation of three public hospitals', *Accounting, Organizations and Society* 20(2/3): 111–45.

Day, P. and Klein, R. (1990) *Inspecting the Inspectorates*, London: Joseph Rowntree Foundation.

Dent, M. (1993) 'Professionalism, educated labour and the state: hospital medicine and the new managerialism', *The Sociological Review* 41(2): 244–73.

Department of Health (1989) *Working for Patients*, London: HMSO.

Dezalay, Y. (1995) 'Introduction: professional competition and the social construction of transnational markets', in Y. Dezalay and D. Sugarman (eds) *Professional Competition and Professional Power: Lawyers, Accountants and the Social Construction of Markets*, London: Routledge.

Exworthy, M. (1995) *Purchasing Clinical Audit: A Study in the South and West Region*, University of Southampton: Institute for Health Policy Studies.

Ezzamel, M. and Willmott, H. (1993) 'Corporate governance and financial accountability: recent reforms in the UK public sector', *Accounting, Auditing and Accountability Journal* 6(3): 109–32.

Grabosky, P. N. (1995) 'Counterproductive regulation', *International Journal of the Sociology of Law* 23: 347–69.

Harden, I. (1993) 'Money and the constitution: financial control, reporting and audit', *Legal Studies* 13(1): 16–37.

Henkel, M. (1991) *Government, Evaluation and Change*, London: Jessica Kingsley.

Hood, C. (1991) 'A public management for all seasons?', *Public Administration* 69(1): 3–19.

Hopkins, A. (1996) 'Clinical audit: time for a reappraisal', *Journal of the Royal College of Physicians of London* 30(5): 415–25.

Laughlin, R. C., Broadbent, J. and Willig-Atherton, H. (1994) 'Recent financial and accountability changes in GP practices in the UK: initial experiences and effects', *Accounting, Auditing and Accountability Journal* 7(3): 96–124.

Miller, P. (1994) 'Accounting as social and institutional practice: an introduction', in A. G. Hopwood and P. Miller (eds) *Accounting as a Social and Institutional Practice*, Cambridge: Cambridge University Press.

Nolan, M. and Scott, G. (1993) 'Audit: an exploration of some tensions and paradoxical expectations', *Journal of Advanced Nursing* 18: 759–66.

Packwood, T., Kerrison, S. and Buxton, M. (1994) 'The implementation of medical audit', *Social Policy and Administration* 28(4): 299–316.

Pollitt, C. (1990) 'Doing business in the temple? Managers and quality assurance in the public services', *Public Administration* 68: 435–52.

—— (1993a) 'The struggle for quality: the case of the National Health Service', *Politics and Policy* 21(3): 161–70.

—— (1993b) 'Audit and accountability: the missing dimension?', *Journal of the Royal Society of Medicine* 86 (April): 209–11.

—— (1995) 'Justification by works or by faith? Evaluating the new public management', *Evaluation* 1(2): 133–54.

Power, M. (1994) *The Audit Explosion*, London: Demos.

—— (1995) *Auditing and the Decline of Inspection*, London: Chartered Institute of Public Finance and Accountancy.

—— (1996) 'Making things auditable', *Accounting, Organizations and Society* 21(2/3): 289–315.

—— (1997) *The Audit Society: Rituals of Verification*, Oxford: Oxford University Press.

Sitkin, S. and Stickel, D. (1996) 'The road to hell: the dynamics of distrust in an era of quality', in R. Kramer and T. Tyler (eds) *Trust in Organizations*, Thousand Oaks, CA: Sage.

Thomson, R. and Barton, A. (1994) 'Is audit running out of steam?', *Quality in Health Care* 3: 225–9.

Walsh, K. (1995) 'Quality through markets: the new public service management', in A. Wilkinson and H. Willmott (eds) *Making Quality Critical*, London: Routledge.

Chapter 3

Clinical audit and conflict

Kevin Healy

Definitions

Socrates (469–399 BC) was sentenced in Athens to drink hemlock for 'introducing strange gods' and 'corrupting youth'. Yet the Socratic method of asking penetrating questions in order to test the assumptions which underlie knowledge provided the basis of all subsequent rational thought. His motto was 'Life unexplained is not worth living'. Perhaps we could now regard his approach to life as an early example of audit.

In present times audit is defined in the *Oxford Reference Dictionary* as 'an official scrutiny of accounts to see they are in order'. Medical audit is further described in the Department of Health document *Working for Patients* as 'the systematic critical analysis of the quality of medical care, including the procedures used for diagnosis and treatment, the use of resources and the resulting outcome for the patient' (Department of Health 1989: 1). The process of clinical audit has evolved within health care since the early 1990s into a multidisciplinary cycle as follows:

1 Define standards for clinical care.
2 Compare actual practice with these standards.
3 Implement change to bring practice up to standard.
4 Repeat the cycle at appropriate intervals.

Conflict is inherent and inevitable throughout this process. An ability to face such conflict constructively is essential for the creative use of audit by clinicians.

In this chapter clinical audit as a source of conflict is explored at a number of levels: personal, interpersonal, departmental, institutional and national. Examples of clinical audit in practice are given, and some of the difficulties that may arise are selectively highlighted. An understanding of the conflicts seen at each step in the process of clinical audit is developed. Conflicts central to the setting of standards, conflicts central to monitoring and observing current practice in relation to these standards, and conflicts inherent in the process of change are examined. Well-recognized psychoanalytic ideas are applied to help in the understanding of the conflicts involved in clinical audit at differing levels. Finally, the value of conflict within the process of clinical audit is explored. It is discussed as a phenomenon that is inherent, inevitable and essential for the process of clinical audit.

On a macro level, audit is a national activity driven by economics, by appealing to rational argument and common sense, and not least by the exigencies of political popularity. Audit can also be understood as a personal activity internally driven by curiosity and by the pleasures of introspection. Within the National Health Service (NHS) the chosen approach and style of working of an individual consultant psychotherapist is intertwined with aspects of his or her personality. The process of audit (that is, looking at what happens, being clear what we would like to happen and taking the steps necessary to have happen what we would like to happen) is certainly threatening to the status quo and may feel threatening to individuals, who may prefer to live with the known and wherever possible avoid change. What do I in fact know about my 'colleagues' or they about me? Do they really know how I behave, what drives me to behave in this way and what sort of service I provide to others, both staff and patients?

Levels of audit

Personal audit

On a personal level, audit is an intra-psychic activity involving both cognitive and emotional elements. Cognitively, it is a process of self-evaluation against preset values. It is linked with self-esteem and other feeling states. It involves a critical look at the self that may potentially be fuelled by harsh judgemental attitudes. Such self-criticism may therefore be constructive or destructive in intent and outcome. A recent article in the *British Medical Journal* (Fonseka 1996), headed 'To err was fatal', describes a personal audit of the author's clinical practice during the past thirty-six years. He presents five situations where a mistake in practice led to the death of a patient. This audit process is presented constructively to readers in terms of the writer learning from these difficult experiences. An example of a more destructive ongoing personal audit might be as given below.

CASE I

Paul is a 31-year-old struggling draughtsman. In his early twenties he suffered a paranoid psychotic breakdown and was hospitalized for eight weeks. He has been reasonably controlled on depot injections of medication since. He has had no further hospitalizations, has been in once-weekly psychotherapy intermittently over the past five years and has taken important steps in getting on with his life. He is, however, very self-critical. He sets high standards for himself and others which are impossible to achieve, observes his failure to meet these standards and deems himself a failure as a consequence. He becomes depressed, paranoid and suicidal. I suggest that he is involved in a destructive self-critical process, a type of personal audit.

Interpersonal audit

One could argue that the practice of psychoanalytic psychotherapy itself may itself be viewed as an audit process involving patient and therapist. The goal to be achieved may be conceptualized by the patient and therapist in different ways. The patient may seek symptom relief or solutions to difficulties, alongside gaining a deeper self-awareness. The therapist may wish to help a patient towards a capacity for concern and thoughtfulness, and/or seek to create a therapeutic space to help the patient feel and think within the treatment. What happens in the here and now of sessions is explored in psychoanalytic psychotherapy through reflection on the states of mind evoked in both patient and therapist during the encounter. Edna O'Shaughnessy (1994) clearly illustrates this active, audit-like process engaged in by an analyst while treating a patient. To a greater or lesser extent, patients and therapists strive to achieve their goals in therapy. Therapy is a continuing process of monitoring what is happening alongside what is desired.

Unit/departmental audit

Most clinical audit takes place within working units, or departments. The work of the department is monitored against set standards. Necessary changes are made to bring practice up to standard. The whole process is repeated. Such, at least, is the theory. Outpatient psychotherapy services have developed around the roles of consultant medical psychotherapists and/or clinical psychologists in the NHS. There are complicated reasons why each of us has chosen this line of work. Our work identity can be understood as one of the layers which helps us contain our more primitive anxieties and feelings. When we audit our work and the work of our department we may feel that aspects of ourselves are exposed. Audit is certainly threatening to the status quo, and personally threatening in that it is a process shared with others either within or between departments. The word 'audit' has its root in the Latin *audire*, meaning to listen, and not in the Latin *audere*, meaning to dare. I would contend that, in fact, both derivations are applicable to the process of clinical audit.

CASE 2: AUDIT OF PSYCHOTHERAPY SERVICES WITHIN A MENTAL HEALTH TRUST

Five medical consultant psychotherapists in a Mental Health Trust directly involved in outpatient work met for one and a half hours every two months over a two-year period to audit our respective outpatient services on five different sites across the Trust. This was initially an interesting, informative and at times exciting activity which potentially had great significance for the way we worked and the services we provided. We developed a process of clinical audit to explore the work of our departments based on an approach suggested by Fonagy and Higgitt (1989).

It soon became clear that there were great differences in the services provided at the different sites. These differences arose from factors such as the time spent in post by individual consultants, the stage of development of the service as a consequence, and the particular clinical and research interest of individual consultants. We examined the work of consultation/ assessment, recognizing this as perhaps our central clinical role in a psychotherapy service. We noted that in none of our departments was adequate prior written information given to patients about what to expect from an assessment/ consultation meeting. Individualized consultant practices and preferences often determined the outcome of assessment, and the types of treatment available and offered to a patient. The latter was also influenced by the network of rotating medical staff, paid and honorary psychotherapists attracted to work in a department. We also examined other activities of our departments that were not directly patient-related and which utilized more that 50 per cent of our time. Such activities included teaching, research, administration and business planning. We looked at our links with primary care.

Over a period of three months towards the end of the second year of our meeting our enthusiasm for audit abruptly vanished. The timing coincided with a period of more general anxiety pervading NHS staff locally and nationally in response to changes in the NHS. We became increasingly aware of competition with others and amongst ourselves for human and financial resources. With increasing competition in attracting patients/customers to our services came a 'them and us' mentality, which began to pervade our discussions. Anxieties about the survival of our services overwhelmed our capacity to think and work alongside each other. Our meetings fizzled out amid poor attendance, changes in venue and changes of time to fit with increasing work pressures. We had earlier been able to address issues of competition, of confidentiality, of access to privileged information, and issues of envy, jealousy and rivalry a number of times early in the course of the two years of meeting. We recognized that these issues were clearly linked to our working together in the clinical audit process. However, we failed to address them openly or adequately within our audit group when they came to the fore again with a fresh intensity.

This situation has been clearly described by Obholzer (1993), who writes of the general forces at play within our society, particularly those produced by uncertainty. He also explores forces specific to the NHS, such as the climatic change involving the development of competition, as well as the resulting rivalry and envy, and consequent 'we/they', 'us/them' situations. He paints a picture of a competitive divided NHS where uncertainty is ever present, change universal and threats to survival all-pervasive.

Institutional audit

CASE 3: AUDIT AND MANAGEMENT STRUCTURES

Within the inpatient psychotherapeutic community in which I work an active process of clinical audit had been in place since 1991. Monthly case presentations to all clinical staff at the hospital explored clinical issues relevant to the case presented. They were also important in raising general issues relevant to similar work throughout the hospital. Alongside this there was a discussion of a suitable topic involving all the clinical staff at the hospital, which lasted for one hour each month. We actively monitored our current practice, and had lively discussions of these observations and of standards to be set. However, we had great difficulty in translating any of this activity into changes in practice. We failed to link our thinking and proposals to the process of managing any consequent change.

The management structure at the hospital had evolved in a time of major national and local change within the NHS. The government had introduced a split in functions in the NHS between those who purchased services on behalf of patients and those who provided services to patients. An 'internal market' was set up, introducing competition between provider units in attracting funding from the purchasing authorities, including Health Authorities and general practitioner (GP) fundholders, for the services they provided. A whole range of new relationships needed to be formed within our own Mental Health Trust and with our purchasers. In the midst of this the senior clinician at the hospital retired. What would happen if we got a new powerful clinical director who did not wish to direct the service in a way that reflected our current working practices and strengths? In the first instance, a 'Hospital Executive Committee' was devised to run the service, with representation from all professional groups in the hospital. As it turned out, however, the constitution of this committee occupied all management thinking space for a considerable time. The power of veto by the clinical director over decisions made by this committee was repeatedly discussed. In retrospect, it would seem that the primary task (Rice 1963) of this committee was to neutralize any threat from the incoming clinical director. It was not an effectively functioning committee that might take forward the aims and objectives of the hospital. It does not seem surprising, under these circumstances, that a management structure designed to neutralize change failed to implement any changes identified by the clinical audit process.

National audit

Audit is now a feature of public life at a national level. The National Audit Office provides independent information, advice, and assurance to Parliament and the public about all aspects of the financial operations of government departments and many other bodies receiving public funds. It does this by examining and certifying the accounts of these organizations, and by regularly publishing reports to Parliament on the results of its value-for-money investigations of the economy, efficiency and effectiveness with which public resources have been used. The Audit Commission has a remit to appoint auditors to all local authorities, Health Authorities and NHS Trusts in England and Wales. Its objective is to promote 'best practice' in local government and NHS bodies, encouraging economy, efficiency and effectiveness in both the management and the delivery of services. It investigates and reports on the impact of legislation, or government action or advice, for local authorities. The commission's strategy recognizes the changes faced by local government and the NHS. It charges the commission to help audited bodies realize the benefits and deal with the hazards of change. The commission has identified five practical objectives which will be the focus of its work in the next few years. These are: helping with change in local government and the NHS; monitoring the performance of audited bodies; making accountability more effective; improving the quality of local audit; and continually improving the quality of the commission's work. Conflict is a very obvious feature of the process of audit at a national level.

CASE 4

The Audit Commission (1996) produced a national report, *Misspent Youth*, based on a two-year study of services involved with young people and crime. The report identifies a number of problems in this area. Many of them stem from the lack of cooperation between the different agencies involved, which are often pursuing different objectives. Crime committed by young people is a major problem, but the system could be improved and resources used better. For example, the youth-court process takes four months on average from arrest to sentence, costing around £2,500 for each young person sentenced. But half the proceedings against young people are discontinued, dismissed or end in a discharge. Monitoring of reoffending after different sentences is rare, and most young offenders receive no intervention to address their behaviour. The report recommends using 'caution-plus' programmes to deal with young people who admit offending a second or third time, thus freeing resources to deal with persistent offenders more quickly, giving them more intensive supervision in the community and piloting preventive services. The report also suggests that local authorities should take the lead, developing multi-agency strategies targeted on areas of greatest risk. Health visitors, mental health services and drug action teams all had a part to play. On the day the report was published a home office minister spent his time viciously savaging it on radio, television and in the other media. He instead wished to highlight the needs of society and government to punish these criminals and to be seen to punish them. The conflict involved with regard to implementing the recommendations of this audit could not have been more obvious.

On a more hopeful note, and returning once more to the NHS, the Department of Health has recently undertaken a National Review of Psychotherapy Services (1996). This indicates a growing demand in the NHS for psychological therapies which complement physical treatments. Demand for counselling and psychotherapy is rising in primary and secondary care as a consequence of both the high levels of distress arising from mental health problems and an increasingly sophisticated level of public awareness and expectation. Yet few understand what such treatment involves, what works for whom and how best to provide comprehensive services of the highest quality. The Psychotherapy Review describes a variety of psychological therapies used to treat mental health problems in adults and children in primary, secondary and tertiary care. It collates for the first time in this country the evidence for the effectiveness of such treatments. It offers practical guidance to purchasers, providers, employers and trainers about how to drive forward the agenda of evidence based practice and how to improve the quality of existing services. In my view, the conflicts in relation to this impressive review will become clearer at local and national levels as the report is considered, accepted and implemented.

Theoretical considerations

As is evident in the cases listed above, conflict is inherent in each step of the process of clinical audit. In this section I attempt to understand why this is so.

Implementing change

In most situations change is difficult. Human beings are notoriously resistant to change even when the change appears to be relatively minor or where those concerned have ostensibly agreed to it.

Managing change inevitably requires managing the anxieties and resistance arising from the change process.

Obholzer (1993) identifies three layers of anxiety that need to be understood before they are addressed. Primitive anxiety refers to the ever present all-pervasive anxiety that besets the whole of humanity. We create rituals to protect ourselves from such anxiety, to provide us with 'a social skin'. As many of the social institutions of the past no longer serve to protect us we imbue existing everyday institutions with protective/defensive functions. They protect us from personal and social breakdown, give us a sense of belonging, save us from feeling lost and alone. Anything that threatens to sever us from the band – redundancy, retirement, migration, institutional change – can flood us with this kind of anxiety. A second category of anxiety arises from the nature of the work we undertake. In response to these anxieties, work can come to become organized not to pursue the primary task, but rather to defend members of the institution from anxiety. A third type of anxiety is personal anxiety, the anxiety we feel when something triggers off elements of past experience, both conscious and unconscious. Our need to have containing institutions – that is, for our institution to protect us from being overwhelmed by these different layers of anxiety – is often at odds with and deflects from the institution's primary task and the changes required to pursue it.

Change, then, not only meets with resistance but can produce staff illness, breakdown and burnout. Yet without change the institution may become increasingly 'off task' and out of touch with the environment it is supposed to serve, putting its very existence at risk.

Jon Stokes (1994) writes of the unconscious at work in groups and teams, with particular emphasis on the contributions of the work of the psychoanalyst Wilfred Bion. He states that Bion distinguished two main tendencies in the life of a group: the tendency towards work on a primary task, described as *work-group mentality*, and a second often unconscious tendency to avoid work on the primary task, referred to as *basic-assumption mentality*. These opposing tendencies can be thought of as the wish to face and work with reality and the wish to evade it when it is painful or causes psychological conflict within or between group members. In work-group mentality members are intent on carrying out a specifiable task and want to assess their effectiveness in doing it. By contrast, in basic-assumption mentality the group's behaviour is directed at meeting the unconscious needs of its members by reducing anxiety and internal conflicts. Bion identified three types of basic assumption. A group dominated by the basic assumption *dependency* behaves as if its primary task is solely to provide for the satisfaction of the needs and wishes of its members. If the basic assumption *fight–flight* predominates, the assumption is that there is a danger or enemy which should either be attacked or fled from. The group is prepared to do either indifferently. The basic assumption *pairing* is based on the collective and unconscious belief that whatever the actual problems and needs of the group, a future event will solve them. The group is focused entirely on the future, but as a defence against the difficulties of the present.

When one is under the sway of a basic assumption a questioning attitude is impossible. Effective work which involves tolerating frustration, facing reality, recognizing differences among group members and learning from experience will be seriously impeded. To pursue the process of clinical audit effectively therefore requires the presence of a work-group mentality.

Stokes argues that individuals are drawn to one profession or another partly because of their unconscious predisposition towards one basic assumption rather than another. Each profession operates through the deliberate harnessing of different sophisticated forms of the basic assumption in order to further the task. He postulates that the basic assumption dependency may be a prominent underlying motivation in the decision to become a health professional. In a group taken over by basic-assumption mentality the formation and continuance of the group becomes an end in itself. Leaders and members of groups dominated by basic-assumption activity are likely to lose their ability to think and act effectively. The functioning of teams can be promoted by the sophisticated use of a basic assumption in the service of work, or impeded and distracted by inappropriate or aberrant use of basic assumptions.

Over time, an equilibrium tends to develop between the basic needs of individuals and the primary task of an institution, leading to fairly static patterns of work and work relationships. Any attempt to change these patterns and relationships is resisted both on an individual level and by the organization as a whole. To upset the equilibrium can lead to a dread of being overwhelmed by anxieties and concerns both of a primitive kind and related to the work in hand. Change, therefore, is often resisted both consciously and unconsciously. Change, however, is a factor inherent in the audit cycle.

Monitoring/observing/being observed

One aspect of the process of clinical audit involves a critical scrutiny of what is taking place. This includes a spectrum of behaviour ranging from listening, to hearing, to perceiving, to noting, to observing, to looking, to inspecting, to examining and to exploring. Again, there are major familial, social and cultural attitudes that govern our ability to look at and observe what may be going on.

Eye contact, for example, can have differing meanings in different societies related to social and sexual roles. It may also have particular personal intra-psychic meanings for a particular individual. Being able to look and take in with the eyes what is actually happening in the world around one is a feature of what Melanie Klein termed 'depressive position functioning' (Segal 1973), and what Donald Winnicott (1965) called 'a capacity for concern'. In this position people and things are permitted to be what they are, and not transformed into the fearful ogres or idolized figures so characteristic of a more primitive and paranoid way of perceiving the world. In other instances, looking may be understood as an active, attacking process. We are all familiar with the phrase 'if looks could kill' and with the concept of a 'penetrating stare' or, when feeling guilty, of not being able to look someone in the eye or in the face. This form of looking would seem more directly connected with the internal world of the looker, and may be more closely associated with less integrated, less mature levels of psychological functioning.

Brazelton and Cramer, in their book *The Earliest Relationship* (1991), describe the eagerness of new parents in looking at their newborn. One of the first questions a new mother asks is 'Can my baby see me?' When parents first lift the baby to face them the eyes of an unmedicated baby will open and search the parents' faces. Few responses on a baby's part have a more powerful impact on parents. An interesting experiment revealed how important sight is to the newborn baby. An alert baby's eyes were covered first with an opaque and then with a clear plastic shield. He swiped frantically at the opaque shield and attempted vigorously to remove it. When it was removed he instantly quieted. When a clear shield was substituted he calmed down to look through it; being able to see seemed to outweigh the disturbing aspects of something covering his face, suggesting a real investment in vision even at birth. This dovetails elegantly with parents' eagerness for visual response from their babies.

On the whole, being observed is generally more problematic for most of us than observing. Being observed, especially if we are being observed in a crisis situation, may evoke the feeling of dread that what we are doing is wrong and will be exposed to the world to be critically judged by others. Certainly this was true of my first experience of medical audit as a young medical student in the 1970s. In the maternity hospital where I worked all perinatal deaths were audited by the consultant obstetricians. The impression created in other workers by these confidential audit meetings was of a setting where the 'guilty consultant would be torn apart limb from limb by colleagues'.

In contrast to this, however, it is also true that observing and monitoring good clinical practice as part of an audit process can have the important effect of raising morale among staff. These factors are all-important in setting up a cycle of clinical audit. To be involved in the audit process, in actively gathering information and observing, has a very different feel from 'being audited'. To look at and confirm good practice can have an important effect on morale, perhaps allowing less good practice to be usefully audited in turn.

The setting of standards and evidence based practice

In 1923 Freud presented his classical model of mental structure, involving three separate but related levels of organization: the id, the location of instinctual drives; the ego, responsible for observing, evaluating and monitoring both the outside world and the id; and the superego, responsible for standard- and goal-setting, and at times a seat of harsh criticism. Clearly, in this description I am drawing attention to a parallel between an organization of mind and a sociological structure, namely that of audit. The tension between ego, the capacity for observation and evaluation, and the superego's 'standard-setting' could be argued to drive the process of clinical audit. This is a model based on conflict that may be recognized or unrecognized, adapted to or denied, constructive or destructive.

We may behave at times as if the standards we set for ourselves and for others are determined by logical, rational thinking. Linked with this is the strong push to introduce evidence-based medicine (EBM) into the NHS as the basis on which investigations and treatment will be purchased and commissioned. Rational, logical thinking underlies the enquiry into what makes for a just healthcare system. The Royal College of Psychiatrists and the British Psychological Society are producing and updating guidelines for good clinical practice. The Health Advisory Service is developing guidelines for purchasers and commissioners of health services. The Mental Health Act Commission develops guidelines in relation to the care of detained patients. The General Medical Council has, since its inception, presented guidelines or rules that define proper medical practice. While we like to think of all these standards as rationally and logically worked out, we need to take account of the importance of familial, social, cultural and religious factors in influencing them. We have personal standards within our interpersonal relationships. There are those with whom we are comfortably on first name terms and those we address more formally. There are those with whom we politely shake hands, those whose hands we warmly clasp, those whose cheeks we kiss politely and those whom we warmly embrace. The setting of standards, however, is not just a rational ego activity.

When standards are set nationally it may feel to individuals at a local level as if they are being imposed on local services without any local choice. Local workers may feel a direct pressure to live up to and act up to other people's standards. Responsibility for and ownership of these standards at a local level may never be achieved. Brazelton and Cramer (1991) describe the impact of the attributions of others on an infant's perception of its own behaviour. They suggest that, through meaning attribution, whole sets of values, of reinforcements, of prohibitions, of emotional colouring contribute to shaping an experience, a behaviour or a trait in the infant's repertoire. When parents attribute meaning to an infant's behaviour they are led to label it 'good', 'bad', 'stubborn', 'smart' and so on. Their consequent pleasure or anxiety will determine the infant's own set of values about his or her capacities, his or her sense of what can and cannot be shared. To a great extent, children's representations of themselves will be moulded by parents' expectations, ideals, predilections and aversions. These are transmitted in great part through mimicry, remarks and actions that reveal to the child how the parents have interpreted his or her intentions.

Mason (1981) writes of the way in which the superego can function in a suffocating manner. He suggests that the upright stance and the development of speech, along with the presence of the superego, are attributes of humanity that have raised it above the animal kingdom. This psychic structure is responsible for our conscience, our morals, our ethics, our religion and our aesthetics. It is the source of all our spiritual aspirations and endeavours. However, as well as protecting and inspiring us the superego can punish, torture, revile and destroy. In fact, a great deal of our life is spent either following the dictates of the superego or attempting with varying success to escape them. Melanie Klein (1933) explored the early intra- and interpersonal transactions that led to superego development. She suggested that the superego represented an internalized composite of external reality and infantile fantasy. I would argue that the same holds for an individual's experience of the audit process. The normal superego becomes the controlling agent of dangerous id impulses. The abnormal or excessively destructive superego is itself felt to be as dangerous and as persecuting as the impulses it is supposed to control. Many disastrous consequences may follow in the presence of such a persecuting superego. An all-powerful, all-knowing, all-present superego creates a sensation in the mind of being watched by eyes from which nothing can escape. These eyes are cruel, penetrating, inhuman and untiring. They record without mercy, pity or compassion. They follow relentlessly and judge remorselessly. No escape is possible, for there is no place to shelter. Their memory is infinite, and threat is nameless. The punishment when it comes will be swift, poisonous and ruthless. Hopelessness is engendered particularly when a feeling that the merciless, implacable quality of the internal watcher cannot be defied. Struggle against it is useless and resistance is futile. The involvement of such a harsh superego will clearly change the nature of any clinical audit process and turn it into a process that is more akin to Paul's audit of himself outlined in Case 1, earlier.

The value of conflict

Conflict is inherent in the process of clinical audit. It is the prime factor that creates the tension necessary to disrupt the equilibrium of a steady state, thus allowing change to occur. In a similar way, the physical conflicts of hunger or thirst and the psychic tension thus produced are prime motivators in encouraging the actions of eating and drinking. Freud (1905) argued similarly that sexual urges actively promote interest in other human beings as a way of satisfying sexual needs. More recently, the need in humans for human attachments has been recognized as a source of conflict and tension, and as a motivation for individuals to engage with other individuals

(Bowlby 1988; Holmes 1993). Conflict can be seen as a driving force behind all human actions and interactions.

Internal psychic conflicts are the stuff of depressive position functioning. The coexistence of loving and hating impulses towards the same internal object relationship (Segal 1973) or the coexistence of concern and ruthlessness towards a similar internal relationship (Winnicott 1963) is an immediate source of conflict.

At times, however, such conflict cannot be tolerated. Instead, a rather different state of mind predominates, in which the individual feels dominated by threats to his or her integrity and survival, a situation described by Klein (1933) as the paranoid–schizoid position, in contrast to the depressive position. At these moments any conflict represents such a threat, whether its source is internal or external. The world becomes a nightmarish place, and the individual struggles to manage by creating the fantasy of divisions between what is felt to be good and what is felt to be bad. Internal and external worlds are split in this way, affording the individual a primitive means of managing or denying unbearable anxiety. Conflict that is managed in this way, however, cannot be addressed psychologically, cannot be thought about without first recognizing the powerful and primitive anxieties that have brought the situation about. In such states the functioning ego is also split. It is less capable of psychological work. It is not a state in which to engage effectively with the process of clinical audit. This may well have been the shared psychic world that undermined the process of clinical audit among the five consultant colleagues in Case 2, earlier.

Wilfred Bion (1962) suggests that thinking is a development forced on the psyche by the pressure of thoughts. He argues that every junction of a preconception with its realization produces a conception. Conceptions will therefore be expected to be constantly conjoined with an emotional experience of satisfaction. Thought, on the other hand, he suggests, arises from the mating of a preconception with a frustration. The model he proposes is that of an infant whose expectation of a breast is mated with a realization of no breast available for satisfaction. This mating is experienced as no breast or an absent breast inside. The next step depends on the infant's capacity for frustration; in particular it depends on whether the decision is to evade frustration or to modify it. If the capacity for toleration of frustration is sufficient the 'no breast' inside becomes a thought, and an apparatus for thinking it develops. A capacity for tolerating frustration thus enables the psyche to develop thought as a means by which the frustration that is tolerated is itself made more tolerable through internal representation. From depressive position functioning arises the capacity for abstract thought and symbol formation. Such a frame of mind and of mental functioning is necessary in order to engage in a process of effective clinical audit.

Stages of development

In classical psychoanalytical theory childhood development is divided into stages of oral, anal and sexual conflicts. These developmental conflicts are responsible for initiating and modifying contacts with individuals in the external world. While these conflicts may at times be problematic, they are seen as necessary in order for development to proceed. Conflict is universal in the world of an adolescent, although it may not be as extreme as is often indicated in psychoanalytic literature (Rutter and Rutter 1993). Conflicts abound in teenagers concerning autonomy, dependency, sexuality, identity and interpersonal relationships. Marriage, pregnancy and parenthood are also largely about conflict and its resolution. The mid-life crises faced by men and women lead on, in time, to perhaps the ultimate conflict of all, the conflict between life and death. Conflict is seen to be an inherent, necessary, essential component of development.

Conflict and clinical audit

Clinical audit is an ongoing process of enquiring and thinking within existing structures, with a sense of ownership by the staff involved, that allows for effective implementation of change where and when indicated. It is a process that meets with enthusiasm in a minority of individuals, and healthy resistance, scepticism or indifference in greater numbers. Some individuals actively oppose the process of clinical audit, perceiving it as something that is driven by their own superegos or more likely by superego values imposed by others. Superego-type audit activity is characterized by a dread or terror in those being audited of being found out, being criticized and being harshly judged. It is often associated with the wielding of a big stick, such as being struck off by the General Medical Council for serious professional misconduct. It may involve the keeping of an attendance register of all those taking part in the audit. It is felt to be imposed by others. Standards are set on high and passed on to be implemented without choice. Those observing or monitoring may be part of a clinical audit department and come from outside the team to monitor the work of the team. Any resulting suggested change in practice is resisted as being imposed from outside. In this type of audit all stages in the cycle are invariably resisted to some extent. It is this type of audit that has been described as 'a form of ritual purification'.

Purchasing authorities can usefully support the process of clinical audit as a tool supportive of the development and maintenance of effective clinical services. However, where actual audit topics are decided by purchasers without consultation with provider units this will usually result in a superego-type audit activity that is not conducive to the growth and development of a clinical service.

In contrast, a clinical audit process that is ego-driven stems from curiosity, a wish to learn about one's working practices and a desire to perform better. Such a process is felt to be involving. Standards set are owned by the participants, monitoring of practice is done by the team members themselves and suggested changes are taken on board with some enthusiasm. Purchasers can be usefully involved in this process through a cooperative dialogue with providers that leads to mutually agreed audit priorities. Such, at least, is the theory. In practice most audits appear to be driven by both ego and superego values.

Main (1989) introduced the concept of a culture of enquiry in describing the functioning of an inpatient therapeutic community. This may continue the Socratic method of asking penetrating questions in order to test the assumptions which underlie knowledge. The process of clinical audit can be considered to be an ongoing 'culture of enquiry'. It is hopefully no longer perceived as 'a strange god', but can be taken on board as an internal process with personal, interpersonal, departmental, institutional and national applications.

References

Audit Commission (1996) 'Misspent Youth': Young People and Crime, London: HMSO.

Benatar, S. R. (1996) 'What makes a just health care system?', British Medical Journal 313: 1567–8.

Bion, W. R. (1962) 'A Theory of Thinking' in Second Thoughts, New York: Jason Aronson.

Bowlby, J. (1988) A Secure Base: Clinical Applications of Attachment Theory, London: Routledge.

Brazelton, T. B. and Cramer, B. G. (1991) The Earliest Relationship, London: Karnac Books.

Department of Health (1989) *Working for Patients*, London: HMSO.

Fonagy, P. and Higgitt, A. (1989) 'Evaluating the performance of departments of psychotherapy', *Psychoanalytic Psychotherapy* 4(2): 121–53.

Fonseka, C. (1996) 'To err was fatal', *British Medical Journal* 313: 1640–2.

Freud, S. (1905) *Three Essays on Sexuality: Standard Edition, Vol. VII*, London: Hogarth Press.

—— (1923) *The Ego and the Superego (Ego Ideal): Standard Edition, Vol. XIX*, London: Hogarth Press.

Holmes, J. (1993) *John Bowlby and Attachment Theory*, London: Routledge.

Klein, M. (1933) 'Early development of conscience in the child', *Contributions to Psychoanalysis*, London: Hogarth Press; reprinted in *Love, Guilt and Reparation*, London: Hogarth Press, 1975.

Main, T. F. (1989) *The Ailment and other Psychoanalytic Essays*, London: Free Association Books.

Mason, A. (1981) 'The suffocating superego: psychotic break and claustrophobia,' in J. Grotstein (ed.) *Do I Dare Disturb the Universe*, London: Karnac Books.

NHS Executive (1996) *NHS Psychotherapy Services in England: Review of Strategic Policy*, London: HMSO.

O'Shaughnessy, E. (1994) 'What is a clinical fact', *International Journal of Psychoanalysis* 75: 939–47.

Obholzer, A. (1993) 'Institutional forces', *Tom Main and After – His Legacy. Therapeutic Communities* 14(4): 275–82.

Rice, A. K. (1963) *The Enterprise and its Environment*, London: Tavistock Publications.

Rutter, M. and Rutter, M. (1993) *Developing Minds: Challenge and Continuity Across the Lifespan*, London: Penguin Books.

Sandler, J. and Dreher, A. U. (1996) *What Do Psychoanalysts Want? The Problems of Aims in Psychoanalytic Therapy*, London: Routledge.

Segal, H. (1973) 'The depressive position', *Introduction to the Work of Melanie Klein*, London: Karnac Books.

Stokes, J. (1994) 'The unconscious at work in groups and teams', in A. Obholzer and V. Z. Roberts (eds) *The Unconscious at Work: Individual and Organisational Stress in the Human Services*, London: Routledge.

Winnicott, D. W. (1963) 'The development of the capacity for concern', *The Maturational Processes and the Facilitating Environment*, London: Hogarth Press.

Chapter 4

Kaizen and the process of audit within an NHS psychotherapy unit

Michael Feldman and Kate Pugh

> Managers must create an environment in which people are enthusiastic to identify deficiencies and work together to right them. Fear must be abolished.
>
> (Smith 1990)

Introduction

This chapter will examine some of the dynamic factors which come into play when practitioners feel themselves subjected to unfamiliar forms of scrutiny, however reasonable the arguments for such intervention. The anxieties and defences mobilized by this process will militate against change and may defeat the aims of the exercise. Consideration is given to a model for the implementation of audit originating from Japanese working practices, where there is an attempt to create a greater sense of ownership among professionals working together to improve the quality of the service for all those involved in it. When it is successful this approach engages the interest, enthusiasm and motivation of staff, and significantly reduces the defensive strategies which may work against change.

The Department of Health issued a circular in January 1991 outlining proposals for the implementation of medical audit. Medical audit was defined as the 'systematic, critical analysis of the quality of medical care, including the procedures used for diagnosis and treatment, the use of resources, and the resulting outcome and quality of life for the patient' (Department of Health 1991). It was stated that an effective programme of medical audit would help to provide reassurance to doctors, patients and managers that the best possible quality of service was being achieved considering the resources available. The detailed practice of medical audit was a matter for the medical profession and would evolve as experience was gained. Close links were to be established between medical audit and existing arrangements for postgraduate medical education.

In his guidelines for medical audit Dr Charles Shaw, director of the medical audit programme (Shaw and Costain 1989), suggested seven main measures that might serve as practical criteria:

1 Health authorities and medical staff should define explicitly their respective responsibilities for the quality of patient care.
2 Medical staff should organize themselves in order to fulfil responsibilities for audit and for taking action to improve clinical performance.
3 Each hospital and specialism should agree a regular programme of audit in which doctors in all grades participate.
4 The process of audit should be relevant, objective, quantified, repeatable and able to effect appropriate change in organization of the service and clinical practice.
5 Clinicians should be provided with the resources for medical audit.
6 The process and outcome of medical audit should be documented.
7 Medical audit should be subject to evaluation.

The advantages of medical audit were endorsed by the Royal College of Psychiatrists (1989) and the implementation of audit in the provision of mental health services has been developing since. Following the implementation of medical audit there was a rapid shift to audit being viewed as a multi-professional function, but in many ways the central dynamics remained unaltered.

With such general agreement on the value of audit and suggestions for its implementation, it might be surprising to encounter the following assessment of the impact of these proposals several years later. In an article reviewing the implementation of clinical audit (Moore 1997), the author quotes Geoffrey Barnes, regional coordinator of clinical audits in the North-West. He makes the point that in spite of the fact that consultants and general practitioners (GPs) have been required to review their performance and improve standards where necessary since the 1991 reforms, 'In practice, many doctors still resist, avoid and blankly refuse to undertake clinical audit or to act on its results, despite massive investment of public funds. . . . The way it is run is sending money down the drain' (*ibid.*).

Demand for change is reinforced by growing acceptance among leading doctors that audit in its current guise has failed. In 1996 the Public Accounts Committee of the House of Commons estimated that by the year 2000 some £834 million will have been spent on encouraging doctors and other health professionals to audit their work. And yet they found that around 14 per cent of GPs and 17 per cent of hospital consultants effectively do no audit, despite receiving funds to do so, and only one-third of the projects which do take place lead to any change in clinical practice. The situation is described by Alan Maynard, professor of health economics at York University as 'a shambles' (*ibid.*). He suggested that clinical audit has been allowed to develop without central direction or local accountability. Doctors decide which treatments are subjects for audit and keep secret the results, usually even from their hospital's managers. Yet many audit projects are nothing more than 'bean counting', where data is collected to no useful purpose. Maynard says: 'the whole question is why should it be run by doctors?' (*ibid.*). He believes that clinical audit needs a national watchdog: 'Locally, doctors should provide audit results to health authority managers so they can compare standards of different services' (*ibid.*).

On the other hand, Moore (1997) quotes Professor Alan Hutchinson, of the Royal College of General Practitioners, who suggests that 'Monitoring by a national watchdog would be the death knell of audit. The professional barriers will just go up' (*ibid.*). Similarly, giving local managers more say would be 'completely contrary' to the principles of audit, according to Richard Dale of the Royal College of Surgeons: 'Managers do not have the knowledge base to choose or judge' (*ibid.*). Allowing patients or managers access to results would simply encourage concealment, says Richard Rawlins, who chairs the British Medical Association's (BMA) audit committee: 'You can't expect doctors to wash their dirty linen even in front of non-medical people in the hospital' (*ibid.*).

Thus one effect of the demand for improvements in medical audit seems to be to increase the pressure for managers to become 'watchdogs' invested with greater powers, and for doctors to feel more threatened, becoming more defensive and hostile, thus frustrating the enterprise. This situation can easily escalate, with increasing polarization, mutual accusation and blame. An alternative approach involves the recognition of some of the dynamic factors at work, taking account of the persecutory anxieties which are almost inevitably evoked by the pressure to change. This approach involves continually involving staff in the organization and management of changes, discussing, clarifying and sharing objectives with them as far as possible, and allowing solutions to emerge from discussions.

When any organization is subject to pressure to change, considerable anxiety is mobilized within the organization and a variety of defensive operations are brought into play. Jaques (1955) and Menzies-Lyth (1959, 1988) have carried out detailed studies on the way social institutions respond to such pressures, using a model derived from psychoanalytic theory.

In 'A psychoanalytic perspective on social institutions', Menzies-Lyth (1988) describes the way in which the job situation seems to contain a 'focus of deep anxiety and distress', and associated with this there is 'despair about being able to improve matters'. The defensive system set up against these feelings can be seen as having two parts: first, there is a fragmentation of the core problem so that it no longer exists in an integrated and recognizable form; and, second, the fragments are projected on to less important aspects of the job situation, which are then mistakenly experienced as the problem about which something needs to be done. In addition, responsibility is usually projected on to unknown others – 'them' – who are seen as the ones to be blamed for the anxieties and difficulties the staff are experiencing, and who are identified as the ones who should do something about the problem. For example, the members of an unsupported community nursing team may blame 'the managers' for providing them with too much paper work, while the predominant underlying anxiety is that their work is under-supervised by their senior staff, leaving them feeling helpless and ineffective with regard to their patients. This core problem is unrecognized and, instead, 'the paper work' becomes the focus for their resentment and anger. This resentment is directed at a non-specific network of unknown managers of a larger network that they can blame for feeling over-whelmed, which results in them not being in a position to request the supervision and support from their colleagues that would make a difference to their work. The task therefore, in audit, is how to bring the focus back to 'the heart of the matter'. For this we might usefully turn to the concept of *Kaizen*.

The Japanese concept of *Kaizen*, a commitment to continual improvement in quality, places the emphasis on *process* rather than outcome as the most effective way of improving a product or service. *Kaizen*, an idea commonly used in Japanese industry and increasingly influential in the USA, is now emerging in use in medical practice as a means of improving health care (Berwick 1989; Irvine 1990). The idea at the heart of *Kaizen* is that poor quality arises from ineffective systems rather than ineffective people. If there is a problem it is because deficiencies in the system lead, for example, to the workers being inadequately trained, poorly supervised, under-resourced, with insufficient time to do the job. Furthermore, one of the crucial defects in the system lies in the fact that there are no ongoing strategies for identifying the problems, and no methods by which they can be remedied. To make *Kaizen* work, then, managers must create an environment in which people are enthusiastic to identify deficiencies and work together to right them: 'Fear must be abolished' (Smith 1990). In this approach 'every defect is a treasure', because once the defect is recognized the work can begin to put it right.

Much of the study on *Kaizen* has come from American business management (Walton 1986; Juran 1983; Crosby 1979) and the authors emphasize data collection and statistical techniques. Initially the steps in the process of the system in question must be charted and measured. This will involve the use of organized data, and indeed this exercise may be revelatory in itself in exposing deficiencies and strengths in the system. An attempt is then made to identify where most improvement can be made, and further assessments and measurements made after these improvements have been implemented. The aim is to shift the whole process towards greater *quality* (Smith 1990; Berwick 1989).

This approach has been used to great effect in industry to improve productivity and could usefully be adapted for application to different branches of medicine to improve service. In the case of many areas of medical practice, including outpatient psychotherapy services, the addition of clinical discussion with the collection and analysis of organized data will be essential to this examination of process to improve quality of service (Feldman 1992).

In the remainder of this chapter this process will be illustrated by offering an outline of the way this might be applied to a psychotherapy service within a postgraduate teaching hospital in south-east London. This will be accompanied by some clinical examples of audit in practice.

Kaizen in psychotherapy

The Maudsley Hospital is a large postgraduate psychiatric teaching hospital with a wide range of clinical services, and important teaching and research functions. The psychotherapy unit is an outpatient service which receives between 300 and 400 referrals a year. Approximately half of these are direct referrals from GPs, and half from the psychiatrists, nurses and other mental health workers both within the Maudsley Hospital and outside it. Patients who are referred are assessed by senior members of staff and, if they are considered suitable, are offered individual or group psychotherapy, or family therapy. There is a strong emphasis on teaching in the unit, with regular seminars on theoretical and clinical material. The patients in treatment are generally seen once a week, either individually or in a group, for a period of nine months, although a few patients are seen for longer periods. All the psychotherapeutic work is regularly supervised by senior members of staff. In addition to the permanent medical staff and senior registrars these are psychiatric registrars who spend periods of their training on the unit, and two senior part-time non-medical therapists have recently been appointed to the staff.

The service lends itself to being considered as consisting of several different 'modules', which represent the process through which patients pass. These modules are *referral, assessment, treatment* and *follow-up*. Within these modules it is possible to delineate broad aims, methods of monitoring routinely collected data, and more complex clinical assessments and discussions relevant to that stage of the process. These are considered, in turn, at the monthly audit meetings, which have been conducted since February 1991 and are held in the unit. Other aspects of the functioning of the unit are also addressed at these meetings, including the teaching functions and the audit process itself. Changes in the broader context within which the psychotherapy unit functions, such as the introduction of the so-called 'market', have emphasized the necessity for continuous review and revision of the unit's work.

Information on all the activities of the unit in the process of referral, assessment and treatment of patients is collected routinely by the secretarial staff and stored on a specially designed computer database, so that it is readily available for simple analyses of data. These data chart the progress of each patient through the unit from referral to assessment to treatment and follow-up. The details of the case will be known only to the therapist and supervisor, and this detailed information, including the nature of the therapeutic relationship, often represents an important input to the audit meeting, supplementing and often illuminating the other clinical and administrative data derived from both the patient's clinical notes and the computer database.

Thus, in each audit meeting part of the input represents the 'routine data' referring to the module under discussion, collated by the secretarial staff as part of the routine work of the unit. When appropriate, more comprehensive data relating to the previous six months are also made available. Thus any trends may form the basis for discussion or provide a starting point for more detailed study. This process is extended periodically to include data on all referrals and across various modules, for example examining the relationship between assessment, treatment and outcome data. Finally, what has evolved as the most important part of the audit meeting is a discussion of the clinical issues which relate to the data of the module under discussion. The clinical dimension enriches the statistical data and gives it meaning, as well as engaging the interest and participation of all the members of the unit, who attend the meetings with enthusiasm. It represents an important focus for teaching and the most immediate means by which actual changes in clinical practice can be brought about. It has become clear that it is in fact the systematic and detailed discussion of clinical cases which engages the interest of the staff, serves to clarify unit procedure and is likely to identify ways in which the service can change.

Thus, in summary, the overall aim of the monthly audit meetings is to address a particular issue relating to one of the 'modules', which concern the broad areas of patient referral, assessment, treatment and follow-up. Examination of the data which is regularly collected might draw attention to a particular trend, or a problem might be highlighted by noticeable delays or difficulties in the 'flow' of patients through the system. On other occasions, the recurrence of a clinical problem, or some difficulty in the unit's relationship with the broader institution, or referrers, might draw attention to an area which needs investigation and discussion. What often emerges is the need to clarify the unit's broad aims in a particular area, and ways in which the quality of the work might be improved. This system is illustrated by examples of this approach to the audit of the unit's work.

Referral: the waiting list

The unit aims to keep few, if any, patients on the waiting list for six months or more. When it emerged that there were three patients on the waiting list for substantially longer than six months it was decided to explore the reasons for this. A number of reasons were considered: on some occasions it was unclear whether a particular therapist had in fact taken on a patient he or she had been considering; in some cases the patient's notes were unavailable and it was difficult to get access to the assessment report. In addition, however, the question was raised whether there were particular characteristics of these patients, or particular features of the assessment report, which gave prospective therapists an unfavourable view of the patient. With some patients the assessor played an active part in encouraging a therapist to take on the patient. Other assessors were less active or, in one or two cases, had left the unit.

A review of the three patients who had been on the waiting list for the longest period revealed that each of them had been offered a treatment vacancy or several offers had been made. Either the patient had turned down the offer or offers, or there were other reasons which had led to the treatment not materializing, and the patient had remained on the waiting list.

Case examples

The first patient, a middle-aged woman with a long-standing difficulty in maintaining employment and in sustaining relationships, had asked specifically to not be taken into treatment after her assessment, when she had been offered individual therapy with an experienced therapist, as she could not commit herself to therapy, but at the same time she requested that she remain on the waiting list as she did not want to be forgotten. The second patient, who had had a severe depressive illness, had written six very apologetic letters to the unit in response to offers of treatment, explaining why she could not commit herself to therapy at present, as if she would if only she could, and that she did not want to let the unit down by refusing therapy. The third patient, an unemployed actress who had not worked for some years, had turned down an offer of treatment on the grounds that she would like 'secure employment in the area' before coming into treatment.

Although the secretarial staff usually draw the attention of the assessor to such cases after a period of time, the particular cases reviewed, which were all assessed by different consultants, highlighted an obvious deficiency in the system, namely that no member of staff had the primary responsibility for monitoring the waiting list, reviewing the cases and making decisions. The patients were therefore allowed to languish on the waiting list, with little or no prospect of being taken on for treatment, re-interviewed and/or discharged.

This discussion led to a number of policy decisions regarding the waiting list:

- The fact that four of the medical files of patients on the waiting list were not available in the unit led to the adoption of a policy that in such cases temporary folders should be available, with the assessment report and unit correspondence.
- It was decided that the waiting list should be distributed to the members of the unit at the beginning of each term and reviewed in a unit meeting.
- A nominated senior registrar was made responsible for monitoring the list and identifying those patients who refuse offers of treatment. It was considered important that the original assessor and the referrer be informed when there had been negotiations between the patient and the unit over an offer of treatment. If it appeared that the patient was very reluctant to engage in treatment the assessor was to be involved in the decision about any further steps which might be appropriate.

Assessment: the decision of group versus individual therapy

An examination of the data available revealed that in the preceding six months, where the patient was accepted for psychotherapy, in 38 per cent of cases he or she was assigned to group therapy and in 62 per cent of cases to individual treatment. This has implications for training, since it was found that there had been an increase in the number of trainee therapists wishing to form groups, and they often had to wait for suitable numbers of patients. Since the waiting list for individual therapy is correspondingly longer, patients were forced to wait longer for treatment.

The meeting focused on the some of the factors which might have led to the assessor's decision to offer the patient one type of treatment rather than another, with the detailed consideration of three cases where individual therapy was offered. The discussion revealed that, among a variety of other considerations, complicated emotional responses to patients seemed to play a part in such decisions.

Case example

> A woman in her thirties had presented with a number of physical complaints and a conviction that she suffered from a post-viral illness, labelled 'ME'. She had been persuaded to come for a psychotherapy assessment by her liaison psychiatrist, who had felt that she had a number of difficulties stemming from her childhood. She had witnessed, at the age of 3, the near-fatal road traffic accident that had left her sister severely disabled. Her defence against the loss of parental attention and concern at this time seemed to be to become the ideal parent to her damaged sibling and to deny her own needs. She now worked as charity worker, having little regard for herself. She conveyed to the assessor a history of enormous emotional deprivation that needed to be 'made good'. The assessor seemed to have been powerfully affected by the pressure the patient placed on him and, without thinking it out very clearly, came fully to accept the patient's view that only rather special one-to-one treatment would be satisfactory for her. In the event, however, the patient had been unable to use individual treatment and had dropped out early. In her treatment, the therapist was treated with contempt as having nothing to offer. The patient retreated into a mental state which re-created her early life experience, where she felt that she was coming to therapy primarily to help the therapist and that this became another, familiar burden.

One issue which emerged in the discussion was the importance of irrational, unconscious factors which operated in the assessor, often under the powerful influence of the patient's conscious or unconscious communication of his or her needs. This sometimes led to the assessor coming to share the patient's fantasy about what would or would not provide a cure. There seemed to be some evidence that the assessor had invested belief in the omnipotent power of individual therapy for this patient as a defence against feeling helpless himself. Any mention of group therapy would have felt like a terrible betrayal of the patient, and both seemed to share the implicit assumption that it would be bound to fail.

There was further consideration of the criteria which different assessors used for assigning patients to individual or group therapy, and of some of the irrational as well as the rational factors which influenced such decisions. Among the issues discussed were the training needs of the institution, concern about the length of the waiting list, and the extent to which such factors should or should not influence the assessor's judgement and decision regarding a particular patient. It was evident that the clarification of some of these issues provided a stimulating and helpful forum for improving the quality of the clinical decisions.

Assessment: family meetings as an integral part of the assessment procedure

The unit receives a large number of referrals for family assessments and therapy, and there is an active and thriving clinic conducted by one of the unit consultants. However, it was noted that in the preceding six months six referrals to the unit which had not specifically requested family assessments had in fact been directed to the family therapy clinic. The meeting considered the appropriateness and value of this procedure. In the three cases which were discussed in detail important matters came to light which might not have emerged so clearly, if at all, in the course of individual assessment.

Case example

A man in his forties, married with three children, was referred by his GP, who had identified marital infidelity by the man's wife as a source of conflict between the couple, causing the husband to be depressed and increasingly withdrawn. The initial decision of the assessor was to offer the couple an assessment in the family therapy clinic over a few sessions. At first it was unclear what the reality of the marital relationship was, but by the third session both the husband and wife made it clear that they knew that no such infidelities had actually occurred. However, the husband ruminated obsessionally about his wife having affairs, and this led to heated arguments and him storming out on many occasions. These sessions revealed a long history of pathological jealousy in the husband that both partners apparently colluded with in order to maintain a relationship otherwise lacking in excitement or intimacy. In the course of the sessions it became possible to discuss the effect, not only on them as a couple, but also on their young children, who were witnesses to these scenes. These discussions led the wife actually to make the decision to separate from her husband, while taking steps to maintain his contact with the children. The man decided that he wished to get help in his own right, and it was agreed that he should receive individual therapy.

The discussion clarified the usefulness of a family assessment in selected cases, as a means of understanding the nature of the problem with which a particular member of the family presents. In the case described above the analysis of the complex marital situation led to the couple being able to face the serious difficulties between them. It then became possible for the man to acknowledge his own problems and to consider addressing them in a clearer way in individual therapy. Among the broader policy issues covered by the topic of the meeting and the three illustrative cases, discussion focused on the desirability, indications and contraindications for redirecting a referral to the family therapy clinic before an individual assessment has been undertaken. It was pointed out that some patients are reluctant to be seen with their families, and the meeting examined the number of cases so redirected who either failed to attend for the family assessment or who dropped out before the assessment was complete.

Treatment: the role of two recently appointed senior therapists on the unit

Two qualified adult psychotherapists had recently been attached to the unit in order to provide long-term therapy for patients with severe and chronic difficulties. The therapists presented some of the dilemmas they felt faced with in providing supportive treatment for such disturbed patients where the prospects of significant change were limited. In the discussion the unit staff were divided in their opinion as to whether such patients should be taken on for individual psychotherapy. Some felt, however, that these patients were being provided with a useful form of 'containment', which reduced demands that would otherwise be made on other services and which prevented deterioration in the patient's situation.

Case example

One of the therapists described a female patient with a very disturbing history of having witnessed repeated violence between her parents, culminating in the murder of her alcoholic father at the hands of her mother. This knowledge was used as a threat that she could hold against her hated mother without her having to move on from this awful past. The patient had five children under the age of 5 and had recently been diagnosed with cancer, necessitating hospital treatment. There was much to suggest that her children were neglected and at risk of physical and sexual abuse from her current partner, who was father of the youngest child. It appeared that she was allowing her partner to turn to her daughter for comfort while she withdrew from him. The therapist felt overwhelmed by the adverse circumstances in the patient's life and her own wish to intervene to ensure the safety of the children. This, together with the patient's inability to think symbolically but always to act, made the therapist feel that psychotherapy was unhelpful. However the patient was intelligent and resourceful, and impressed the assessor with how she had survived against the odds, which had led to the original decision to offer her therapy.

The discussion revolved around the question of what service it was felt the unit should be providing to the hospital and the community. Some participants argued that it should offer dynamic psychotherapy only to those patients who seemed to be capable of change within the relatively brief time for which treatment was generally available. Another view was that even when the outlook seemed unfavourable some patients had been able to make surprisingly good use of the therapy provided. It was also argued that, even when the period of individual psychotherapy was limited to nine or twelve months, where the patient seemed able to make some use of this it was often possible to offer him or her a further period of group therapy or, in some cases, to refer the patient outside the institution for longer-term therapy.

It was also strongly argued that the unit should not have too narrow a view of its role and function within the institution. It could be seen to have an important function in containing patients who were severely damaged and disabled, and only capable of very limited psychic change. While there may not be any significant improvement in the such patients in the short term, long-term supportive psychotherapy often seemed to prevent any deterioration, preserve those social relationships they had, and limit attendance at other hospital departments as well as their GPs.

With the diminishing role of senior social workers in psychiatric teams able to take on such patients, the psychotherapy unit was increasingly being asked to perform such a function in the hospital, and it might be appropriate to do so. It was important to review these policy issues, to preserve a useful role in relation to a difficult group of patients, but also to protect the core functions of the psychotherapy unit, which were to provide teaching for the trainees and to treat patients judged suitable for dynamic psychotherapy. Finally, it was agreed that the cases treated by the therapists should be varied, and that the therapists should not be expected to carry too large a load of these long-term, very difficult patients.

Follow-up: long-term treatment of severely traumatized patients

From time to time the unit was concerned with patients who were judged at assessment, or after a period of individual or group psychotherapy, to be suitable for intensive treatment in a residential setting. This opinion might be based on the depth and severity of the patient's psychopathology, the setting in which he or she lived, and/or behaviour which was damaging to the patient or others. In the meeting it was noted how difficult it had become to secure funding for residential psychotherapy placements. There was no precise record of the number of such patients, but it was decided that in future such cases should be more systematically documented.

Case example

In the meeting a patient was discussed who had completed eighteen months in once-weekly group therapy. She had contacted the unit again and, after a further assessment, had been considered suitable for inpatient psychotherapy in a specialist therapeutic community hospital. She was a single woman in her forties who lived alone and isolated while abusing alcohol and drugs and earning money by working as a prostitute, allowing herself to be beaten. This reflected a childhood dominated by extreme cruelty, abuse and neglect. She had been abandoned by her mother at birth, and had suffered severe physical harm and neglect in her first foster placement by the age of 1. She spent her childhood in a series of institutional homes. In adult life she seemed incapable of allowing herself any comfort, for example having no furniture in her unheated flat, and she could not develop relationships in which she would be cared for in any way. In therapy she had participated for the full eighteen months of treatment but was very disturbed by the ending of therapy, particularly in relation to the female group therapist, whom she idealized.

There was agreement that this patient would best be treated in a residential therapeutic community, where her damaging behaviour could be contained. The female therapist had already ascertained that the Health Authority would not fund such a placement and believed that the patient's ongoing treatment should be provided by the Maudsley Hospital services. In the course of the discussion the suggestion was made that the unit's resources could be mobilized to provide for such patients by setting up a long-term group meeting twice weekly, which would continue for three years or more, conducted by experienced members of the unit. While some of the difficulties and disadvantages of this undertaking were considered, the meeting decided to set up such a group, and suggested research baseline interviews and follow-up assessments to monitor the success of the project.

Conclusion

This chapter offers a model for audit, based on the broad concept of *Kaizen*, that aims for improved quality of service by concentrating on process rather than outcome, and by involving all members of a psychotherapy unit in discussion, review and evaluation of the work. It illustrates this with examples of audit meetings from a psychotherapy outpatient service in south London that holds monthly meetings on referrals, assessments, treatment and follow-up, and makes use of appropriate statistical data as well as detailed clinical material. The clinical cases illustrate the extent to which detailed, focused discussion of patients often served a valuable function in the audit process, focusing on important aspects of the service that would not otherwise have been apparent.

The model described did seem, in practice, to allow for the examination of the way the service was operating, and its possible defects, without stimulating persecutory anxieties. The problems which were identified allowed constructive discussion of ways in which the process could be improved. Moreover, the audit meetings themselves proved stimulating and educational, and attendance and morale were high.

It is implicit in the concept of *Kaizen* that the process of audit and the conduct of the meetings themselves should be kept under review. The senior members of the unit should try to avoid, as far as possible, the imposition of rules or procedures on to the process, as these are liable to be used defensively to avoid dealing with the issues at 'the heart of the matter'. Maintaining a culture which is open, experimental and flexible will facilitate adaptation to changes – within the unit itself, in the parent institution, or changes taking place in the broader political and economic context.

At a recent audit meeting the potential impact of the hospital joining the so-called internal market was discussed. It began to appear that the unit would have to direct a good deal of attention to 'marketing' – considering, for example, the number of referrals from GP fundholding practices; evaluating the costs of consultations, judging the implications for the unit's survival of treating a greater proportion of patients in group or individual psychotherapy, etc. There was some despondency over the loss of the 'luxury' of being able to consider the process and ways of improving the service, being forced instead merely to respond to external demand on the service. However, it was then recognized in this meeting that this response to the major external changes and pressures was precisely the 'stuck' situation described by Menzies-Lyth (1988), where central issues were sidelined and persecutory anxieties began to dominate.

Further discussion in the meeting, involving most of the members of staff, led to a broader and more constructive approach, and to ways in which the audit data and the audit process which was in operation could adapt to the new circumstances. It seemed important to consider ways in which changes might be made in the unit's functioning and the process of audit which would take account of the need for the unit to remain viable, while maintaining a concern for the quality of the training and the clinical service which the unit could provide.

One function of audit is to clarify 'the task', the importance of which is described by Menzies-Lyth:

> unless the members of the institution know what it is they are supposed to be doing, there is little hope of their doing it effectively and getting adequate satisfaction in doing so. Lack of such definition is likely to lead to personal confusion in the members of the institution, to interpersonal and inter-group conflict and to other undesirable institutional phenomena.
>
> (Menzies Lyth 1979)

The attention given to the various aspects of the unit's work lends itself to continuing attempts to clarify 'the task', illuminating the work that is actually taking place, with its limitations and defects, and pointing to areas in which progressive changes can be made.

Audit as described in this paper also has important implications for staff morale. The morale of a unit is the capacity of the group to maintain a belief in itself on the basis of a 'cruelly accurate appreciation of reality' (Hinshelwood 1987). Morale is more stable when there is an objective and measurable output, and it is therefore understandable that psychiatric practice should look to outcome measures as a prop against an erratic morale while ignoring the emotional factors that affect the system of group beliefs (*ibid.*). This chapter argues for attention to process rather than outcome as a means of improving patient care and a staff group's sense of effectiveness. Hinshelwood (*ibid.*) points to two crucial ingredients of morale in an institution: integrity and effectiveness. The audit meetings described in this chapter serve to increase both these aspects in the working group. The ongoing discussion of working practices within the structure described encourages a sense of cohesiveness and a coming together, as opposed to the fragmentation that threatens the demoralized workplace. The use of routine data and frank exposure of the clinician's struggles with clinical cases allows a realistic appraisal of effectiveness which hopefully avoids both despair and omnipotence in its assessment of the unit's work.

References

Berwick, D. M. (1989) 'Continuous improvement as an ideal in health care', *New England Journal of Medicine* 320: 53–6.

Bion, W. R. (1970) *Attention and Interpretation*, London: Tavistock Publications.

Crosby, P. B. (1979) *Quality Is Free: The Art of Making Quality Certain*, New York: McGraw-Hill.

Department of Health (1991) 'Medical audit in the hospital and community health services' (circular).

Feldman, M. M. (1992) 'Audit in psychotherapy: the concept of Kaizen', *Royal College of Psychiatrists: Psychiatric Bulletin* 16: 334–6.

Hinshelwood, R. D. (1987) *What Happens in Groups*, London: Free Association Books.

Irvine, D. (1990) *Managing for Quality in General Practice*, London: Kings Fund Centre.

Jaques, E (1955) 'Social systems as a defence against persecutory and depressive anxiety', in M. Klein, P. Heimann and R. E. Money-Kyrle (eds) *New Directions in Psychoanalysis*, London: Tavistock Publications; 1971.

Juran, J. M. (1983) *Managerial Breakthrough*, New York: McGraw-Hill.

Menzies-Lyth, I. E. P. (1959) 'A case study in the functioning of social systems as a defence against anxiety: a report on the nursing service of a general hospital', *Human Relations* 13: 95–121.

—— (1979) 'Staff-support systems: task and anti-task in adolescent institutions', in R. D. Hinshelwood and D. Manning (eds) *Therapeutic Communities: Reflection and Progress*, Routledge & Kegan Paul.

—— (1988) 'A psychoanalytic perspective on social institutions', in E. Spillius (ed.) *Melanie Klein Today*, London: Routledge.

Moore, W. (1997) *Guardian*, 12 February.

Royal College of Psychiatrists (1989) Preliminary Report on Medical Audit. *Psychiatric Bulletin* 13: 577–80.

Shaw, C. and Costain, D. (1989) 'Guidelines for medical audit: seven principles', *British Medical Journal* 299: 498–9.

Smith, R. (1990) 'Medicine's needs for "Kaizen": putting quality first' (editorial), *British Medical Journal* 301: 679–80.

Walton, M. (1986) *The Deming Management Method*, New York: Perigree.

Chapter 5

The Manchester experience

Audit and psychotherapy services in north-west England

Frank R. Margison, Ruth Loebl and Graeme McGrath

Introduction

This chapter describes the development of audit processes within an inner-city National Health Service (NHS) psychotherapy service. The basic assumptions about the purpose of audit have been discussed elsewhere in this volume (see Introduction and Chapter 1). The project adopted the Department of Health's definition of medical audit: 'The systematic, critical analysis of the quality of medical care, including the procedures used for diagnosis and treatment, the use of resources and the resulting outcome and quality of life of the patient' (cited in de Lacey 1992: 458).

The project team has drawn heavily on two key reviews of the literature (Fonagy and Higgitt 1989; Parry 1992). Both papers draw attention to the relative paucity of applications of research and audit in clinical settings but make recommendations for the optimal application of existing knowledge. The Fonagy and Higgitt paper, in particular, draws attention to advantages of audit in psychotherapy such as confidentiality leading to open examination of practice, cyclical reviews leading to incremental gains in practice, clinician choice of topic leading to greater likelihood of change, and improvement in team cohesiveness. However, they also draw attention to possible disadvantages, including the risk of the audit process being seen as repetitive and dull leading to poor compliance, excessive use of highly qualified and experienced clinical time in meetings, bias inherent in peer review, and fears about confidentiality and intrusion into clinical practice.

These authors make some salient points about facilitation of audit to avoid splitting between an interested group of clinicians and those who feel alienated by the process. They suggest that implementation may be improved if:

- evidence of existing poor quality can be demonstrated;
- audit starts with small projects;
- overcomplex computer packages are avoided;
- access is restricted to clinicians rather than managers;
- feedback is included (particularly about good aspects of care);
- flexibility is maintained and institutionalization occurs as late as possible.

These suggestions guided the Manchester project team and led to a key decision to constitute a separate project group whose primary task was to develop a shared administrative and audit system tailored to clinicians' needs. This small team is linked to a larger team of clinicians who are free to follow their own inclinations in setting audit topics while still being supported by the project team. In the event, this has proved to be a highly successful strategy, but there is a continuing tension between the Department of Health's definition requiring analysis to be systematic and the necessity of developing projects as the need arises.

Analytic approaches

Clinical audit can also be defined by the way in which it differs from other analytic approaches such as:

- randomized controlled trials (RCTs);
- service evaluation (i.e. the application of social research procedures in assessing conceptualization, implementation and utilization of social interventions);
- operational research (i.e. improving cost-effectiveness by the use of mathematical models);
- service audit (i.e. describing service processes and outcome);
- quality assurance (i.e. monitoring processes by which treatment is delivered according to predefined standards);
- total quality management (i.e. a management-led commitment to continuous improvement in quality by improvement in processes).

Within the project described here a broad view of the task of clinical audit was adopted so as to include elements of most of these overlapping methods, including quality measures, in an attempt to reconceptualize and develop systems, and clinical standard-setting.

Conventionally, audit has dealt with input, activity and output as they relate to particular abstract areas relevant to quality, for example:

- How comprehensive is the coverage?
- How relevant is the intervention?
- How acceptable and accessible is the treatment intervention?
- How equitable and effective are the treatments?
- How efficiently is the treatment delivered?

While there is widespread acceptance of the audit cycle (i.e. topic selection, setting a standard, observing practice, comparing practice with standard, implementing change, reviewing standards, observing practice, etc.), the literature suggests that at times clinicians may become paralysed by the setting of impossible standards where criteria cannot be met within existing resources. For example, analysis of seventy-one clinical audits in the Australian Clinical Review (1981–87) showed that 70 per cent of studies could identify problems, and potentially could induce change and improvement, yet improved outcome was noted in only ten of these studies (de Lacey 1992). There are particular problems in assuming that the process of computerization in itself will lead to good audit. Crombie and Davies (1991) drew attention to the fallacy of an assumed common core of data which covers audit and administration. In the design of this project we tried to remain aware of the tendency to become all-inclusive.

In August 1987 the psychotherapy section of the Royal College of Psychiatrists was asked to comment on a series of consultative papers on Performance Indicators. One of the authors (Frank Margison) was extensively involved in these discussions. It became clear that psychotherapy services presented particular conceptual and practical problems in developing measures which could be used to compare departments. In summary, the difficulties were:

1 Lack of definition and differentiation between treatment types under the broad heading of psychotherapy.
2 Problems in defining appropriate activity and outcome measures.
3 Problems in using measures appropriate for short-term change (e.g. symptom resolution to assess long-term therapy aimed at more global change).

4 The lack of generalization from 'research' to practice.

These difficulties were also seen in the context of a more general reluctance to embrace the recent emphasis on audit. Fears commonly expressed by clinicians included:

- a concern that excessive standardization might be enforced on clinicians and patients;
- threats to confidentiality and the private nature of the consultation in psychotherapy;
- the risk that the doctor–patient relationship might be impaired or intruded upon;
- concern that cost would become the primary criterion, with little emphasis on quality;
- medico-legal concerns such as actions for negligence when therapy is compared against external standards;
- lack of trust in peers.

A report was written which summarized an approach to data collection. Within this chapter we will describe the way in which the Gaskell House Psychotherapy Centre undertook to develop some of these ideas. Support was obtained from the Department of Health and North-West Regional Health Authority for a project coordinator who would facilitate two parallel developments reported in detail here: first, the development of a multidisciplinary audit group which would systematically address issues of quality arising in the department; and, second, the development of a computerized audit and administration system whose specification would be enhanced by the clinical audit process.

Extensive consultation also took place through the Service Evaluation Group of the UK division of the Society for Psychotherapy Research, during which it became clear that, while it was desirable to have uniformity of standards and core measures, it was unlikely that all departments would wish to use precisely the same methods of collecting data. However, considerable interest was expressed in the development of a computer-supported system to assist audit activities in psychotherapy departments around the country. Progress had already been made towards an administration system using a card index which tracked patients' progress through the department and prompted staff to follow up the patients who had missed appointments. This part of the project was therefore designed to build on the established body of good practice within clinical audit (see the discussion below).

This chapter also aims to give a practical account of the ways in which audit principles can be introduced and carried through in a working department, not all of whose members were initially as enthusiastic as the project team about introducing computerized systems.

The people

Pre-audit survey of psychotherapy provision in the North-West

Prior to establishing our two local audit projects we surveyed the level of psychotherapy provision in most of the surrounding districts. This was both to assist the team in identifying the role of a specialist service and to identify items of information which might be gathered routinely in an administrative system. A pilot version of the questionnaire designed to elicit psychotherapy resources was developed. This covered six main areas:

- general and managerial aspects of the service;
- physical resources;
- staff resources;
- training resources;
- identified future training needs;
- priority developments for the future.

In the context of this chapter, the most striking feature of the completed questionnaires was that established services found it relatively easy to collect information even when the service was quite diffuse and extensive. Those districts which had very little service and no strategic development plan found it impossible to complete adequately because of the difficulties in drawing a boundary around what could legitimately be called psychotherapy if a district does not define its service in those terms. The structural properties of the 'psychotherapy service' need, therefore, to be defined before any systematic audit process can be undertaken.

Further points of note arising from this exercise in relation to the project reported here are summarized below:

1   *Structural measures*:

- There was a general lack of seminar, teaching and video facilities for psychotherapy in many departments.
- Many departments had a shortage of consultation rooms and rely on ad hoc use of other facilities.
- Most departments did not have well-developed planning structures. A planning remit was non-existent or ambiguous for many districts, and there was also confusion about responsibility for psychotherapy outside specialist departments.
- The relationship between specialist units and the voluntary sector tended to be unclear.

2   *Therapist provision*:

- Marital, family and child psychotherapy specialisms were almost totally lacking.
- Training plans for *existing* staff tended to be ambiguous, and where they were in place the emphasis was on consolidating skills rather than developing new skills in the light of evidence of effectiveness.
- Despite this, most staff saw themselves as competent across more than one sub-specialism of psychotherapy.
- The data available for planning services was almost totally lacking, and most departments had difficulty defining activity and the balance between modes of therapy.

As a result of this study some particular points were incorporated into the development of the computerized administrative and audit system to assist departments in gathering relevant information:

- An extra module defining level of skill across the main types of therapy was incorporated into the 'therapist's details' section, which in turn could be linked to a therapist by patient-activity analysis, allowing more specific monitoring of skill mix by patient activity.
- Even well-developed departments have experienced great difficulty in identifying the number of patients treated by each mode of therapy, and trends in their data. A basic information system to run a department would need to have the capacity to measure total numbers in the different types of therapy, numbers on waiting lists and numbers recently taken on for therapy.

In the course of the survey it became clear that this level of information was important at the clinical level and was required quite independently of the need for managers to manage contracts.

Since the completion of this project the need for 'billing' systems to manage complex contracts with fundholding practices has been recognized. There is perhaps an argument for integrating this type of information system with clinical systems, but the caveats raised earlier in the chapter (about data security, ownership, confidentiality) still apply, and the slow rate of improvement in technology which might allow integration across systems still makes it difficult for departments to engage in collaborative audit.

Psychotherapy audit programme: introducing audit

Reliability of psychotherapy assessments

A particularly important point in the management of resources within a psychotherapy department is the assessment and allocation of a patient to a mode of treatment. The cost of treatment is clearly a function involving a number of sessions as well as type of treatment. The project team was concerned about the consistency of decision-making among assessors, as they play a key 'gatekeeping' role in resource allocation.

Resource management is extremely complex as there are several interacting factors. Howard and colleagues (Sperry *et al.* 1996) have shown that there is a negatively accelerated curve if length of treatment is plotted against change, i.e. a law of diminishing returns. However, the slope of such a curve varies according to whether the change measures distress, symptoms or interpersonal adjustment. Hence the number of sessions required depends partly on the outcome desired as well as on the difficulty of the case. In some modes of therapy the patients treated may stay in therapy for a time that is convenient for that modality rather than receiving treatment tailored to individual need. For example, some groups have fixed lengths or pre-planned breaks when members tend to leave.

A further complication in many departments is the need to plan the workload of staff, who may be attached for fairly short periods. This has led to many departments offering fixed-length therapies, which have the advantage of predictability and a safe structure within which a patient can work on given tasks, but there is clearly a loss of flexibility as a consequence. The most difficult issue is to know what is 'enough', particularly when diffuse goals like 'improved relationships' or 'greater confidence' are sought.

Ideally, a system would match resources offered with type of problem, expected difficulty and outcome. In the interim an alternative approach had to be developed which would allow comparison between and within departments. The method developed relies on case vignettes which elicit ratings of suitability for different subtypes of therapy (long-term individual psychodynamic, short-term focal individual psychodynamic, structured short-term individual, analytic group, structured group, family or marital therapy, psychotherapy day programme, psychotherapy inpatient programme, and other). Each is rated on a 1–7 Likert scale, where 1 equals 'totally unsuitable' and 7 means 'ideally suitable'.

In addition, the respondent is given the opportunity to describe the 'ideal' treatment and what would probably be offered 'in practice' given resources currently available. Finally, the raters were asked to use a 0–100 scale of global dysfunction for (1) symptoms and distress and (2) disability. After the ratings for the seven cases described had been filled in, a group discussion was held to explore the nature of the decision-making and problems arising.

The results of the initial pilot study are presented here based on a workshop for staff involved in the main psychotherapy departments in this region and some preliminary data from lay raters. The seven case vignettes were prepared giving extensive background information, details of the current problem, response during the interview and the therapist's response. Care was taken to exclude overt cues about the therapy eventually offered. Two examples are summarized briefly here. Each case vignette would have been about five pages of typescript.

CASE I

This involved a 36-year-old divorced woman with recurrent relationship problems. Warm feelings were noted in the countertransference and the patient was thought to be psychologically minded. There were pervasive guilt feelings but these were not disabling. Her mother had been chronically ill during the patient's childhood. (The assessor had actually thought her suitable for a dynamic approach and she in fact did very well in brief dynamic psychotherapy, although these facts were not known to the raters.)

CASE 7

This involved a 46-year-old divorced woman referred with depression after her husband left her. Several statements about suicide had been made. There was a history of long-standing marital violence. Alternating idealization and denigration of the therapist was noted. Her aim for therapy was to 'sort things out'. Little or no awareness was apparent on trial interpretations (the assessor in fact thought her unsuitable for a dynamic approach but offered supportive therapy with the possibility of couple therapy if her husband returned).

The other five case vignettes covered a range of different actual outcomes and levels of difficulty, and a mix of socio-demographic details.

Even on this pilot data, clear discriminations could be seen between patients on overall suitability. This was reflected also in the distribution of scores for each type of therapy. A striking finding was the close similarity between ratings of suitability for long-term individual dynamic therapy and short-term focal dynamic therapy. In discussion it became clear that patients who were thought suitable for short-term dynamic therapy were indeed thought to be suitable for long-term therapy, but a differentiation would have been made in terms of the level of exploration necessary to achieve particular goals. For the more 'difficult' patients there was a wider spread of ratings, which also revealed personal preferences amongst the therapists, for example for day programmes or for structured brief therapy.

Discrepancies between ideal therapies and those actually offered were difficult to analyse systematically. Two main differences were apparent. First, some therapists clearly held the view that 'more was better', i.e. that individual therapy ideally involved more than one session per week, but that this was rarely available in NHS settings. Second, some therapists suggested day programmes as the 'actual' therapy, but with the ideal situation being a year or more individual therapy if resources permitted. In discussion it seemed that experienced therapists tend to follow a decision tree of assessing overall suitability, then matching the individual's preferences and needs to resources available. This model is quite different from the assessment of the suitability of each therapy for each individual patient according to likely costs and benefits which the 'rational decision-making' model would suggest.

Despite the limitations of this exercise, there did seem to be a reasonable consensus on overall suitability and also on the preferred type of therapy for most of the examples, given the expected finding that individual therapists would tend to show some bias towards the types of therapy they were most familiar with. In actual fact, the biases apparent between departments were not very marked, but did occur most obviously where the patient was complex and of uncertain suitability. Major differences occurred between ratings of suitability for brief structured therapy (such as cognitive analytic therapy), as some therapists experienced in that field rated this type of therapy much higher than others who had little experience.

The exercise fulfilled most of the primary aims, i.e. discussion took place between units on clinical issues exploring differences and similarities in key decision-making. Furthermore, some clarification was gained about the nature of expert knowledge being used in this task, and this is being incorporated into the advanced training programmes in the region.

The process of clinical decision-making emerged as a complex mix of 'probabilistic expertise' based on detection of specific cues about suitability, while also using a pattern-matching mode – that is, 'recognizing' a type of patient the assessor associates with particular therapies. To some extent this is appropriate (for example identifying cues related to long-term relationship dysfunction as opposed to recent crisis, which does predict outcome), but it is in danger of becoming a self-fulfilling prophecy by pre-selecting patients merely on the basis of similarity to patients already being treated. A third mode of decision-making which only came out in discussion was a subtle mix related to resource utilization. Decisions were based on knowledge about effectiveness, the need to maintain the basic service infrastructure (e.g. where vacancies threaten the continued viability of a therapeutic group) and, finally, a discussion of likely costs, risks and benefits with the patient. This model is a rational one when relatively little is known about predictions of outcome, but indicators of risk need to be taken into account where differentiation of outcome by type of treatment is unclear, and where the patients' engagement in therapy can be maximized by them taking part in a decision-making process.

What became clear during the course of this work was that clinicians use a sophisticated set of judgements which involved the interaction of risks, patient preference and desired outcome. This complexity has not been taken into account in previous attempts to apply research findings in clinical practice.

Audit of assessment letters

Assessment letters are written after a new or existing patient attends for an extended assessment, where the outcome of the assessment determines the patient's subsequent treatment. Although it is often written in the form of a letter, usually addressed to the referrer, the full assessment may not actually be sent to anyone, but a copy is always retained in the case notes. The assessment letter may be all that is available in the notes to allow a therapist to decide if it is appropriate to take the patient off a waiting list and into therapy. Since the assessment is such an important stage in the administration of patients in psychotherapy the letter must be very detailed and must contain all the salient facts about the case, the patient's history and current situation, and the suggested mode of treatment if further psychotherapy is thought appropriate. This need for a lot of detail means that assessment letters can be very long, and it is difficult to ensure that *all* relevant details are included.

The audit started when the problem of defective assessment letters was raised, where it was thought that not all the necessary information was being recorded in every assessment letter. In the first instance, criteria were set by identifying a list of items which were thought by the group of clinicians to be important in assessment. We identified that some items were 'taken for granted' and were therefore not available when another therapist (who had never met the patient) was making a decision whether to take on the patient for a course of therapy. Forty sets of case notes were studied, and information was judged to be absent, mentioned, described adequately, described well or not applicable. Each item was then examined for the pool of patients and it was decided to dichotomize the scores into generally adequate or generally inadequate reporting. A review of all items then took place to decide which, if any, could be discarded. In this case it was decided that none should be discarded but that some might be relevant only for a proportion of patients. In this way a list of agreed items was confirmed. Further discussion then took place about how to achieve better recording. The possibility of a checklist was considered but the raters all agreed that the clinical 'feel' of a letter was an essential part of the communication process. It was agreed that some key items of information would be included in the computerized system but that the narrative format of the letters would continue.

Results

An agreed policy was defined, which was to state all necessary items, highlighting which ones had previously been recorded inadequately, for the attention of all clinicians carrying out assessments. A variety of different methods of prompting were discussed but it was left to individual clinicians to decide whether to use a pro forma. The Psychotherapy Patient Administration and Audit System (PSYPAS) system incorporates into its assessment form and life history form many of these crucial items to improve recording. The results of the initial development of relevant assessment items is given in Table 5.1, and information about which items were included in the database and which were recorded more frequently at the re-audit. The audit was repeated in 1993/4 after the implementation of the computerized system. It can be seen that many items were included and the recording of information improved on almost all of the items.

Of the fifteen items which had been highlighted as particularly poorly recorded, ten were included in the database and all showed definite improvement in recording (although one – outside interests – did not seem to capture the relevant clinical sense and so is marked as possible). Those items which were not incorporated in the database were much more difficult to re-audit, but three (coping style, use of symbols and dreams, and risk predictors) appeared to be better recorded in a small case-note sample, and two (family history and whether the patient had been given information about the waiting list) were not apparently altered from the case-note review.

Taken at face value, this confirms the effectiveness of incorporating desired items into a checklist. However, the limited information on a checklist about, for example, early family environment, is unlikely to be as informative as a narrative account, and we would strongly recommend combining both checklists and letter formats to improve the recording of relevant information.

Table 5.1 Summary of changes after audit

Information	Poor prior performance (from case-note review)	Included in database	Improved on re-audit
Demographic			
Age		*	*
Gender		*	*
Ethnic origin	*	*	*
Referrer		*	*
Occupation		*	*
Civil status		*	*
Health professional		*	*
Date seen	*	*	*
History			
Presenting complaint		*	*
Current psychiatric diagnosis		*	*
Previous psychiatric history			
Relevant medical history		*	*
Family history	*		
Medication	*	*	*
Abuse of medication		*	*
Illicit drugs	*	*	*
Alcohol abuse	*	*	*
Self-harm	*	*	*
Violence	*	*	*
Early history			
Childhood experience		*	*
Family atmosphere			
Parents and siblings		*	*
Early loss			
School history			
Peer relationships			
Abuse	*	*	*
Adult history			
Relationships – work			
Relationships – friendships			
Relationships – sexual			
Children	*	*	*
Adult losses			
Interests	*	*	•
Coping style	*		•

Table 5.1 continued

Information	Poor performance (from case-note review)	Included in database	Improved on re-audit
Material from session			
Behaviour in session			
Symbols/dreams	*		•
Able to use feeling language			
Able to use interpretations			
Experience of previous therapy			
Decisions			
Suitability for preferred therapy			
Alternative options			
Focus/problem areas		*	*
Recommended therapy		*	*
Predictions about progress			•
Risk factors	*		•
Administrative information			
Times not available		*	*
Preference re. gender of therapist		*	*
Other professionals involved		*	*
Medication and prescribing		*	*
Contact if review needed		*	*
Waiting-list information	*		

Notes:
* = definite
• = possible

The technology

The Psychotherapy Patient Administration and Audit System (PSYPAS): introduction and aims

The patient administration system described here evolved out of manual paper-based administration systems in use in several psychotherapy services in the North-West and Merseyside regions. A system based on index cards had proved to be effective when staff commitment was high, but it was impossible for such a system to be fail-safe, and missing data was not apparent until it was needed and found to be absent. Much clerical time was spent in maintaining the records, which were often found to be rather out of date, and confidence in the system slowly declined. Although in theory it would have been possible to derive audit and research information straight from the cards, in practice both the inaccuracy of the information and the length of time it would take to collate the patient data prevented any audit work being done using the index cards as source material. Administration work could take place with difficulty, but usually demanded that the cards at a particular stage within the system had to be examined one by one, and action taken as a result of this lengthy procedure. Updating the psychotherapy waiting lists was an immense task, involving rewriting the entire lists by hand.

One of the initial aims of the PSYPAS project was therefore to increase the efficiency of patient administration by replacing the index-card system with a computer-based database system to administer the progress of patients through a Psychotherapy Department. As the programming work developed, it started to become obvious that this program not only would be a very attractive substitute for manual administration systems, but would also be useful for other psychotherapy practitioners. This has proved to be true, and PSYPAS has become an interesting facility which will appeal to many existing and potential psychotherapy services around the country.

Table 5.2 illustrates the model of how patients progress through the service, from referral to assessment, followed by waiting, treatment and the closure followed by re-assessment or discharge. However, this representation was modified several times (including the addition of a 'hold' facility) in order to capture the complexity of a real department. If this prior work is not done the system will inevitably fall into disuse because the clinicians will have the experience that the model 'does not fit'. We also built in a facility for a patient to have an additional form of treatment, but a different model would be required to reflect the complexity of a multi-modal treatment approach such as a therapeutic milieu day unit.

Table 5.2 A flow diagram of the service

Main pathway↓	Alternative pathway	Action required	Information at this stage
REFERRAL received (Confirm with referrer and or GP) ↓ or →	Not suitable for psychotherapy →	Contact referrer &/or GP and CLOSE AND DISCHARGE	Narrative account from referrer
Contact letter, questionnaire and information pack sent ↓ or →	No response →	Contact patient with repeat questionnaire Contact referrer & GP Continue main path or CLOSE AND DISCHARGE	
Questionnaire received: Consider for ASSESSMENT ↓ or →	No assessment offered →	Contact patient and referrer & GP with explanation and CLOSE AND DISCHARGE	Questionnaire covering demographic, life history, problem areas and previous treatment
ASSESSMENT appointment offered (*) ↓ or →	Refused or did not attend (DNA)→	HOLD, Contact referrer & GP, and patient Continue main path or CLOSE AND DISCHARGE	
ASSESSMENT dates, attendance, notes, assessment report, life history report → or ↓	Dropout	HOLD, Contact referrer & GP, and patient Continue main path or CLOSE AND DISCHARGE	See Assessment table Plus Assessment report Life History report Life events

Table 5.2 continued

Main pathway↓	Alternative pathway	Action required	Information at this stage
Consider TREATMENT options ↓ or →	No treatment offered→	Contact referrer & GP Refer elsewhere (HOLD until accepted) or Reassess go to * (second opinion) or CLOSE AND DISCHARGE	
TREATMENT offered ↓ or →	Not accepted→	Contact referrer & GP Reassess go to * (review) or CLOSE AND DISCHARGE	
TREATMENT accepted: WAITING ↓ or →	Offer review when requested, confirm after 6 months →	Contact referrer & GP as required	Assessment measures repeated
TREATMENT appointment offered (Repeat assessment measures) ↓ or →	Refused or DNA →	HOLD Contact patient and referrer & GP ↓ Continue main path (To reassess go to * then treatment continues or alternative treatment offered) or CLOSE AND DISCHARGE	

Table 5.2 continued

Main pathway↓	Alternative pathway	Action required	Information at this stage
TREATMENT in progress ↓ or →	Treatment suspended or DNA (review needed or other specific action)	HOLD (include review date, action taken and response awaited) Contact referrer & GP ↓ Continue main path (To reassess go to * then treatment continues or alternative treatment offered) or CLOSE AND DISCHARGE	Process narrative Session notes (? extra assessment measures)
TREATMENT completed (for this Course of Care) Repeat assessment measures ↓ or →		Contact referrer & GP	Assessment measures repeated
Follow-up appointment(s) Repeat assessment measures ↓ or→	No follow-up appointment or DNA	Contact referrer & GP with end of therapy report Reassess (go to *) or CLOSE AND DISCHARGE	Assessment measures repeated
CLOSE course of care ? REASSESSMENT Go to * and continue next course of care or↓		Contact referrer & GP with progress report	End of therapy report
DISCHARGE		Contact referrer & GP	

A second aim of introducing a computer-based administration system was to address the lack of patient-related data for use in research, audit or simple management of the department. There was a hope that implementing such a system would also provide statistical and activity information required by the Trust and the Health Authority from each therapist. More important, while using the index-card records it was not possible to determine simple information about how many therapists were associated with the psychotherapy service, which patients were seen when and by whom, or who was supervising all these cases. A positive outcome of the project has been that the situation in this crucial area of administration has been rectified.

A final aim of this part of the project was to use the formal procedure needed to develop a computer program of this sort to create actual procedures and forms for use within a service. The 'best practice' which would be the outcome of discussion in order to produce the best database system could be applied both within our own service and in others, perhaps services containing clinicians with less experience. Procedures and forms have indeed emerged, and are likely to be suitable in many situations: the administrative procedure would serve as a model for a psychotherapy service where none exists at present, for example, or a form we have devised could be used as an aid to assessment carried out by trainees.

During the course of the development work on PSYPAS it proved very valuable to elicit comments and opinions from other psychotherapists around the region and beyond, particularly the staff of the Liverpool Psychotherapy and Consultation Service, who had been actively involved in developing a shared system and who had piloted a system specification. The developing system was demonstrated and presented, in various stages of completeness, at several seminars and to other psychotherapy services. An early version was shown to the annual meeting of the Society for Psychotherapy Research, then at the Computers in Psychiatry annual meeting at Keele University.

Overview of the system

Three separate functions of a pychotherapy department are catered for by the PSYPAS system:

- *Patient administration* is handled by the core system, which stores information about each patient referral, and the subsequent progress of that patient through some or all of the stages of assessment, waiting, treatment, close and discharge. Reports can be generated to highlight possible situations where the system has not been updated as the progress and status of the patients change in real life. Waiting lists can be printed as and when updated versions are required, and linked to a regular departmental review. Patient-centred records are created, which store all the relevant information about various stages in the patient's care in an easily accessible yet secure form. Separate records on all therapists associated with the service provide essential information required to manage the department.
- Routine *standard letters* can be printed at every stage of the psychotherapy process, sometimes addressed to the patients and sometimes to the referrers and GPs. This reduces administrative time in producing standard letters, and prompts clinicians to be more rigorous in informing external referrers, clinicians, doctors, therapists and/or GPs of the progress of a patient within psychotherapy and at the close of therapy.
- *Standard reporting processes* are possible since there is potential within the system for a great deal of information to be collected either routinely and systematically or on an ad hoc basis. This information can then be output in a variety of forms, either those provided as standard by the program or in any way that a clinician requires using the program's standard database interrogation procedures. Assessment and life history data can be displayed graphically; questionnaires issued and scored over a period of time can be tabulated and the results plotted on a graph; or a computer record can be made of session notes and consultations, as well as details of the staff working within the psychotherapy service. Standardized clinical information within a service and across the country is achievable, and data can be output in a variety of forms to a number of different software products, for statistical or graphical manipulation.

Design of the system

One major difficulty encountered was in integrating new software with the existing software chosen by professional information technology (IT) managers, who have tended to purchase large systems to run on mainframe computers to which local clinicians have little access. A remarkable array of software is utilized, with a seemingly haphazard link between the needs for information management, physical resources such as computers and the inevitable need to link data across districts – and the implementation of this system in 1990 was inevitably influenced by the state of NHS information management at the time. Given this complexity, the PSYPAS system was designed according to the following characteristics:

- The system should be capable of running on the then standard personal computer (the most common machine found in local services at the time being 286 processors with only 1 megabyte of memory).
- The database should run within an existing software system used extensively in the NHS, preferably with easy access to graphics and word-processing facilities for easy report development. The system should be capable of stand-alone or network implementation.
- The database should be defined so as to allow easy manual comparisons with other departments where systems cannot easily merge data electronically.
- The software should allow for transfer of data files into other software packages and, where possible, between departments.

The project adopted SmartWare II, which was then a standard software package used extensively within the NHS. It fulfils these basic criteria, and a software development could be designed which was user-friendly for the time and menu-driven, but also with the capacity for extensive data interrogation by more skilled staff and easy transfer of data into other software systems. Current systems have improved considerably and all of the criteria listed above are easily achieved by many standard packages with simplified report-writing capacity.

First steps

The first thing to develop was a model of the administrative path of a patient when referred to a psychotherapy service. Once this had been established and verified by comparison with other psychotherapy departments it became possible to design the core databases and programs, which allowed relevant and accurate data to be collected at the appropriate points within this model. This work was carried out in close cooperation with the Liverpool Psychotherapy and Consultation Service, with preliminary system specifications drawn up with the Liverpool University Department of Computer Science.

At the same time as the core administrative procedures were being developed, a research data set was also being discussed with other clinicians around the country. There is always a balance to be attained so that enough data is collected but superfluous data which will not be used is eliminated as far as possible. A minimum data set was discussed and PSYPAS includes the results of that discussion. New techniques also had to be devised so that performance and outcome can be measured as methodically as possible, and the ongoing discussion over performance indicators and outcome measures influenced the design of some of the databases. When the system was reviewed in late 1996 most of the items on the database were still considered to be relevant, although some items could now be specified in a more precise way given the experience of the preceding six years.

The system was left sufficiently flexible to add new outcome measures as they were devised, but the main information system incorporates simple scales on three agreed focal areas and a 0–100 scale on symptoms and functioning to allow comparisons with other departments in terms of case mix and severity. Some of these limitations are related to general problems in devising sensitive and reliable outcome indicators and are not specific to this programme.

However, some limitations of the software had to be taken into account in some circumstances, combined with the difficulty of *defining* some of the clinicians' requirements, let alone the technical difficulty of implementing them. Dealing with therapy groups turned out to pose an insurmountable problem, given the capacity of the systems to manage complex interrelated data and the requirements for confidentiality. A pared-down version of the specification was implemented but the development of a fully integrated system which will manage group therapy turned out to be too complex a task and requires further work. Part of the task is conceptual as it is not clear whether the group or the individual members should be the main element being described. This decision, like many in psychotherapy research, is not primarily technical but depends on the assumptions of the therapists. For example, a therapist may pay particular attention to the 'group as a whole'. The level of recording of data will be fundamentally different if the therapist sees the group as a 'matrix', which would require entries at the individual, group, therapist and subgroup level.

Modern database design will make some of the technical problems easier to solve, but the underlying concept of what is the 'appropriate unit of analysis' is based on a value judgement on the part of the user which is in turn affected by theoretical assumptions.

In other areas the limitation turned out to be one of confidentiality, security and confidence in the system. System security is maintained by having the main file server inaccessible and by the use of passwords. These aspects of system security with back-up procedures have been sufficient to date, but in recent discussions about redesigning the system it is clear that the standards for data security need to be higher now that the file server is part of a Trust-wide system which is ultimately linked to the NHS network. In our view, any modern system should have data encryption as an automatic process rather than an optional facility, and expert advice is needed about password security to prevent unauthorized access. Although the system we designed had the capacity to record notes of individual sessions, we decided not to implement this module as staff did not feel sufficiently secure about the system.

Software implementation

The system is based around twelve separate databases and a program written in the SmartWare II Project Processing language. Use is also made of the spreadsheet module within SmartWare II, which allows quite sophisticated graphical output. Three core databases contain information about referrals, courses of care and therapists, and these three are the only databases which are essential for the system to administer patients. Peripheral databases contain information about appointments, assessment, life history, questionnaires (including two breakdown databases), consultations, groups and session notes. All of these databases changed and evolved as examples were presented to clinicians throughout the project, and feedback was incorporated into the database design. Discussions on minimum data sets allowed new fields to be added and unwanted fields to be removed from most databases.

All records are centred on the patient except for the therapist and consultation records, which are based on therapists. All personal information which identifies a patient is kept in one particular database; all the others are linked to this one by an index number, allocated consecutively by the system as referrals are entered. This enables sharing of research and audit information without risk of loss of confidentiality, and also allows the system to have added security by removing this single database from the system at the end of a day or at weekends, when the risk of theft or tampering with the system is increased.

The software program is simply designed to locate and display the correct record from the appropriate database when the user selects a menu option and enters the patient's or therapist's number or surname. Once the record is located, the user is guided through data entry or amendment with comments and rules to help avoid input of incorrect data. However, there is limited checking for consistency, of dates for example; there is no verification that the waiting end date is after the waiting start date. These checks may be incorporated as time allows.

The PSYPAS program allows controlled access to all the databases by running a menu system under four main headings: Administration, Patient details, Letters & reports and Questionnaires. All options are protected by passwords, and the system also has a screen-blanking facility so that an unattended screen does not continue to display patient details. Most of the data manipulation takes place under the Administration heading; it is here that a user would find the option to move an assessed patient on to a waiting list or to close a course of care and discharge a patient, for example. The Patient details heading allows direct access to all the patient-centred records within the databases, requiring just the patient's name or index number and, occasionally, a course of care number. All letters, reports, graphs and statistics are available under the Letters & reports option, and the Questionnaire facility gives a way to record the issue and return of routine questionnaires, together with scores and breakdowns where appropriate, and can also display these results graphically.

The implementation of all these options took place quite gradually, with the introduction of core administrative needs first. More difficult operations were developed alongside the main implementation, and as users began to become familiar with the system they pointed out flaws and unmet needs as they went along. The core system of referral, administration, assessment, waiting, treatment, close, discharge is now well tested and established, as are the text of letters and the format of reports covering these areas. Appointments are generated routinely, and we have collected assessment and life history data on about 2,000 patients. The text and format of letters and reports can be changed simply, for example to allow for changes in the style of headed note paper used by the Trust. Questionnaires are likely to be comprehensively tested with a current research project which will involve gathering questionnaire information from patients on our waiting lists and those who are undergoing therapy.

A particularly interesting software development is the facility to view graphs immediately, taking data entered on individual assessment ratings, aggregated life history information and questionnaire results. The information is collected from databases using a cross-tabulation and transferred to a spreadsheet, from where a graph is generated. All this is done without requiring user input. After the graph is displayed it can be printed and then the user is returned to the database module at the main operational menu headings. This type of direct visual feedback is likely to encourage users to engage with the data collection and also to review progress of patients regularly.

Software development was undertaken by the project coordinator (Ruth Loebl), with assistance from the staff of Gabriel Scientific Consultancy (GSC) in Stockport. GSC is an established company which supplies and supports SmartWare II, and has now agreed to publicize, market and support PSYPAS. Programming was done on an ad hoc basis, as and when problems emerged during specification, testing and the pilot phase. In retrospect, the system has been remarkably robust in that there have been no system failures over a six-year period, no lapses in security, and the work of the department has gradually assimilated the checking procedures built in to PSYPAS as part of our routine clinical work. The effectiveness of the software system in other departments has not been evaluated formally, but the lack of an agreed support system and the limitations on 'customizing' the system by staff who are not expert in this software language suggest that a strategy for implementing a system across several departments with dedicated software support would be necessary if the goal of information sharing were to be fully realized.

One of the difficulties encountered by other departments has been managing the transition from the previous system to the new version. The project manager for this department (Ruth Loebl) had previous experience elsewhere in industrial settings, and the advice that about half of the resources dedicated to the development of the system should be given to the implementation period turned out to be well founded. As practical advice to any team thinking of developing a computerized audit system, we would suggest that the time taken to implement a system and the problems in the transition period far exceed the time involved in designing and writing the software.

Practical steps towards implementation

As we are a working psychotherapy service, the introduction of brand-new technology and the replacement of index cards with computerized records had to be achieved with the minimum disruption to existing procedures, with as little duplication as possible so that staff would not become hostile because of additional workload, and the new system had to engender confidence in its security, confidentiality and, especially, its accuracy. Once the software was thought to be in a form where the core procedures worked without serious fault we created a schedule for gradual introduction in parallel with existing systems as a pilot. The project coordinator (Ruth Loebl), who was responsible for the software programming, undertook to duplicate some of the administrative work and thus to spotlight where the new program needed adjustment. Throughout the project the emphasis was always on adapting the system to mirror the work of the department, while scrutinizing the work of the department to ensure that current administrative practices were not inefficient.

The first phase of the pilot was to enter all new referrals to the service into PSYPAS and produce the covering letter which accompanies a preliminary questionnaire. This had the added advantage of relieving the clerical staff of the task of producing this letter themselves, while reassuring the coordinator that no referrals were being missed. Once it was established that the computerized system was adequately coping with referrals, existing patients on the waiting lists were added to the system. This entailed a great deal of data entry, since the computer files had to be created right back to the point of referral so that data would be complete. At this stage it became evident how inaccurate the existing manual index cards had become. At this stage it was also possible to print and review the department's waiting lists from PSYPAS. Although some corrections needed to be done to replicate the paper lists with the system version, each time the lists are reprinted this corrective work becomes more manageable. Initially we had expected that the waiting list would eventually become self-correcting, but in practice it has been an aspect of the service which requires a high level of maintenance because it tends to be used by inexperienced staff.

At the point when the project coordinator left the service each of the main functions was overseen by a senior member of staff, and more recently the administration of the department has moved to a more integrated level, where the job definition of one of the administrative staff mirrors the design of the system so that she regularly uses the self-checking procedures within PSYPAS to ensure that therapists continue to keep all of the information up to date. Therefore the implementation of PSYPAS for psychotherapy patient administration has been successfully achieved without compromising accuracy or overloading clerical staff with unreasonable additional data entry, although to some extent we avoided these problems by employing the project coordinator for both data entry and intense scrutiny of each stage of implementation of the software to ensure that accuracy was not compromised. In this respect, it would have been impossible to manage had she not also been the main software programmer.

Implementation for research and audit

There are two competing aspects of a patient administration and audit system. The financial and contracting requirements of the NHS require sophisticated systems in their own right. We have retained some elements for ease of use, but this is now a specialized field for professional data managers. However, the small clinician-developed system has a definite advantage in implementing and developing research and audit. Inevitably, there is a compromise between the two sets of needs. As will be seen in the section on validation, there is considerable overlap between service design, audit and quality control (Parry 1996).

The parts of the system in Manchester which relate to research and audit, as distinct from quality assurance and service evaluation, are:

- appointments;
- assessment and life history reports;
- questionnaires;
- consultations;
- session notes.

These are not part of the core system of patient administration and so were not vital to the pilot phase of testing. In fact, we did include the appointments options in the pilot phase, because of the simplicity of the implementation and the usefulness of being able to print appointment letters straight after data entry. The contents of assessment reports and life history reports were the subject of one of our early audit projects, as a set of criteria for data collection was readily available. Further development was done after consultation with other psychotherapy services, and two revised databases were set up to deal with assessment and life history. About five months into the pilot phase the project clinical leader (Frank Margison) started to collect data for input into these databases and checked their ease of use. There are now over 2,000 records available for analysis, generated by all of the assessing therapists. As a result of this pre-audit work it is now possible to audit effectively areas such as patient mix, ethnicity and communication with referrers, because of the early work which allows precise indicators which can be used to set performance standards with regular monitoring.

One of the advantages of having such monitoring information readily available has been the relative ease of checking progress towards becoming a service which reflects the ethnic mix of the population served by the department, and the system has been able to demonstrate that once patients have been referred there is no apparent bias in treatment allocation. It also shows that there is still a low level of referrals from ethnic minority groups; the solution to this will clearly lie at the level of the referrers rather than in the behaviour of the staff or patients once the referral is made.

A validation exercise

Can the system support audit in the department?

The *process* of audit is much more difficult to validate than the *outcome*. There is always a tendency to assess the usefulness of a strategy against preconceived ideas of what needs to be assessed and measured. In this project we undertook a rather different approach. Fonagy and Higgitt (1989) suggested a list of possible audit topics and different measurement strategies. The list was broad but not intended to be exhaustive. We have used a validation check which involved listing the possible topics and then describing the contribution that this project has made to the investigation of these topics.

While this is clearly not an independent validation, it seemed useful to assess the project in this way as a form of convergent validity check. The results are incorporated into Table 5.3; they show that the project has covered all but one of the suggested topics at some point and that for most topics the PSYPAS system will directly support ongoing audit.

Table 5.3 Validation of audit

Items	Suggested measurement method	How dealt within this project
Speed of response in dealing with referrals	Time	Routine reports available
Range of therapies	Review	District review questionnaire
Quality of initial assessment	Expert review	• Improved assessment and life history forms
		• Assessment letter audit
		• Methods for cross-validating assessment outcome, diagnosis, defined problems
Clarity of diagnosis and formulation	Expert review	• Statement of key problems
		• Clinical audit meeting
		• Review of assessment letters
		• Action to set up a weekly referral and assessment review group
Type and length of therapy	Standard measures and review	Routine report available
Quality of records	Standard measures and review	• Standardized assessment records
		• Rating of completeness of information
		• Optional session reports
		• Additional peer review
Level of training of therapists	Review of CVs	Routine reports of therapist skill/experience level

Table 5.3 continued

Items	Suggested measurement method	How dealt within this project
Level of supervision	Review of frequency/type	1990 review of patients in therapy and 1991 review of supervisor activity
Adequacy of primary-care liaison	Review of medication	Regular contact letters about patient status
Handovers	Sample and review	PSYPAS produces lists of cases on the point of closing or end of course of care and can generate a random sample
Managing crises	Expert review	No specific mechanism (but covered here by psychotherapy audit)
Negative responses	Review attempted suicides	Select cases where measures show no or negative change
Follow-up	Case-note review	• Random list of closed cases generated • Routine reports to prompt action if no contact recorded by a stated date

Does the department do what it thinks it does?

Validating primary diagnosis

The breakdown of referrals by primary diagnosis is broadly consistent with the views of referrers and the specialists in the team (Margison and Stewart 1996). Relatively few patients are referred with a primary diagnosis of psychosis or severe depression. Many referrals have a primary problem of depression and/or anxiety. Some problems such as poor self-esteem and relationship difficulties do not appear as diagnostic labels, and so the degree of agreement cannot be measured precisely from this exercise. However, having identified that the global pattern of referral was consistent with the views expressed by referrers and specialists, it was then possible to carry out an audit of those cases falling outside the expected groups.

All cases with a diagnosis of psychosis were chosen for this audit and identified from the PSYPAS system. The computerized records were then checked, including the list of associated problems and the therapist's summary view. All of these cases were found to have particular reasons for the referral to the service. For example, some involved a patient request for a second opinion about diagnosis, some were assessments to check whether psychotherapy might be an adjunct to medication to reduce relapse rates. This audit was a powerful validation both of the appropriateness of cases referred and that exceptional cases were identified as such, and typically would include a particular reason for the assessment which was made clear in the assessment letter as well as in the therapist's assessment. It was also noted that most of these patients falling outside the normal diagnostic categories were not actually taken on for therapy within the department as the request was typically for a further opinion.

Multiple diagnoses

A further check on internal validity was to look at the overlap of diagnoses when more than one entry was made at a particular point in time. The most common overlap of diagnosis was, as expected, an overlap of a neurosis (principally depression and/or anxiety) linked with a personality disorder; one of the recognized forms of comorbidity. Just under half of all cases had some form of multiple diagnosis, and half of these cases (about 25 per cent of the total) had a dual diagnosis of personality disorder and an episodic illness diagnosis; this confirms the expected difficulty in assessing outcome. In particular, it is known from several studies that the presence of personality disorder has an important bearing on the likely impact of therapy.

Conclusions

Developing a structure for departmental audit

In this chapter we have described the way in which a project team, working closely with the other clinicians in a department, introduced a flexible structure to further audit activities. The validation process has shown that the system can support a range of audit topics and that data are increasingly being used to inform the clinical processes involved in running a service.

The system is a valuable training tool in that it helps trainees to monitor their caseload, to evaluate outcome on clinically relevant topics systematically and to carry out their own explorations of the data set to support audit. Most trainees have been able to carry out, or at least be involved with, the ongoing audit project, and the ease of access of computerized information makes it feasible for quite sophisticated questions to be answered, quality criteria to be set, and the process of change to be monitored and reviewed within the six to twelve months that the trainees work in the department.

The work on developing outcome measures is now sufficiently advanced for routine application in the department's brief therapy work, and it will be extended gradually into long-term therapy. The measures are idiographic and use the shared definition of problem areas of patient and therapist, with two global measures of symptoms and severity. The department is currently involved in developing a core outcome measure which can be given routinely to all patients attending the department, but in the interim the idiographic measures are useful in maintaining and evaluating a focus on agreed goals of therapy.

At the same time, the quality of work can now be systematically and repeatedly evaluated as described in the main text, above. Qualitative evaluation of the care of particular patients has been improved considerably by the establishment of regular audit meetings. The opportunity to select random cases fulfilling specified characteristics has been greatly enhanced by the use of the computerized database. Quantity of work and the maintenance of specified standards for waiting times are now routinely subject to audit and review, and the audit project has been successful in bringing into the institutional life of the department the capacity for self-scrutiny by therapists.

Despite the caveats mentioned at the beginning of the chapter about confidentiality, ownership and ease of use, the department has undergone the transition towards routine audit of practice. However, the system is still in a developmental phase; a number of problems still require resolution. Almost all patients now have a computerized assessment schedule, but the compliance with rating change at the end of therapy is still far from complete.

By having a system which allows systematic appraisal of patient involvement in the department, we have been made painfully aware of the limitations of our service. These aspects of 'process' are easy to measure but not always easy to change. From audit carried out across the whole psychiatry department we know that we have a relatively low failed attendance rate, but the number of patients referred who actually complete a planned course of therapy is still much less than 50 per cent, as some are not considered suitable, some decline therapy, some drop out and some require only advice at the initial interview. This in itself is not necessarily a 'bad' figure, as some patients require only advice or a second opinion, but we do not have sufficient information to know why treatment non-compliance occurs. Perhaps because of the long waiting time between assessment and the start of therapy, some patients fail to engage. It may be that some of these patients have improved and no longer need therapy, but the failure to engage them in the service is still a cause for concern.

The ability to raise systematic questions about the performance of our department can be an uncomfortable experience, and we have often been surprised at our inability even to guess at the level of some parameter without using the systematic audit system. The nature of these questions may still be fundamentally odd for such a personal engagement as psychotherapy. Even clinicians who are familiar with the system, have observed its benefits and are not averse to measuring change in systematic ways still find that there is a profound difference between the experience of meeting a patient for a session and observing that same patient in a disembodied form as part of an audit task.

It is our view, however, that this tension between different world-views can be creative and does not necessarily destroy the essential psychotherapeutic process, but the difficulties need to be acknowledged at the level of different assumptions about the world rather than of technical hitches to the implementation of a system.

The future

The audit systems described here have been designed to support a wide range of future audit projects. Recent audit topics have included a review of the workload and case mix of all staff; comparisons of the view of the main problem of referrer, patient and assessor; and a revision of the waiting-list system. If we were to redesign the computerized system we would make several changes. The software used to design the system has been adequate for our needs, but modern systems have a greater capacity to link with the main hospital administration, there are improved and simplified 'query languages' which are more intuitive to clinicians, and the graphical representations of data need to be modernized. All of these are inevitable with the rapid progress in computing, but the main system has proved to be extremely robust and the basic conceptualization of how patients progress through the department still provides a good basis for analysis.

We have known since the outset that patients do not follow neat pathways through the course of their care. We built in a 'hold' system to cater for all of these eventualities. This is regularly reviewed, and there are fields to cover review date, reason for 'hold' and action to be taken. We have been surprised at just how many patients fall into this ad hoc category (approximately 15 per cent) and by the enormous range of possible reasons – from patients being admitted for concurrent surgery, administrative and contracting issues, and delays when the patient fails to contact. In any revision we would redesign the flowchart so that a range of specified actions can occur (and will be prompted if they do not occur) while the patient is actively in therapy. Contrary to our image of ourselves running a discrete service with clearly defined beginnings and endings, we have found that a large proportion of patients require the sort of liaison with colleagues that might be expected in a general psychiatry clinic. Complying with the requirements of the Care Programme Approach has led to a considerable rethinking of the role of a psychotherapy service in a broader mental health service, and the audit systems we have developed will continue to reflect that changing role.

Acknowledgements

We acknowledge the help and support of the following individuals: Debra Kirby-Mayers, Project Administrator; Sarah Davenport, Consultant Psychiatrist, Mental Health Services of Salford; Else Guthrie, Senior Lecturer in Psychiatry, University of Manchester; Alistair Stewart, Consultant Psychiatrist, Oldham; Alan Horne, Principal Psychotherapist, Gaskell House; and Michael Goepfert, Liverpool Psychotherapy and Consultation Service.

We are also grateful for the support and help of the clinical teams of Gaskell House and other centres in the region; advice from other regional centres via the Society for Psychotherapy Research Service Evaluation Group; advice from Jenny Firth-Cozens, Yorkshire Regional Audit Coordinator; members of the North-West and

Merseyside Project Team based at Liverpool University Department of Computer Science and the Liverpool Psychotherapy and Consultation Service; and Gabriel Scientific Consultancy, Stockport.

The work was supported by a grant from the Department of Health, administered through the North-West Regional Health Authority.

References

Crombie, I. K. and Davies, H. T. O. (1991) 'Computers in audit: servants or sirens?', *British Medical Journal* 303: 403–4.

de Lacey, G. (1992) 'What is audit? Why should we be doing it?', *Hospital Update*, June: 458–64.

Fonagy, P. and Higgitt, A. (1989) 'Evaluating the performance of departments of psychotherapy', *Psychoanalytic Psychotherapy* 4: 121–53.

Margison, F. R. and Stewart, A. (1996) 'General practitioner and psychotherapy referrals to a specialist psychotherapy service', *Psychiatric Bulletin: Journal of Trends in Psychiatric Practice* 20: 418–21.

Parry, G. (1992) 'Improving psychotherapy services: applications of research, audit and evaluation', *British Journal of Clinical Psychology* 31: 3–19.

—— (1996) 'Service evaluation and audit methods', in G. Parry and F. N. Watts *Behavioural and Mental Health Research: A Handbook of Skills and Methods*, Hove: Erlbaum (UK) Taylor and Francis.

Sperry, L., Brill, P. L., Howard, K. I. and Grisson, G. R. (1996) 'From clinical trials outcomes research to clinically relevant research on patient progress', *Treatment Outcomes in Psychotherapy and Psychiatric Interventions*, New York: Brunner Mazel.

Chapter 6

Audit and survival

Specialist inpatient psychotherapy in the National Health Service

Bridget Dolan and Kingsley Norton

> And how this audit stands, who knows save Heaven?
>
> (Hamlet: Act III, Scene iii)

Introduction

The role of purchasers within the National Health Service (NHS) is to identify local health needs and meet these in the most cost-effective way. This has to be achieved with finite resources and infinite demands. Since there is no technological fix, scientific method or means of philosophical enquiry for determining purchasing priorities (Klein 1993), decisions regarding which services to purchase and which to ration or cut will be heavily influenced by 'value-for-money' arguments. It is not surprising, then, that the advent of the NHS internal market has made purchasers question whether they should pay for psychotherapy at all (Fahy and Wessley 1993; Healy 1994). Dynamic psychotherapy already has an image problem in today's NHS (Rubin 1994; Marks 1994), and if dynamic psychotherapy services cannot produce evidence of their quality and cost-efficiency their continuing survival in the new NHS will be jeopardized.

Audit in psychotherapy

Although it has been argued that audit has been a part of medical practice since 1518 (Shaw 1990), it is only since the early 1990s that 'medical audit' and 'clinical audit' have found their way, as new terms, into the everyday vocabulary of the NHS. For many, the word audit evokes an official examination of accounts. Auditors are called in to find out who has been fiddling the books or to deal with and distribute assets following bankruptcy. It is unsurprising, therefore, that the advent of audit in the NHS has been viewed with suspicion. Many perceive it as a device to provide ammunition for blaming rather than as a tool to aid and improve clinical practice or service provision.

The etymology of audit lies in *audire*, the Latin for 'to hear'. Simply, an auditor is one who hears. However, auditing is not such a simple one-step process. It is a multi-step procedure, often concentrated on a cycle which is dynamic and, potentially, continuous. In this conception what is heard also needs to be evaluated and, following this, changes need to be implemented if there is to be any improvement of the quality of care to patients. Thus audit is most constructively seen as contributing to a cyclical process of improvement rather than as a device to find out what people are doing wrong (Spender and Cooper 1995).

The audit cycle can be described as measuring how what is happening matches up with what should be happening and, if necessary, refining systems to correct any mismatch. However, this presumes that it what should be done is already known, i.e. that acceptable standards exist against which to measure practice. One of the difficulties in implementing the audit cycle in psychotherapy is that in many areas there are no accepted or adequately defined standards against which to compare practice. For example, when auditing clinical outcomes the paucity of outcome data and, where it does exist, the lack of generalizability of findings mean that for much audit in psychotherapy the first stage required is to set standards for the institution.

This chapter describes how one specialist inpatient psychotherapy unit, Henderson Hospital, has begun to address these issues within its own institution. The studies described are part of an ongoing audit process within the unit, and represent the first attempts to set standards for the unit which will provide the basis for future ongoing cyclical reviews of practice through the audit loop.

Henderson Hospital and audit

Henderson Hospital,[1] comprising an inpatient and outreach psychotherapy team, has responded to a number of challenges posed by the purchaser–provider split since 1991. Some of these challenges are peculiar to the tertiary nature of the unit and its provision of a national service. Potentially, the hospital has to negotiate individual contracts with all UK purchasers of health care (albeit most referrals are from south-east England). The need to market the 'product' of specialist inpatient psychotherapy has become paramount, with issues of quality and cost-efficiency being pre-eminent in persuading purchasers to buy the 'product', thereby maximizing the hospital's potential for continued existence in the health service marketplace.

Medical audit, and later multidisciplinary clinical audit, served initially to increase the staff team's anxiety about the survival of Henderson Hospital in the marketplace. The additional tasks implicit in the audit process were unwelcome. Being used to hearing undeserved complaints regularly from our client group of severely personality disordered patients, even knowing these were often the result of unconscious projective mechanisms, did not lift the communal spirit. It was as if audit would inevitably reveal some central flaw in the service. Like our client group, the staff team seemed to believe that any discovered imperfection, no matter how slight, would have the effect of invalidating, if not annihilating, the whole Henderson edifice. Even the impressive treatment outcome study results from past research work (see Warren and Dolan 1996) offered little solace and no protection from the imagined insidious force of audit. Paranoid perceptions prevailed.

Feeling that we were likely to be damned if we did and damned if we did not embrace audit, we chose the former. At the time it seemed that audit and survival were indivisibly linked, and that any audit undertaken would not only be heard by those inside the institution but also scrutinized by an external 'audience', i.e. the purchasers. This realization meant that special attention was paid to the 'audience' of the audit when devising audit projects and systems.

As a consequence, the unit has engaged in audit at a number of different levels for a number of different audiences, commensurate with national catchment area and tertiary-level status as well as internal institutional needs.

Local-level/internal audit

A range of internal audit projects have been carried out within the hospital which were driven by the need perceived within the unit itself. Some of these audits relate to specific aspects of the clinical programme such as auditing the procedures for filtering new referrals, the conduct of weekly 'surgery' time and the accuracy of the computerized clinical database. Other audit projects, although driven by factors specific to Henderson, may have more general relevance in other units, such as the appraisal of new staff induction procedures or the audit of nursing procedures (the latter carried out jointly with the King's Fund Centre). Essentially, the audience for each of these projects has been the Henderson itself, both patients and staff.

Regional-level audit

As it is a tertiary service, patients reach Henderson Hospital only through other professionals or organizations. Thus a large proportion of audit has explored the interface between the hospital and its surrounding catchment area of the host region (formerly South-West Thames). Such audit is in response to two stimuli: first, the need to improve communications between the various outside agencies so that an appropriate and efficient service is offered to patients; and, second, the need to demonstrate to this outside audience that we are indeed providing a service of acceptable quality, and seeking to identify and improve any shortfalls, where practicable. The regional audience for such audit is demonstrated by the fact that one such project (described in detail below) was funded by the local Regional Health Authority (RHA), with results disseminated to interested parties regionally or wider. Findings from that audit led to the development of an outreach service in 1995, which is itself currently being audited (again funded by regional monies) as part of an ongoing audit cycle (Dolan and Murch 1994).

Supra-regional-level audit

The regionally funded audit project at Henderson has itself been audited in a national 'meta-audit' survey commissioned by the Department of Health to evaluate the progress and impact of audit activities funded by regional audit grants (CASPE 1995).

At a supra-regional level Henderson Hospital has fed into other national audits. In particular, the Reed Committee (which, on behalf of the Department of Health and the Home Office, was conducting a national review of services for mentally disordered offenders) represented a national and centrally organized audit which, importantly, included the needs of personality-disordered patients. Henderson played a part in this audit process both by being audited as a small part of the much larger range of relevant personality-disorder services and by contributing a review of the relevant international literature on the treatment of personality disorder (Dolan and Coid 1993).

The audit process, at all three of these levels, continues to have an impact on the institution, and there has been much to learn from it, in terms of both staff responses to the audit activity and those of external bodies such as purchasers of the service. We shall discuss these issues in relation to some specific audit projects, and outline the growth and development of the institution which has resulted from the use of audit as part of our armoury in the struggle for survival within the NHS.

Audit projects from Henderson Hospital

In 1990 we anticipated that the introduction of the purchaser–provider system into the NHS would leave many specialist units, which had previously enjoyed regional or national central funding, vulnerable within the developing internal market (Dolan and Norton 1990). There were already a number of research studies showing the efficacy of Henderson Hospital in terms of reducing the number of subsequent inpatient admissions, reducing subsequent offending over five-year follow-up (Copas and Whiteley 1976; Copas *et al.* 1984), reducing distress from psychological symptoms (Dolan *et al.* 1992), improving self-esteem and reducing rule-breaking behaviour (Norris 1983). However, all these studies had taken a behaviour- or symptom-focused psychiatric/psychological approach to outcome. Issues of the quality of service clearly extend beyond such quantitative research data; thus it seemed important also to validate the service in terms of satisfaction of the service users themselves. In the first instance, we set out to examine the views of one category of service user who we believed would already be anticipating difficulties with the internal-market system – this being made up of the professionals who referred patients to our service.

Local-level audit

Referrer satisfaction survey

This initial review surveyed 80 professionals from within the local health region who had referred an admitted patient to Henderson Hospital in the period 1986–90. All referrers had been included, regardless of the length of time their client stayed in therapy. The survey asked the referrer: (1) whether they thought their client had been helped by the admission; (2) how satisfied they were with the service offered; (3) to identify specific positive or negative aspects of the service; (4) to suggest improvements in the service and (5) whether they would refer another client for treatment or assessment in the future.

The views of the 66 (82.5 per cent) professional referrers who responded were compiled. The majority felt that admission had been helpful to their client. Only 18 per cent felt admission was unhelpful, although many of these clients had prematurely dropped out of therapy. Three-quarters of respondents expressed their general satisfaction with the service provided. Particularly positive aspects of the Henderson service were commented upon by 28 respondents (48 per cent), mostly relating to the totality of the service provided and to the group assessment procedure. Only 10.6 per cent said they were not satisfied with the overall service. Specific aspects of service with which referrers were dissatisfied included: (1) the discharge procedure and time to discharge summaries being received; (2) the process of assessment taking too long; and (3) the model of therapy used at Henderson (specifically, two referrers felt clients should be given psychotropic drugs, which are never prescribed on the unit). Despite some areas of dissatisfaction, 94 per cent of previous referrers said they would continue to refer suitable clients in the future – it is noteworthy that this included some of those who felt that their recent client had not been helped by admission. (For a fuller report on this study, see Dolan and Norton 1991.)

Impact and importance of the referrers survey for the unit

The main audience for this audit was intended to be Henderson Hospital itself. The project aimed to identify internal issues which could be addressed in the unit to improve our interface with referrers. In response to these audit findings, changes were implemented in the discharge procedure and a system was set up to monitor when discharge information and discharge summaries were sent. From Henderson's point of view, the efficiency of the procedure markedly improved. The survey also made us aware of the need to convey to professionals more accurate or more specific information about the treatment model offered in the unit. It was particularly surprising that something as fundamental as being a psychotropic drug-free unit had not been conveyed accurately to referrers even within the host region. If referrers were not to be given false expectations of the type of treatment their patients would receive at Henderson the communication of such information had to be improved.

One response stemming from this was to design a new brochure, with the help of the Henderson patients (known as residents). This comprised a folder-type cover into which could be slotted a variety of loose-leaf infills, which included information about the unit in three alternative versions for patients, professional referrers and managers; 'typical' residents, by means of short case histories; the selection procedure for choosing new residents; teaching and training provided by Henderson staff; and research and other relevant Henderson publications. It was anticipated that as needs changed these loose-leaf infills could be updated. It is perhaps an example of the iterative audit process that this brochure had a life of only five years before it was decided that the administrative task of filling the cover for the 1,000 or more copies distributed each year was far too labour-intensive. In 1996 the brochure returned to a printed and stapled book format.

For any specialist tertiary-level service professional referrers are the main source of 'business', and this small postal survey, which was not particularly resource-intensive or excessively time-consuming, produced important initial information for the unit on how we were perceived by our referrers. The audit thus had a secondary advantage which had an impact on the regional 'audience' in that it also provided a marketing opportunity, informing those professionals who had not recently referred a client that we were still in business and reminding them that we continued to be a resource they could use. Indeed, we capitalized on this aspect in the wider national sphere by preparing the report for publication in the *Psychiatric Bulletin* (Dolan and Norton 1991), which again provided a means of 'marketing' the unit to an audience of 7,000 psychiatrists who regularly receive this publication.

Regional-level audit: costs of service usage

It is generally accepted that personality-disordered patients have notoriously high service usage and tend to suck in services in a reactive and unproductive way (Perry *et al.* 1985). The severity of their aberrant and antisocial behaviour also means they are not adequately contained in outpatient settings, and many have a history of repeated failed contacts with psychiatric, social, forensic, penal and probation services (Skodol *et al.* 1983). However, the actual *costs* of such service usage had not been calculated for severely personality-disordered patients within the UK.

Despite the encouraging findings from our first survey of referrers, we were aware that in the 'new' NHS 'quality' was not only
about user satisfaction and good treatment outcomes but that 'value
for money' was becoming of increasing importance for survival. The
view of psychotherapy as an unaffordable luxury was particularly
pertinent for our client group of personality-disordered individuals,
who professionals often believe untreatable, or at best view with
pessimism, and who are consequently often seen as less deserving of
resources. Indeed, in 1992 the number of referrals to Henderson
Hospital fell by 25 per cent compared with the two years prior to the
implementation of the purchaser–provider split and the resulting
extra-contractual referral (ECR) system. Only 36.4 per cent of the
ECRs had funding of their treatment agreed in the first year of
the new system. The net effect was that the hospital, which prior to
the NHS reforms had been running at close to full bed occupancy,
had as many as 10 of its 29 beds unoccupied at one point in 1992
(Dolan and Norton 1992).

In 42 per cent of those ECR cases where funding was refused the
reason stated for the refusal was financial. Thus it seemed that many
patients were being refused specialist treatment because their
District Health Authority (DHA) was trying to save money. As the
new contracting system meant that tariffs were produced for hospital
admissions and treatment, it was now easier to establish the annual
costs of the healthcare service usage of our patients. In view of the
impact of financial concerns on the referral rates, we believed that it
was important to explore the value-for-money aspects of the service
in more detail.

To begin assessing this issue we calculated the service-usage costs
of a cohort of 29 patients in the one year *prior* to their admission to
Henderson Hospital. Data on mental health and forensic service
usage in the one year prior to admission to Henderson were collected
retrospectively from three sources: case notes, including information
provided by the referrer; the 'social history form', a questionnaire
completed by all admissions, concerning family, personal and clinical history; and self-report from current residents on a form
specifically asking about the previous year's usage of services.

Financial costs were calculated on the basis of tariffs for 1992/3
requested from the four Thames RHAs, and the average figure was
used. At that time the average cost was £153.20 for a general acute
psychiatric inpatient bed; £173 for a bed in a close supervision unit;
£586 for an outpatient treatment package; and £71 for a day hospital

per day. Average costs of prison detention – £386 per week – were obtained from the Home Office.

In the previous year 21 of the 29 residents (72 per cent) had been inpatients for a total of 293 weeks; 3 (10 per cent) had been in close supervision units for a total of 20 weeks; 23 (86 per cent) had used outpatient services; and 3 (10 per cent) had attended a day hospital for a total of 404 days. Table 6.1 shows the total one-year cost for these 29 patients to be £423,115 (i.e. £14,590 per patient), representing, per capita, a considerable drain on NHS and Home Office resources. Although the use of average figures provided by the four Thames RHAs provides only a rough guideline to national charges, 75 per cent of Henderson referrals come from these four regions. Since the calculation of service usage excluded those costs arising from general practitioner (GP), social services, probation service, and medical or surgical interventions, often precipitated by these patients' frequent impulsive and self-damaging behaviour, these overall costs are likely to be underestimates.

Table 6.1 Estimated costs of mental health and prison service use of twenty-nine residents in the year prior to admission to Henderson Hospital

Service	Units	No. of units	Unit costs (£) min.	mean	max.	Total cost (£) mean
Inpatient beds	days	2,051	73	153.20	242	314,213
Secure psychiatric beds	days	140	111	173.00	258	24,220
Total inpatient costs						338,433
Outpatient assessments	each	6	86	179.00	429	1,074
Outpatient therapy	episodes	16	357	586.00	1,075	9,376
Day hospital	days	404	36	71.00	123	28,684
Total outpatient costs						39,134
Prison	weeks	118	404	386.00	744	45,548
GRAND TOTAL						£423,115

At the time, we argued that those personality-disordered patients who are not treated are likely to continue to be high service users and remain extremely costly to their purchasing DHAs and to the nation as a whole. In order to demonstrate the impact of Henderson Hospital treatment on these costs we applied an audit standard of a 41 per cent reduction in service uptake to these costs. This standard was extrapolated from previous outcome studies at Henderson Hospital, which had shown that 41 per cent of all treated patients were free of psychiatric admissions and conviction in the three years after discharge from Henderson Hospital (Copas *et al.* 1984). On this basis, a 41 per cent reduction in the £423,000 total costs would represent a saving of £173,477 (or £5,982 per patient) per year (Menzies *et al.* 1993). After four years these savings would have outweighed the £675,990 cost of funding the 29 patients' admission to Henderson Hospital.

Impact and importance of the cost of service usage study for the unit

At a time when so much of the NHS was becoming finance-oriented, the effect of being able to produce such figures for purchasers and managers was tremendous. The 'expensive luxury' tag had long haunted the Henderson Hospital service. Now, for the first time, it was clear that it was not that the treatment we offered was costly but that the patients themselves were an extremely costly group. Purchasing bodies could now be made aware that such patients would be a drain on their health service resources (and costly to the nation as a whole) regardless of whether specialist treatment was funded. As a result, it was now easier to justify the input of such specialist resources, which could potentially reduce this cost in the future.

The impact on the audience was substantial. Many purchasers who had previously been sceptical now agreed that our service had demonstrated its worth. In some ways it was even galling that this 'audit' study seemed to be so influential in producing favourable responses from purchasing authorities towards the Henderson Hospital and, thereby, in making future contracting for the unit more secure. As researchers, the study seemed to us to have many methodological shortfalls and to be less robust than the comprehensive three- and five-year follow-up outcome studies which were already available (see, for example, Copas *et al.* 1984). The response to the report showed how it was important to speak to purchasers in the new NHS language of value for money rather than trying to convince them by referring to the number of significant p values and asterisks in our academic research papers! The audience obviously needed audit to be presented to them in a form they could hear.

Closing the audit loop: subsequent cost offset

Despite the favourable response to our 'costs' paper, as it stood it could hardly claim to be audit, as the standards established for general service costs now needed to be used as a true reference point for our current outcomes to see if the current Henderson Hospital treatment performed as well as predicted – that is, whether it produced a 41 per cent reduction in costs over subsequent years. Therefore, subsequent to the publication of the first report the study of service usage continued, with one-year follow-up data collected for 24 of the 29 residents in the original sample (i.e. 83 per cent).

Information on each patient's service usage in the one year subsequent to discharge was obtained from the referrer (in 17 cases) and/or the GP (in 14 cases), and from the client him- or herself (in 7 cases). Costs were calculated using the same methods as earlier, with the new tariffs for 1993/4. The average cost of services used by these 24 residents in the one year prior to admission was £13,966 per person (Table 6.2).

Table 6.2 Service usage in the one year prior to admission: twenty-four residents at 1992/3 tariffs

Service	Units	No. of patients	No. of units	Unit mean (£)	Total cost (£)
Inpatient beds	day	17	1,568	153.20	240,218
Secure psychiatric beds	day	2	140	173.00	24,220
Outpatient assessment	each	6	6	179.00	1,074
Outpatient therapy	episode	12	12	586.00	7,032
Day hospital	day	3	404	71.00	28,684
Prison	week	4	88	386.00	33,968
TOTAL COSTS					£ 335,196
COST PER PATIENT					£ 13,966

Table 6.3 shows the services used in the one year subsequent to discharge. Four subjects had further inpatient admissions, one of whom was readmitted to Henderson. Two people had outpatient assessments, 12 had outpatient treatment and 1 attended a day hospital. None of the residents spent time in prison or a secure psychiatric unit during the year. The average cost of services used was £1,308 per person. This represents an annual saving post-discharge of £12,658, which is a 90 per cent reduction in costs compared with the pre-treatment year. This 90 per cent reduction far exceeded the 41 per cent target set in the first study, albeit that study had a small sample of patients.

Table 6.3 Service in the one year following admission: twenty-four residents at 1993/4 tariffs

Service	Units	No. of patients	No. of units	Unit mean (£)	Total cost (£)
Inpatient beds	day	3	73	179.00	13,962
Henderson Hospital	day	1	50	110.00	5,500
Outpatient assessment	each	2	2	166.00	322
Outpatient therapy	episode	12	12	790.00	9,480
Day hospital	day	1	28	70.00	1,960
TOTAL COSTS					£31,390
COST PER PATIENT					£1,308

Any calculations on this basis must, of course, account for the actual costs of treatment within Henderson Hospital. These 24 patients were treated in the unit for an average of 231 days (one patient left after only one day, while another stayed for a full year); thus the average cost of their treatment at Henderson was £25,641 (231 × £111/day). Should the cost offset continue at a similar rate for subsequent years the cost of admission to Henderson would be recouped in under two years and represent savings thereafter. (A full report of this study is available; see Dolan *et al.* 1996.)

Impact and importance for the unit of conducting the follow-up cost offset study and closing the audit loop

As with the first costs study, this re-audit of service usage after treatment confirmed the impact of our specialist treatment in a particularly relevant aspect of personality disorder – the heavy demand for services. Again it is noteworthy that the two published papers describing this study (Menzies *et al.* 1993; Dolan *et al.* 1996) are the most frequently requested reprints from the hospital. Workers in other units often enquire about the audit methodology and the possibility of replicating the investigation within their own services.

Regional-level audit: service audit

With the initial audit studies successfully completed, there were wider questions to be asked about the interface of Henderson Hospital with other services. Liaison with primary and secondary healthcare professionals is important both at the point of referral and at discharge from Henderson. Given the national catchment area, many discharged residents who require further therapy will continue to be under the care of both primary and secondary service professionals. Improving liaison with primary and secondary health-care teams, both during and after Henderson treatment, may lead to better management of the patient in the community and pre-empt those crises which could lead to further admissions.

Therefore a project was designed to audit the experiences and progress of all patients (including those not admitted) following their referral to Henderson Hospital. The audit intended to identify specific areas of deficit and of good practice in inter-service liaison, and develop procedures to improve these interfaces in future cases. A subsidiary aim of the project was to develop a methodology for audit which could be more widely applicable to other areas of mental health and potentially to other healthcare services. This more ambitious project required a full-time audit coordinator, and thus funding was sought for this from the local RHA.

Audit methodology

The project used the combined methods of qualitative interviewing and survey research. Because of the one-year time frame of the study it was necessary to track cases retrospectively through the referral to discharge process to allow one year to have elapsed since discharge for the admitted patients.

The audit sample consisted of 50 consecutive patients referred from April 1991. These patients, their referrers and their GPs formed the audit sample. The average age at referral of the patient sample group was 27 years (range from 17 to 49 years), and 30 (60 per cent) were male. Thirty-eight of these referrals were made by psychiatrists

(76 per cent); of the remainder, 6 were made by social workers (12 per cent), 2 by GPs (4 per cent), 1 by a probation officer; 1 by a psychologist, 1 by a community mental health nurse and one was a self-referral (2 per cent each).

Approximately half of the referrals (23 – 46 per cent) were admitted to Henderson Hospital following referral; the reasons for non-admission are shown in the table below. The average length of stay of the admitted patients was 6.1 months, although stays ranged from 2 days to 12 months.

Table 6.4 Outcome of 50 SW Thames referrals

Outcome of referral	Number of referrals (%)
Admitted to Henderson	23 (46%)
Accepted but did not attend admission	5 (10%)
Did not attend assessment	10 (20%)
Assessed but not offered admission	4 (8%)
Not offered an assessment	2 (4%)
Referral withdrawn by the referrer	6 (12%)

Users' views of the service

This audit aimed to examine the service users' perceptions of the quality of the service provided by Henderson Hospital, and the perceived strengths and weaknesses of the referral, assessment, admission, discharge procedure. A survey methodology was used to collect quantitative data; however, to assure that questions used in the survey were relevant to the service users, qualitative interviews were initially conducted with five professional referrers, five GPs and five referred patients. Once these interviews had been used to establish the most important issues for service users, a postal questionnaire was sent to the entire audit sample.

Selection of interview subjects

Ten professionals (five referrers and five GPs) from the audit sample were selected for interview. The referrers interviewed represented three different professional groups (three psychiatrists, one social worker and one probation officer). None of the selected professionals refused; however, one GP preferred to be interviewed over the telephone rather than in person. It was felt inappropriate for the audit coordinator to visit the patients alone, so these interviews were conducted over the telephone. All five patients interviewed had attended a selection group; however, they had different referral outcomes – two were admitted, one was turned down for admission, and two were accepted but had cancelled their admission.

Semi-structured interviews

All interviews consisted of open-ended questions regarding the service users' experience of the referral, assessment, admission, discharge process. Interviews were semi-structured, with some specific introductory questions, following which the direction of the interview was determined by each interviewee's answers. The service users first described their experience of the Henderson referral-to-discharge process and specifically asked them to identify any strengths, weaknesses or problems which they felt existed in the system. All interviews were recorded, with the permission of the interviewee, and these recordings were later transcribed. Transcriptions were subsequently studied by the audit coordinator (who conducted the interviews) and a psychologist (who was not present at the interview), and relevant issues raised by interviewees were categorized.

Issues raised at the interviews

The professionals

As anticipated, the interviews identified several issues for the audit of which the audit team were previously unaware. For the professionals, the main area of concern was their knowledge (or lack of knowledge) regarding services provided by Henderson. It was apparent that even one frequent referrer was not as knowledgeable about the range of care provided by Henderson as might be desirable. For example, one consultant psychiatrist thought that a patient of his (who had spent a year at Henderson) had not attended an outpatient aftercare group because she lived too far away, when in fact no such aftercare service was provided at that time. Several professionals were unclear about funding arrangements and actual costs of admission to Henderson. It was apparent that the audit would need to assess the quality and accessibility of information provided by Henderson.

In general, the GPs interviewed knew very little about the service provided by Henderson Hospital, even when, as in two of the cases, they had actually made the referral themselves. One GP said he felt it was not appropriate for him to know too much as he would normally refer his patients on to the catchment-area consultant psychiatrist and he expected the psychiatrist, as a specialist, to know about Henderson and make the decision about referral. However, all but one GP were keen to know more about the treatment a patient might expect to receive at Henderson.

Interviews showed how experiences of the Henderson assessment procedure and selection interview often differed between interviewees. For example, the social worker said that she had felt some confusion about her role in the selection interview; she had accompanied her client to the interview expecting also to be interviewed but she was not invited into the group. Had she known this would be so she felt she would not have attended as she would have preferred her client to have felt more independent from her. In contrast, the probation officer interviewed felt that she should have been encouraged to accompany her client because of the distress he felt after taking part in the selection interview. She felt it would have been beneficial for her to have been there to support him during and after the interview.

Interviews also revealed instances of a lack of communication between Henderson and the other professionals involved with the patient. One GP was unaware that her patient had been admitted to Henderson until a member of the patient's family informed her. She said it would have been useful to have known at the time. Some professionals also commented on the quality of information provided by Henderson following assessment. One psychiatrist said that he had expected a more detailed psychodynamic report following the selection interview.

The patients

Interviews with patients revealed that there was often a misunderstanding about what would happen at the selection-group interview. It seemed that most interviewees thought it was a chance to have a look around the hospital and had not expected to be asked to talk about themselves and their problems with a group of residents and staff. It seemed that, in general, the selection procedure was very anxiety-provoking for patients. However, one interviewee noted that had he known before attending what would happen at selection the whole process would have been even more anxiety-provoking and he may not have turned up!

The two ex-residents both felt that some kind of specific aftercare from Henderson would have been helpful in making the adjustment to the outside world. Both said they had found support in an informal network of ex-residents but noted that not everyone who left Henderson had kept such contact or had access to it. A common theme in all interviews was the need for provision of accurate information about Henderson Hospital.

The survey questionnaire

Following analysis of the interview themes a survey questionnaire was developed for each of the three groups of subjects (referrers, GPs and referred patients) based upon the issues raised at interview. Each questionnaire was divided into four sections, focusing on referral, selection, admission and discharge.

Fifty-two questionnaires were sent out to referrers (two patients had more than one professional involved in the referral) and 38 were returned (73 per cent), of which only 30 were answered (58 per cent). Of the 38 respondents, 22 (77 per cent) were psychiatrists, 3 (10 per cent) were GPs, 2 (7 per cent) were social workers, with 1 probation officer, 1 psychologist and 1 other therapist. In 14 cases (47 per cent) the referrer's patient had subsequently been admitted; 5 (17 per cent) did not attend the selection assessment; 5 (17 per cent) had not been offered admission; 4 (13 per cent) had cancelled the referral; and 2 (7 per cent) had not attended admission.

Information was available on the current GP of 32 of the 50 patients in the audit sample, and questionnaires were sent to these doctors. Twenty-one (66 per cent) were returned; however only 12 of these (38 per cent) had been answered.

Several of the questionnaires sent to patients were returned as unknown at the address given. Attempts were made to establish recent addresses of these patients from the relevant Family Health Service Authorities, but finally only 23 questionnaires were sent out which were not returned undelivered. Nine of these (39 per cent) were returned completed. In order to increase the patient survey numbers the procedure was modified and questionnaires were distributed to 20 current residents at Henderson Hospital, of which 11 (55 per cent) were answered and returned.

Survey results

Responses to the questions on the survey questionnaires are shown in Tables 6.5, 6.6 and 6.7. Not all respondents answered each question. Results shown are the percentage of the total sample of respondents who answered the question. Figures may not add up to 100 per cent as 'don't knows' are not shown.

Referrers' responses

In the main, the referrers felt that they had enough information on aspects of the treatment at Henderson (80 per cent), and over two-thirds of the referrers indicated that they had enough information about the process of referral and assessment and the types of client best suited to treatment at Henderson. However, although this indicated the adequacy of clinical information provided, over half of the referrers felt they needed more information on the costs and outcomes of treatment at Henderson Hospital and information on waiting lists. The need for information on these items reflects the current emphasis on such quality issues within the NHS.

Most referrers (73 per cent) thought that referral to Henderson Hospital could be valuable for patients even when they were not admitted, although in one-third of cases (37 per cent) the referrer felt the referral had been a 'last resort'.

Of those referrers who had a patient assessed at a selection group only two-thirds (67 per cent) could remember having been sent a selection-group report (although all were sent one) and only half found it useful. This indicated a need for Henderson to examine the reports sent after selection and to consider whether they could be made more useful (or memorable) to referrers. The majority of referrers whose patient was refused admission did remember being told why admission was refused.

Only a small minority (13 per cent) felt the waiting time for admission was too long for their patient. However, it was worrying that only 50 per cent of referrers could remember being informed of the admission. The survey asked referrers about the utility of a mid-treatment progress report on their patient. Although at present Henderson does not supply such reports, one referrer said they had received it! However, around half of referrers (43 per cent) said such a report would be useful.

Only 50 per cent of referrers whose patient was admitted remembered being told about the patient's discharge and only 57 per cent remembered being sent a discharge summary. However, of those who did remember receiving such a summary, the majority (88 per cent) found it useful. Overall, half of the referrers said that admission was beneficial for their patient and only 14 per cent felt it had not helped. No referrers felt that the admission had been detrimental to the patient. (NB It should be remembered that the length of stay of this sample of patients varied from two days to twelve months.)

The area which showed most deficit in the survey was the after-care arrangements. Only one-quarter of referrers felt the aftercare arrangements were sufficient and 43 per cent of referrers felt that Henderson should have liaised more on future management of the patient. Almost half of referrers (47 per cent) felt that Henderson should provide the aftercare, although one-third (33 per cent) thought that aftercare should be provided by other agencies. The referrers suggested a range of possible aftercare options, with the largest number (40 per cent) preferring outpatient group therapy.

Table 6.5 Referrers' survey results

WHAT IS YOUR VIEW OF INFORMATION PROVIDED ON...? (ranked responses)		
	More needed (%)	Enough provided (%)
Costs of treatment	53	40
Outcome of treatment	53	40
Waiting lists	53	40
Re-referral process	43	50
Admission procedure	37	57
Discharge procedure	37	57
Assessment and selection	30	63
Characteristics of patients	27	67
Facilities provided	23	67
Referral process	20	73
Treatment model	10	80
	Yes (%)	No (%)
Referral		
Was referral valuable even without admission?	73	17
Was referral a 'last resort' for your patient?	37	47
Selection Group		
Did you receive a selection-group report?	67	10
Was the selection group report useful?	50	43
Were you told why your patient was not selected?	80	–

Table 6.5 continued

*WHAT IS YOUR VIEW OF INFORMATION PROVIDED
ON...? (ranked responses)*

	Yes (%)	No (%)
Did your patient have enough information before the selection group?	58	15
Admission		
Was the waiting time to admission too long?	13	75
Were you informed of the admission?	50	21
Mid treatment		
Did you receive a mid-treatment progress report?	7	–
Do you think you should be sent a mid-treatment report?	43	21
Discharge		
Were you told of your patient's discharge?	50	14
Did you receive a discharge summary?	57	7
Was the discharge summary useful?	88	–
Should Henderson have liaised with you on the future management of your patient?	43	21
Overall view of admission		
Was admission beneficial?	50	14
Was admission detrimental?	0	64
Aftercare		
Was the aftercare arranged sufficient?	21	36
Do you think aftercare should be provided by Henderson?	47	17
Do you think aftercare should be provided by other agencies?	33	23
What form should the aftercare take?		
Individual outpatient	23	
Outpatient group	40	
Day patient	27	
Other	13	

GPs' responses

In common with the referrers, the GPs indicated that they had sufficient information on the treatment model, admission and discharge,
but particularly required more information on outcome of treatment, waiting lists, client characteristics and the selection procedure.
Only 8 per cent of GPs had enough information on treatment
outcome.

One-third of GPs said that the referrer had not told them that they had referred the patient to Henderson Hospital, and a small number (17 per cent) did not know the outcome of referral. Almost one-third (29 per cent) did not know that the patient was admitted to Henderson, although 86 per cent were told at discharge. Of the 71 per cent who received a discharge summary, all found it useful and only 14 per cent felt they should have had more information about the patient's treatment and progress.

Slightly fewer of the GPs than of the referrers (43 per cent) thought that admission had been beneficial for the patient, although, again, none thought it had been detrimental. The GP sample also indicated that aftercare should be provided by Henderson Hospital, with only 8 per cent feeling it should be provided by other agencies. Again, the most frequently recommended aftercare type was out-patient groups (50 per cent).

Table 6.6 GPs' survey results

WHAT IS YOUR VIEW OF INFORMATION PROVIDED ON...? (ranked responses)		
	More needed (%)	Enough provided (%)
Outcome of treatment	75	8
Waiting lists	67	–
Characteristics of patients	58	25
Assessment and selection	58	17
Costs of treatment	53	40
Referral process	50	25
Facilities provided	50	33
Treatment provision	33	33
Treatment model	25	33
Admission procedure	25	17
Discharge procedure	25	17
	Yes (%)	No (%)
Referral		
Did the referrer inform you of your patient's referral?	58	33
Do you know the outcome of the referral?	75	17
Selection group		
Were you informed of the selection-group outcome?	20	20

Table 6.6 continued

WHAT IS YOUR VIEW OF INFORMATION PROVIDED ON...? (ranked responses)	Yes (%)	No (%)
Admission		
Were you informed of the admission?	71	29
Discharge		
Were you told of your patient's discharge?	86	14
Should you have been informed?	71	14
Did you receive a discharge summary?	71	–
Was the discharge summary useful?	100	–
Should Henderson have provided you with any other information about your patient's treatment and progress?	14	57
Overall view of admission		
Was admission beneficial?	43	43
Was admission detrimental?	–	100
Aftercare		
Was the aftercare arranged sufficient?	14	57
Do you think aftercare should be provided by Henderson?	58	8
Do you think aftercare should be provided by other agencies?	8	17
What form should the aftercare take?		
Outpatient group	50	
Individual outpatient	33	
Day patient	33	
Other	8	

Patients' responses

The survey of patients showed that the vast majority felt that more information would be needed on all aspects of the Henderson Hospital and the admission and discharge process. The only feature on which respondents seemed adequately informed was the length of stay.

Although all patients were made aware that they had been referred to Henderson, one-third were not told anything about the unit and in only 50 per cent of cases did the referrer discuss the referral with the patient. Most patients said they would have liked more information at that time, although some general information was given.

Three-quarters of the patients said they knew about the selection group before it happened, although the majority of this information had come direct from the Henderson, either from the brochure or by being told on arrival; very few (20 per cent) had been told what to expect by their referrer. Once the patient had been admitted to the Henderson there was a generally positive report on the process of admission and the information handed over. (At present, on arrival new admissions join a special group called 'unit reception', where two existing residents greet the new community member and explain rules and other aspects of the unit to them.) Similarly, of the two-thirds of discharged residents who attended the leavers' group (a special weekly group for residents to prepare for leaving), the majority (67 per cent) found it helpful.

In common with the professional referrers, two-thirds of the residents felt that aftercare should be provided by Henderson, although this was not exclusive, as 56 per cent thought outside agencies should also provide aftercare. The residents showed no overall preference for the type of aftercare, with one-third each recommending outpatient groups, outpatient individual work and day-patient attendance.

Table 6.7 Residents' survey results

WHAT IS YOUR VIEW OF INFORMATION PROVIDED ON...? (ranked responses)	More needed (%)	Enough provided (%)
Admission procedure	70	30
Treatment model	65	30
Type of residents	65	30
Selection process	65	25
Discharge procedure	60	30
Facilities provided	55	40
Length of stay	20	80
Referral Do you know who referred you to Henderson Hospital?	100	–
Did they tell you they had made referal?	100	–
Did they tell you anything about Henderson Hospital?	65	35
Did they discuss the referral with you?	50	50
Would you have liked more information?	75	25
Did they say why Henderson Hospital might be helpful?	75	25
Were you given enough general information?	20	60

Table 6.7 continued

WHAT IS YOUR VIEW OF INFORMATION PROVIDED ON...? (ranked responses)

Selection group

Did you know what the selection group was for before it happened?	75	25
If NO, would you have found it helpful to have been told?	100	–
If YES, how did you know?		
GP told me	0	
Referrer told me	20	
Brochure	35	
Letter	25	
Told on arrival	30	
Other	10	

Admission

Did you find unit reception group helpful?	80	10
Was the information given to you on arrival helpful?	75	15
Overall, did you find admission helpful?	70	10

Discharge (The following results are from audit sample only)

Did you attend the leavers' group?	67	33
If yes, did you find it helpful?	67	33

Post-discharge follow-up and support

Do you think aftercare should be provided by Henderson?	67	33
Do you think aftercare should be provided by other agencies?	56	33
What form do you think aftercare should take?		
Individual outpatient	33	
Outpatient group	33	
Day patient	33	
Other	22	

The varied views of the residents towards preparation for leaving and possible types of aftercare are shown in the responses on this issue in the open comments part of the survey, which are all shown in Appendix 1. Some saw aftercare and continuing contact with Henderson Hospital as essential, while others felt that it was important to separate from the unit and stand on their own feet. Others preferred an intermediary option, such as occasional visits to the unit or provision of a halfway house. Some responses also highlight the difficulty of providing aftercare when residents discharge themselves from Henderson impulsively or in an unplanned way at an early point in their stay.

Impact and consequences of the survey results for the unit

The study highlighted several areas of information still needed by users of the service. In response to this the hospital brochure, which had been changed after the 1991 audit survey, was again reviewed, and changes were made to the content and clarity of the information distributed.

However, the major issue arising was the perceived need for aftercare following inpatient treatment at Henderson Hospital. In particular, 43 per cent of referrers wanted better liaison with Henderson at discharge and over aftercare. Only 21 per cent of referrers thought our aftercare arrangements were sufficient; 40 per cent felt that Henderson should provide an outpatient group follow-up service. The majority of ex-residents thought that more aftercare should be provided by Henderson Hospital.

The unit responded to these findings by proposing to develop an outreach service, which would provide a multidisciplinary peripatetic assessment, treatment and supervision service for patients with personality disorder; this was to include not only those who had been discharged from Henderson Hospital but also other personality-disordered patients who, for whatever reason, were deemed inappropriate for inpatient psychotherapy. Treatment and support are provided in group and individual settings. In addition, a major part of the service is supervision and joint working with local community mental health teams who require support and help with managing personality-disordered patients within their local facilities. The service aims to provide the following:

1 An *assessment* service for personality-disordered patients throughout the region where local teams require second opinions or specialist advice on management of difficult cases.
2 A *supervision* and *joint-working* service for local teams who require support and help with managing personality-disordered patients within their own local facilities (whether outpatient, day-patient or inpatient settings).
3 A *treatment* service for those severely personality-disordered

patients who are appropriate for management by the outreach service team in an outpatient setting.

4   An *aftercare* service for those who have completed specialist inpatient treatment and require further outpatient follow-up treatment.

In establishing the Outreach Service, Henderson aims to extend the existing inpatient specialist (tertiary) treatment to secondary (general psychiatric) and primary-care levels. It is hoped that this will evolve into a service which extends the therapeutic community model of working into community services and will disseminate specialist skills through joint working with teams local to patients' usual residence. Thus clinics are held at several sites throughout the region which are accessible to patients, and the specialist approach aims to cascade expertise in the management of difficult clients down to local teams and emphasizes the need for clear communication between professional groups.

Obviously, proposing such an innovative service at a time of budgetary limitations and cutbacks in the NHS would have been unrealizable had there not been the audit information to back up the proposal with evaluative/cost-offset figures alongside it showing the value of the existing inpatient service. In addition, the proposed service was in line with the recommendations of the interdepartmental government Reed Review of Services for Mentally Disordered Offenders (Reed 1994). This had emphasized the dearth of services for personality disorder nationally and recommended that the Care Programme Approach be implemented for those with severe personality disorder leaving hospital, with patients being treated in the minimum level of security and as close to their own homes as possible. The report specifically encouraged purchasing authorities to ensure planning for the health needs of personality-disordered patients in purchasing plans.

The three district purchasing consortia in the South Thames (West) region agreed contracts to fund the Henderson Outreach Service in 1995. An ongoing audit of the service (again funded by regional audit monies) will establish standards for this new service and continue the audit cycle in the future.

Conclusions

A democratic therapeutic community approach, which is often seen as occupying a marginal position with reference to mainstream medical model approaches, might be thought to have had difficulty in accepting clinical audit, especially when it is seen to derive from the 'parent' NHS itself. Yet perhaps the success in implementing audit in Henderson Hospital stems from the daily iterative process, where patients and staff are given space to voice concerns and to suggest and develop new ideas. Thus, although we perhaps did not realize this at first, questions about quality were not a new development in Henderson Hospital. When the staff or residents fail to meet the expected standards they are quickly informed of this by their fellow community members.

So far, Henderson Hospital has survived. Whether it would have done so without its audit findings and their broadcast is not known. That we have successfully bid for and obtained external funding for some of our audit projects and were able to budget for a marketing and information manager were important external-reality achievements which lessened our paranoia and existential anxieties. There was something out there waiting to hear us, but it was not all bad, or so we now think. The Henderson Hospital service has developed, albeit slowly and not to the extent that we would wish. Our audit projects have led to improvements in the service and in the way we are perceived, both locally and nationally.

The findings of the audit have empowered the Henderson Hospital to achieve what it required from other agencies, in that local purchasers have been supportive of the development of our outreach service. Nationally, professional referrers seem more aware of the service offered, and at supra-regional level the Department of Health has supported the Henderson Hospital's bid for supra-regional funding and the development of additional units based on the Henderson Hospital model outside south-east England. Only time will tell ultimately how this audit will stand.

Note

1 For detailed descriptions of the unit and the clinical approach, see Whiteley 1980; Norton 1992, 1996; Norton and Dolan 1995; for a compilation of key papers, see Dolan 1996.

*Appendix I: Specific comments from residents
and ex-residents on aftercare and follow-up*

Q. How could the discharge aftercare arrangement be improved?

'More help with housing.'

'Staff kept saying you should try to go without further therapy for a time after leaving. I think this is wrong.' – (and to question on what form aftercare should take – 'I don't know, but I don't think ex-residents should keep coming back to the Hospital itself.')

'Very difficult to answer. Transition back into society is hard. Some aftercare should be available.'

'Maybe arranging to get together once a month for 3–6 months, just to help build up one's confidence, and encourage support, especially to those most in need.'

'Perhaps one day a week at "H" for a period of time, so that adjusting to the "outside" again might be much smoother.'

'Allow to visit once a week socially.'

'Very difficult to know what you are going to need until after leaving and adjusting to being back in the outside world again. Maybe some sort of informal contact point at Henderson would be helpful, even for a limited period. Say 6 months after leaving, for ex-residents and NHS professionals etc. because not many know what the Henderson was about.'

'I think maybe more help could be given with housing and a better quicker system for any reports needed.'

'I think that an ex-ressie should be able to return for a one day group 3–6 months after discharge.'

'A halfway house would be ideal.'

'Provide something like a halfway house for residents to go to – no groups but support for when you leave.'

'Try helping more with accommodation and discuss aftercare arrangements. I know I will dread leaving.'

Q. Do you have any other comments on follow-up and support?

'People who are voted out should be given follow-up care and more definite housing help.'

'It is extremely difficult to explain Henderson to outsiders – I found this quite isolating after discharge. I believe access to support should be available – with people who understand the experience.'

'For me, I did miss the support for the first few months, with staff, as well as residents. At times I felt alone and isolated.'

'Not really because I feel at present it is correct. After treatment you should be capable of arranging your own help outside and separate from the Henderson.'

'I have been left very much on the outside – I have been told, why not get a job! (This proves to me that I am not treatable.) I fell apart without drugs yet when I'm on them – I can't get treated at "H"! (It's ridiculous!)'

'Wasn't given a second chance – received no support or forgiveness.'

'Yes I think that former residents who have not stayed the full one year duration should be allowed aftercare or some support.'

'Henderson is a complete experience in itself and I don't

think formal aftercare by Henderson would be particularly helpful but as above I think maybe more liaison between Henderson and other services after leaving could be helpful. As an ex-resident it is very hard to find an appropriate "place" within the standard psychiatric services or whatever after leaving because you seem to either have to cope alone or become a "patient" again. Doesn't seem to be much in-between outside of Henderson. Liaison/support informally might help overcome this.'

'I think there should be more and better communication between the Henderson and Outside services. The confidentiality rule gets in the way too much.'

'I would like to see a more complete follow-up to make sure ex-residents are coping OK !!!'

'More of it.'

References

CASPE (1995) *A Review of Audit Activity in the Nursing and Therapy Professions*, London: CASPE Research.

Copas, J. and Whiteley, J. S. (1976) 'Predicting success in the treatment of psychopaths', *British Journal of Psychiatry* 129: 388–92.

Copas, J. B., O'Brien, M., Roberts, J. C. and Whiteley, J. S. (1984) 'Treatment outcome in personality disorder: the effect of social, psychological and behavioural variables', *Personality and Individual Differences* 5: 565–73.

Dolan, B. (1996) *Perspectives on Henderson Hospital*, London: Henderson Hospital.

Dolan B. (1996) 'Assessing change: lessons from the literature', in *Understanding the Enigma: Personality Disorder and Offending*, SHSA, London.

Dolan, B. and Coid, J. (1993) *Psychopathic and Antisocial Personality Disorders: Treatment and Research Issues*, London: Gaskell.

Dolan, B. M. and Norton, K. (1991) 'The predicted impact of the NHS bill on the use and funding of a specialist service for personality disordered patients: a survey of clinicians' views', *Psychiatric Bulletin* 15: 402–4.

—— (1992) 'One year after the NHS bill: the extra-contractual referral system at Henderson Hospital', *Psychiatric Bulletin* 16(12): 745–7.

Dolan, B. M., Evans, C. D. H. and Wilson, J. (1992) 'Therapeutic community treatment for personality disordered adults: changes in neurotic symptomatology on follow-up', *International Journal of Social Psychiatry* 38(4): 243–50.

Dolan, B, Warren, F., Norton, K. and Menzies, D. (1996) 'Cost-offset following therapeutic community treatment of personality disorder', *Psychiatric Bulletin* 20: 415–17.

Fahy, T. and Wessley, S. (1993) 'Should purchasers pay for psychotherapy?', *British Medical Journal* 307:'576–7.

Healy, K. (1994) 'Why purchase psychotherapy services?', *British Journal of Psychotherapy* 11(2): 279–83.

Holmes, J. (1994) 'Psychotherapy: a luxury the NHS cannot afford?', *British Medical Journal* 309: 1070–1.

Klein, R. (1993) 'Dimensions of rationing: who should do what?', *British Medical Journal* 307: 309–11.

Marks, I. (1994) 'Psychotherapy: a luxury the NHS cannot afford?', *British Medical Journal* 309: 1071–2.

Menzies, D., Dolan, B. and Norton, K. (1993) 'Funding treatment for personality disorders: are short term savings worth long term costs?', *Psychiatric Bulletin* 17: 517–19.

Norris, M. (1983) 'Changes in patients during treatment at Henderson Hospital therapeutic community during 1977–1981', *British Journal of Medical Psychology* 56: 135–43.

Norton, K. (1992) 'Personality disordered individuals: the Henderson Hospital model of treatment', *Criminal Behaviour and Mental Health*, Vol. 2: 180–91.

Norton K. (1992) 'A culture of enquiry its preservation or loss', *Therapeutic Communities*. Vol. 13(1): 3–26.

Norton K. (1996) 'Management of difficult personality disorder patients', *Advances in Psychiatric Treatment* 2: 202–10.

Norton K. and Dolan B. (1995) 'Acting out and the institutional response', *Journal of Forensic Psychiatry* Vol. 6(2): 317–32.

Perry, J. C., Lavori, P. W. and Hoke, L. (1987) 'A Markow model for predicting levels of psychiatric service use in borderline and antisocial personality disorders and bi-polar type II affective disorder', *Journal of Psychiatric Research* 21(3): 213–32.

Reed, J. (1994) 'Report of the working group on psychopathic disorder', London: Department of Health/Home Office.

Rubin, P. C. (1994) 'Psychotherapy: a luxury the NHS cannot afford?', *British Medical Journal* 309: 1071–2.

Shaw, C. (1990) *Medical Audit: A Hospital Handbook*, London: King's Fund Centre.

Skodol, A. E., Buckley, P. and Charles, E. (1983) 'Is there a characteristic pattern to the treatment history of clinic outpatients with borderline personality disorder?', *Journal of Nervous and Mental Disease* 171(7): 405–10.

Spender, Q. and Cooper, H. (1995) 'The hinterland between audit and research', *ACPP Review* 17(2): 65–73.

Warren, F. and Dolan, B. (1996) 'Treating the untreatable?: TC treatment of severe personality disorder', *Therapeutic Communities* 17(3): 205–16.

Whiteley J. S. (1980) 'The Henderson Hospital: a community study' *International Journal of Therapeutic Communities* Vol. 1(1): 38–57.

Chapter 7

Audit and research

Mary Target

Introduction

This chapter will consider the usefulness of both audit and research studies in a child psychotherapy service, in principle and in practice. As with other contributions in this volume, points will be illustrated from the author's own work, in this case as part of a clinic within the voluntary sector dedicated to child psychoanalysis – the Anna Freud Centre, formerly the Hampstead Clinic, in London.

The context

There has traditionally been a reluctance among psychotherapists, perhaps particularly child psychotherapists, to use audit and empirical research methods to investigate the effectiveness of their treatment. This is partly because psychodynamic therapists have tended to believe that their effectiveness is best demonstrated by clinical case reports. These are presented in the literature to support a theoretical perspective, a procedure followed by Freud and by most analysts since, and only recently seriously challenged within the psychoanalytic world (e.g. Tuckett 1994; Widlöcher 1994; Shapiro 1994). A further important reason for antagonism towards empirical outcome research and audit studies in this area is the question of how to assess improvement in therapy; practitioners usually see symptom change as an inadequate or even irrelevant measure of outcome, and believe that any attempt to quantify process or outcome variables is misguided and fruitless.

It is natural, and common to all forms of treatment, to assume that if a treatment was associated with improvement in a particular case it has caused the improvement and that this supports the theoretical model on which the treatment is based. However, this assumption is in fact valid only if (1) the treatment has been shown to work across other cases also and (2) the theory offers the only plausible explanation for the changes observed. It has been found that a treatment may indeed be effective but that the improvement is not accounted for by the theory. Examples of this can be found in the literature on cognitive behaviour therapy for children (e.g. Kearney and Silverman 1990), where the changes observed did not correspond to the theoretically therapeutic mechanisms. Such a finding is possible only if there are tight predictions of what clinical change (in this case, in depression and obsessive-compulsive symptoms) can be expected to follow from what psychological changes (altered behavioural contingencies or cognitions) or processes in the therapy (work at a behavioural or cognitive level). Such studies relating process and outcome are difficult to implement in psychodynamic work with children, but *not* impossible, as has been shown by Heinicke and Ramsey-Klee (1986), who linked treatment intensity and aspects of psychodynamic functioning, and by Moran and Fonagy (1987), who related conflictual themes in the analytic material of a severely diabetic girl to improvements in metabolic functioning. (These studies are described in more detail later.)

The notion that what is essential about psychodynamic work cannot be measured has contributed to a situation which is usually seen as practical problem, but which in fact turns on an issue of principle. As outcome studies rapidly gather to support the efficacy (at least in a research context) of all other important forms of therapy (Target and Fonagy 1996), child psychoanalysis and psychoanalytic psychotherapy are at an increasing disadvantage in the struggle for credibility and resources within the medical system and wider society. However, this issue of professional survival is not the most important one. There is a very legitimate demand for evidence from patients and their families, who are asked to give up a much larger amount of time than would be required for other forms of therapy, as well as from those who are asked to fund this intensive treatment. We have an obligation to try to show *whether*, *in what ways* and *in which cases* psychoanalytic treatment benefits children and adolescents, and if possible how these benefits compare with those available using alternative therapeutic models.

In what follows I will describe what attempts have been made at evaluation in the area of psychoanalytic psychotherapy for children and young people, and will then argue that well-conducted audit studies have provided important information about the questions posed above, and can be used as a basis for well-focused research studies which might otherwise not be feasible for reasons of scale, cost or acceptability to clinical services.

Research on child therapy outcome

While there have been some systematic studies in the past decades of the outcome of the psychoanalysis across groups of adult patients (e.g. Kernberg *et al.* 1972; Wallerstein 1989; Sashin *et al.* 1975; Weber *et al.* 1985a, 1985b; Kantrowitz *et al.* 1987a, 1987b; Kantrowitz *et al.* 1990a, 1990b, 1990c), there is very little information even on the short-term outcome of psychoanalytic treatment for children. This is in large part a reflection of the more general fact that research in the field of child therapies has very much lagged behind the adult literature, in terms of both number of studies and quality of design (e.g. Barnett *et al.* 1991). This lag has been greater still in the area of psychodynamic therapies, partly because of the traditional antagonism among psychodynamic clinicians towards empirical evaluation mentioned above, but also because of specific methodological difficulties in the design of studies of long-term, intensive treatments, where choosing a suitable control group poses practical and ethical problems, and the treatment goals are relatively difficult to operationalize (usually what is sought is a change in unconscious psychic structure shown through subtle but pervasive personality changes, as opposed to change in more specific symptoms). For these reasons, evaluations of psychodynamic therapies for children have most often been conducted by behaviourally oriented clinicians, as a comparison condition for a trial of behaviour or cognitive behaviour therapy (Shirk and Russell 1992); they have also generally been administered in the form of brief group therapy (to maintain comparability with the other treatment being evaluated) rather than longer-term, individual sessions as would be used in clinical practice (Kazdin *et al.* 1990; Silver and Silver 1983).

Possibly partly for these reasons, *meta-analyses* of child-therapy outcome studies have found psychodynamic and interpersonal therapies to be less effective than behaviourally oriented techniques (Casey and Berman 1985; Weisz *et al.* 1987). Weisz *et al.* (1987), for example, found an effect size exactly twice as great for behavioural therapies (0.88 v. 0.44, $p < 0.05$). A further factor contributing to the difference has been identified by the authors of these meta-analyses, who found in both cases that the difference was reduced to non-significance once outcome measures very close to techniques practised in the behaviour therapy sessions were excluded from the comparison. Nevertheless, it remains a challenging fact that across the three studies, which included some variant of brief psychodynamic therapy, the mean effect size was negligible (0.01). This fact tends to be more memorable for some influential reviewers than the positive findings of individual studies reported later. If the negative findings of the three earlier studies are to be convincingly attributed, as argued by Shirk and Russell (1992), to the use of therapeutic procedures in research studies which would never be expected to be effective in clinical practice, then we must demonstrate the superior effectiveness of the techniques which *are* used clinically. So far, the evidence from meta-analyses of routine clinical work is very dispiriting for psychodynamic therapy, as it is for child therapies of *all* orientations (Weisz and Weiss 1989; Weisz *et al.* 1995), but the very small number of research studies of outcome for this sort of therapy which do use normal clinical procedures give reason to be optimistic, and are summarized below.

The earliest systematic study was begun in the 1960s. Heinicke (1965; Heinicke and Ramsey-Klee 1986) reported an investigation of treatment outcome in a group of children aged 7–10 with developmental reading disorders linked to emotional symptoms. These children received psychoanalytic psychotherapy, either one or four sessions per week for two years. Greater and more sustained improvement was found in the group receiving more frequent therapy. Outcome was measured in terms of the referral problem (reading level) and general academic performance, together with a standardized version of Anna Freud's psychodynamic Diagnostic Profile (Freud 1962).

This study attempted to do two important things: (1) to isolate the impact of treatment frequency, which is of interest in a variety of therapies, and particularly – for practical and theoretical reasons – in psychodynamic treatment; and (2) to measure change in both objective, service-relevant ways and ways consistent with the theoretical perspective. In all these respects, the study was innovative. There were difficulties with it, reflecting the methods prevalent in all outcome research in the 1960s, when the basic design was planned. Thus diagnostic characteristics of the sample were poorly described, the projective tests and diagnostic interview were of unknown reliability, and the therapy was not described in full detail, simply stated to be analytically oriented. The study did, however, clearly raise the possibility that for certain children, perhaps those with comorbid emotional and developmental disorders, intensive psychotherapy may offer more profound benefits than the same type of treatment offered once a week.

Moran and Fonagy carried out a series of studies which overcame the problems of diagnosis and outcome measurement, by choosing a group of physically ill children where difficulty in treating the medical condition was thought to be due to severely self-destructive behaviour, sabotaging the treatment. The group chosen suffered from so-called brittle diabetes, and the studies assessed the effectiveness of adding psychoanalytic treatment to the existing medical care.

The first study (Moran and Fonagy 1987) explored the relationship between metabolic control and the content of psychoanalytic sessions in a single-case study of an adolescent girl. Process reports were rated for the presence of psychodynamic themes; the association of certain themes with subsequent improvement, demonstrated through independent measures of diabetic control, was shown using time-series analysis. The second study (Moran et al. 1991) compared two matched groups of eleven diabetic children with highly abnormal blood-glucose profiles and histories of regular admissions to the hospital. All patients were offered inpatient treatment; for the treatment group fifteen weeks of intensive (three or four sessions per week) psychoanalytic psychotherapy was added. The children in the treatment group showed considerable improvements in diabetic control, maintained at one-year follow-up; those in the comparison group had returned to pre-treatment levels of metabolic control within three months of discharge from the hospital.

The third study (Fonagy and Moran 1990) involved a series of experimental single-case investigations. The effect of brief psychoanalytic treatment on growth rate (measured by changes in height and bone age) was examined in three children whose height had fallen below the 5th percentile for age. In each case, treatment was linked to accelerated growth and a substantial increase in predicted adult height.

A further, ongoing research project should be mentioned – although it did not involve random allocation between groups – because of its attempt to assess outcome in clinically meaningful ways, and for its attention to particularly needy (and costly) children. Lush et al. (1991) compared 35 children in psychotherapy who were fostered or adopted with 13 similar children for whom psychotherapy had been recommended but did not start. The children mostly received weekly sessions for at least one year. For ethical reasons, children could not be randomly allocated to treated and untreated groups; the study was naturalistic. A further drawback from a scientific point of view was that because no measures suitable to the assessment of psychodynamic change existed, measures were developed specially for the study, of unknown reliability or validity. Promising results have been reported on the first 20 children to be treated: 16 cases made 'good progress', as judged by therapists' ratings and generally confirmed by parents' and external clinicians' opinions. An informal comparison was made with 7 similar (but not matched) control children; none of these had improved during the same period.

Finally, Smyrnios and Kirkby (1993) have reported a comparison between 12 sessions of focal psychodynamic psychotherapy and open-ended, non-focused psychodynamic treatment (with a Kleinian orientation) with children aged 5 to 9 years who suffered from emotional disorders (anxiety and depressive symptoms). The mean number of child sessions was 10 for the time-limited condition, and 27 for the unlimited condition. A further, minimal-contact control condition involved assessment and feedback sessions only, with encouragement to the families to work at the goals by themselves. The groups were small, beginning with 10 children per condition, which had fallen to between 6 and 8 by the time of the four-year follow-up. The authors report that, although pre- to post-treatment gains were significant for each condition, by follow-up children in the open-ended condition no longer showed a significant improvement over the pre-treatment levels of symptomatology. Goals were found to be equally well attained at post-treatment and at follow-up in each of the conditions. Teachers' ratings of social adjustment did not show significant improvement for children in any condition, either at post-treatment or at follow-up (there were trends towards improvement for all conditions, and the insignificant results may well reflect the small numbers involved). Essentially, children in the minimal-contact control group showed improvements almost as great as those in the two treatment groups, and on one measure the time-limited treatment group did better than the open-ended one. The authors conclude that it may be most cost-effective to offer assessment and feedback rather than treatment to children such as those in this study.

There are several problems with this study, some acknowledged by the authors. Some of these were as follows: those in the open-ended group were treated by a different therapist, thus therapist skill or commitment may not have been equal in the different conditions; follow-up assessments were biased in favour of the briefer conditions and were not confirmed by the children's teachers; families in the minimal-contact condition were in fact offered regular therapy sessions, so this group was not untreated; the small sample size (down to an average of seven per group at follow-up) casts doubt on generalizability and may have prevented certain trends from reaching statistical significance. Despite these cautions, the study examined highly important questions of whether evaluation alone may be as helpful as treatment and whether offering more treatment produces better outcome. Although the authors intended to investigate the importance of the number of treatment sessions, it may be that the goal-oriented approach of both the time-limited and the minimal-contact groups was helpful, and was the major difference between these groups and the open-ended one. It may also be, as the authors suggest, that the minimal-contact condition inadvertently mobilized a useful sense of agency in the children and parents, by helping them to clarify their goals and then encouraging the family to believe that it could work towards them by itself.

The place of audit studies of child-therapy outcome

Research projects are very costly and complex to mount, especially for long-term, intensive treatment. It is probably not realistic to hope to answer the most important questions – which therapy benefits which children and in which ways – through a randomized controlled trial (RCT) of this form of treatment across all types of clinical problem, if only because the cost of an adequate sample size and long-term, intensive control group (together with the serious ethical objections to this) would be completely prohibitive. This form of research study, with the requirements of manualization, monitoring of treatment process, etc., has also generally felt alien within a psychoanalytic setting, as was suggested earlier, and has generally led to considerable opposition among the clinicians whose work was at issue. Nevertheless, the Anna Freud Centre has long been firmly committed to systematic research, originally to the clinical and conceptual study of groups of cases and more recently, under the leadership of Dr George Moran, Mrs Anne-Marie Sandler and Ms Julia Fabricius, to empirical data collection which can answer questions of effectiveness in ways understandable to the wider world of treatment evaluation in child mental health.

Following George Moran's pioneering work with Peter Fonagy on the efficacy of psychoanalytic treatment in brittle diabetes, described earlier, it was decided that the Centre would undertake a major chart review of the outcome of all cases treated at the centre since 1952. This was a large-scale, very detailed audit of all treated cases, and is offered here as an example of how this type of study, which does not intrude on ongoing clinical work, can nevertheless begin to answer vital questions about the effectiveness of a form of treatment and can produce specific hypotheses for controlled, prospective research studies. It can also, importantly, feed creatively into theoretical development (see Fonagy and Target 1996).

In the study 763 cases already treated at the Anna Freud Centre in either intensive (four or five sessions per week) or non-intensive (one or two sessions per week) psychoanalytic treatment were systematically reviewed (Target 1993; Fonagy and Target 1994, 1996; Target and Fonagy 1994a, 1994b). In coding these records (many covering hundreds of pages), we decided to use standardized behavioural and psychiatric, as well as psychoanalytic, descriptions of the children treated. This allowed much readier comparison between these children and those included in studies of other treatments. Naturally, it made the data of far less psychodynamic interest; on the whole, we did not code the dynamic psychopathology or details of the analytic process, e.g. transference, interpretative work, and so forth. This was not only because we were deliberately aiming to speak to the wider mental health community, rather than to preach our effectiveness to the psychoanalytically converted, but also because to code all the charts for these features of psychopathology and process would have required a vast amount of time from analytically trained clinicians prepared to apply their expertise to the very different discipline of empirical research. Despite this problem, we did in fact try to code a subsample of the charts in this way, using the categories of Anna Freud's Diagnostic Profile (Freud 1962) to code psychopathology at the beginning and end of treatment, and using categories drawn from the Hampstead Index (Sandler 1962), but we found that these could not be coded reliably by two staff members trained at the centre – that is, they could not agree adequately on whether these features were present or not. We therefore decided to work on establishing psychoanalytically based measures which could be used reliably, in parallel with collecting more 'objective' material which could be coded with very high reliability by research workers. The data-collection procedure used has been described in greater detail elsewhere (Fonagy and Target 1994: app.), but it was essentially as described below.

The basis for the study was the extensive documentation on over 800 cases of child psychoanalysis and psychotherapy completed at the Anna Freud Centre over its first forty years. These cases represented children from toddler to adolescent phases of development and all domains of childhood psychopathology: emotional disorders, disruptive disorders and developmental disorders. Approximately 90 per cent of the cases were included; we excluded cases only where treatment was not recommended or did not start following assessment, where the families were known to researchers or, very rarely, where the case was barely documented. The remaining sample was unusual in that most patients (76 per cent) had received full psychoanalytic treatment (four or five times a week) and 40 per cent had been treated by experienced staff members as opposed to trainees.

The material available in most charts included, at a minimum:

- a standard diagnostic profile, based on at least two social-history interviews with parents, a full report of two interviews with the child, projective and cognitive psychological tests, and school reports, often supplemented by observations from the centre's nursery school, toddler group and baby clinic;
- weekly process reports;
- reports of interviews with parents during treatment.

We collected information on over 200 parameters on each of the 763 cases meeting selection criteria for the study, including demographic, diagnostic, clinical and treatment variables. Our main findings were as follows:

- Attrition was low compared to reports of other treatment approaches. Overall, 18 per cent of patients withdrew from treatment within six months, and, as this made it unlikely that an analytic process would have been established and resolved, these children were excluded from further analysis of treatment outcome. We did carry out analyses in an attempt to find out what distinguished early dropouts from other patients, with limited success (for example, adolescents, more disruptive children and those in non-intensive treatment were significantly more likely to break off treatment early; see Fonagy and Target 1996).

- Children with pervasive developmental disorders (e.g. autism) or learning difficulties did not do well, even with prolonged, intensive treatment. Children with serious disruptive disorders also had relatively poor outcomes, unless they also had quite high levels of anxiety.
- Younger children improved significantly more during psychodynamic treatment, and gained additional benefit from four or five sessions per week.
- Anxiety disorders, particularly with specific rather than pervasive symptoms, were associated with a good prognosis. However, among children with emotional disorders in general, severe or pervasive symptomatology responded very well to intensive treatment (four or five sessions per week) but did not usually improve in non-intensive psychotherapy, although this is of course the form of therapy, if any, most often provided to children such as these.
- Predictors of improvement varied considerably between subgroups of the full sample, and by subdividing the sample according to diagnostic group and developmental level it was possible to predict a majority of the variance in outcome within the subgroups.[1]

Using audit as a springboard for research

The retrospective review of treated cases described above enabled us to examine predictors of good and poor outcome across hundreds of cases of children and adolescents treated in psychoanalysis or psychoanalytic psychotherapy. Although work on this scale clearly does not allow us to examine cases in depth and retrospective investigation greatly restricts what can confidently be said about process and outcome, the study produced some clear-cut and relatively robust conclusions of clear clinical relevance. The most important limitation of this investigation, common to any audit, was that there was no untreated control group. This and other defects from a scientific perspective can now be addressed in further studies, which are in fact in progress or being set up at the time of writing. One, which is underway uses some of the same cases in a long-term follow-up, comparing treated cases with those referred but not treated and with their non-referred siblings. This will provide a strong test of the changes recorded in the audit study. We will be able to compare the adult functioning and resilience of treated and untreated children originally referred with similar problems, and will be able to track the development of treated and untreated children from the same families. The first comparison provides a traditional control group to examine the effects of treatment; the second allows an intriguing glimpse at the complexities of individual development, at the questions of whether the particular child referred from a family was really the most disturbed, whether psychoanalytic treatment offers the possibility of restoring that child to the path of normal development, as Anna Freud believed, and to what extent the two siblings then follow comparable pathways through life. We are hoping, by using well-established measures of relevant aspects of adjustment and resilience, to be able to obtain much information of interest to psychoanalysts and to the wider world of developmental psychopathology.

The second study, currently being established, is the first prospective, randomized controlled study of the outcomes of psychodynamic and cognitive behavioural therapies for severely disturbed children, of the kind which our audit suggested were particularly responsive to intensive therapy. The prospective study therefore starts from a specific hypothesis, derived directly from a detailed audit, about the group for which long-term, intensive treatment may be especially needed, and will test it with all the rigour required by the standards of present-day outcome research.

This continuing work is an effort towards expanding the repertoire of psychoanalytic evaluation methodologies, from one originally dependent on hypothesis-generating techniques (case studies, refined and expanded to a large-scale, systematic audit) to one which is able to evaluate rival psychoanalytic hypotheses. We hope to do this with minimum damage, and much potential benefit, to the subtle and complex therapy we are evaluating and trying to help maintain.

Acknowledgements

I am very grateful to the staff of the Anna Freud Centre for fostering my early efforts in both audit and research, in a spirit of open-mindedness and friendship. I am particularly indebted to Professor Peter Fonagy for giving me the opportunity to work with him on numerous projects and ideas, including those described here, and to Dr George Moran for making this possible.

Note

1 Inspired by our first reports of these findings in 1994, the Child and
Adolescent Ambulatory Psychiatric Clinic in Heidelberg has undertaken
a similar retrospective study, with many findings matching ours. It found a
similar superiority in the effectiveness of intensive treatment, as well as a
separate benefit from longer treatment. The clinic also found the same
pattern of declining responsiveness to intensive treatment with age.
Interestingly, it found an interaction between gender and treatment
intensity (wherein girls were more likely to benefit from intensive treatment, after controlling for the age effect); we did not find this.

References

Barnett, R. J., Docherty, J. P. and Frommelt, G. M. (1991) 'A review of
psychotherapy research since 1963', *Journal of the American Academy of
Child and Adolescent Psychiatry* 30: 1–14.

Casey, R. J. and Berman, J. S. (1985) 'The outcome of psychotherapy with
children', *Psychological Bulletin* 98: 388–400.

Fonagy, P. and Moran, G. S. (1990) 'Studies of the efficacy of child psychoanalysis', *Journal of Consulting and Clinical Psychology* 58: 684–95.

Fonagy, P. and Target, M. (1994) 'The efficacy of psycho-analysis for children with disruptive disorders', *Journal of the American Academy of
Child and Adolescent Psychiatry* 33: 45–55.

—— (1996) 'Predictors of outcome in child psychoanalysis: A retrospective
study of 763 cases at the Anna Freud Centre', *Journal of the American
Psychoanalytic Association* 44: 27–77.

Freud, A. (1962) 'Assessment of childhood disturbances', *Psychoanalytic
Study of the Child* 17: 149–58.

Grünbaum, A. (1984) *The Foundations of Psychoanalysis: A Philosophical
Critique*, Berkeley, CA: University of California Press.

Heinicke, C. M. (1965) 'Frequency of psychotherapeutic session as a factor
affecting the child's developmental status', *Psychoanalytic Study of the
Child* 20: 42–98.

Heinicke, C. M. and Ramsey-Klee, D. M. (1986) 'Outcome of child
psychotherapy as a function of frequency of sessions', *Journal of the
American Academy of Child Psychiatry* 25: 247–53.

Kantrowitz, J., Katz, A. and Paolitto, F. (1990a) 'Follow-up of psychoanalysis five to ten years after termination: I. Stability of change', *Journal of
the American Psychoanalytic Association* 38: 471–96.

—— (1990b) 'Follow-up of psychoanalysis five to ten years after termination: II. Development of the self-analytic function', *Journal of the
American Psychoanalytic Association* 38: 637–54.

—— (1990c) 'Follow-up of psychoanalysis five to ten years after termination: III. The relation between the resolution of the transference and the

patient–analyst match', *Journal of the American Psychoanalytic Association* 38: 655–78.

Kantrowitz, J., Paolitto, F., Sashin, J. and Solomon, L. (1987a) 'Changes in the level and quality of object relations in psychoanalysis: follow-up of longitudinal prospective study', *Journal of the American Psychoanalytic Association* 35: 23–46.

—— (1987b) 'The role of reality testing in the outcome of psychoanalysis: follow-up of 22 cases', *Journal of the American Psychoanalytic Association* 35: 367–86.

Kazdin, A. E., Siegel, T. C. and Bass, D. (1990) 'Drawing on clinical practice to inform research on child and adolescent psychotherapy: survey of practitioners', *Professional Psychology: Research and Practice* 21: 189–98.

Kearney, C. A. and Silverman, W. K. (1990) 'Treatment of an adolescent with obsessive-compulsive disorder by alternating response prevention and cognitive therapy: an empirical analysis', *Journal of Behavior Therapy and Experimental Psychiatry* 21: 39–47.

Kernberg, O., Burstein, E. D., Coyne, L., Applebaum, A., Horwitz, L. and Voth, H. (1972) 'Psychotherapy and psychoanalysis: the final report of the Menninger Foundation's Psychotherapy Research Project, *Bulletin of the Menninger Clinic* 36: 1–275.

Lush, D., Boston, M. and Grainger E. (1991) 'Evaluation of psychoanalytic psychotherapy with children: therapists' assessments and predictions', *Psychoanalytic Psychotherapy* 5: 191–234.

Moran, G. S. and Fonagy, P. (1987) 'Psychoanalysis and diabetic control: a single-case study', *British Journal of Medical Psychology* 60: 357–72.

Moran, G., Fonagy, P., Kurtz, A., Bolton, A. and Brook, C. (1991) 'A controlled study of the psychoanalytic treatment of brittle diabetes', *Journal of the American Academy of Child and Adolescent Psychiatry* 30: 926–35.

Sandler, J. (1962) 'The Hampstead Index as an instrument of psychoanalytic research', *International Journal of Psycho-Analysis* 43: 287–91.

Sashin, J., Eldred, S. and Van Amerowgen, S. T. (1975) 'A search for predictive factors in institute supervised cases: a retrospective study of 183 cases from 1959–1966 at the Boston Psychoanalytic Society and Institute', *International Journal of Psychoanalysis* 56: 343–59.

Shapiro, T. (1994) 'Psychoanalytic facts: from the editor's desk', *International Journal of Psychoanalysis* 75: 1225–32.

Shirk, S. R. and Russell, R. L. (1992) 'A reevaluation of estimates of child therapy effectiveness', *Journal of the American Academy of Child and Adolescent Psychiatry* 31: 703–9.

Silver, L. and Silver, B. (1983) 'Clinical practice of child psychiatry: a survey', *Journal of the American Academy of Child and Adolescent Psychiatry* 22: 573–9.

Smyrnios, K. X. and Kirkby, R. J. (1993) 'Long-term comparison of brief versus unlimited psychodynamic treatments with children and their parents', *Journal of Consulting and Clinical Psychology,* 61: 1020–7.

Target, M. (1993) 'The outcome of child psychoanalysis: a retrospective investigation', unpublished doctoral thesis, University of London.

Target, M. and Fonagy, P. (1994a) 'The efficacy of psycho-analysis for children with emotional disorders', *Journal of the American Academy of Child and Adolescent Psychiatry* 33: 361–71.

—— (1994b) 'The efficacy of psychoanalysis for children: developmental considerations', *Journal of the American Academy of Child and Adolescent Psychiatry* 33: 1134–44.

—— (1996) 'The psychological treatment of child and adolescent psychiatric disorders', in A. Roth and P. Fonagy (eds) *What Works for Whom? A Critical Review of Psychotherapy Research,* New York and London: Guilford Press.

Tuckett, D. (1994) 'The conceptualisation and communication of clinical facts in psychoanalysis', *International Journal of Psycho-Analysis* 75: 865–70.

Wallerstein, R. S. (1989) 'The psychotherapy research project of the Menninger Foundation: an overview', *Journal of Consulting and Clinical Psychology* 57: 195–205.

Weber, J., Bachrach, H. and Solomon, M. (1985a) 'Factors associated with the outcome of psychoanalysis: report of the Columbia Psychoanalytic Center Research Project (II)', *International Review of Psychoanalysis* 12: 127–41.

—— (1985b) 'Factors associated with the outcome of psychoanalysis: report of the Columbia Psychoanalytic Center Research Project (III)', *International Review of Psychoanalysis* 12: 251–62.

Weisz, J. R. and Weiss, B. (1989) 'Assessing the effects of clinic-based psychotherapy with children and adolescents', *Journal of Consulting and Clinical Psychology* 57: 741–6.

Weisz., J. R., Donenberg, G. R., Han, S. and Weiss, B. (1995) 'Bridging the gap between laboratory and clinic in child and adolescent psychotherapy', *Journal of Consulting and Clinical Psychology* 63: 688–701.

Weisz, J. R., Weiss, B., Alicke, M. D. and Klotz, M. L. (1987) 'Effectiveness of psychotherapy with children and adolescents: meta-analytic findings for clinicians', *Journal of Consulting and Clinical Psychology* 55: 542–9.

Widlöcher, D. (1994) 'A case is not a fact', *International Journal of Psycho-Analysis* 75: 1233–44.

Chapter 8

Evaluating the outcome of a community-based psychoanalytic psychotherapy service for young people

One-year repeated follow-up

Geoffrey Baruch, Pasco Fearon and Andrew Gerber

Introduction

This chapter describes the findings of an audit of a community-based psychoanalytic psychotherapy service for young people aged between 12 and 25 years which started in 1993. The central focus of the audit and of this chapter is the evaluation of mental health outcome. Elsewhere, Baruch (1995) has described in detail the process of managing the audit and incorporating it into the clinical sphere at the Brandon Centre. Three main factors prompted the audit: first, purchasers' demands for providers of psychotherapy services to demonstrate the effectiveness of their interventions; second, increased competition from new youth-counselling projects for financial support, and hence the need for an established professional psychotherapy clinic like the Brandon Centre to demonstrate empirically the quality of its work; third, a genuine need to know the impact of psychoanalytic psychotherapy on the centre's patient population as a whole.

The model of outcome evaluation we use as part of the Brandon Centre audit is based on that proposed by Fonagy and Higgitt (1989). The main elements are:

- reliable and valid measures;
- using different sources of information, including the patients themselves, the therapists, significant others in the patient's life;

- assessments taken at the beginning of treatment, during treatment, at the end of treatment and at follow-up.

This model represents a compromise between, on the one hand, the need to implement an approach which is acceptable according to current standards governing the assessment of outcome in psychotherapy research (see Fonagy and Higgitt 1989; Roth and Fonagy 1996) and, on the other, the need to maintain the integrity of psychoanalytic psychotherapy as practised in a community-based setting.

Regarding current standards, there is widespread agreement among those working on the evaluation of change of children and young people in psychotherapy about the need to use consistent and accurate measures which take into account the full symptomatic presentation with age. As development proceeds, this presentation often changes predictably without the impact of treatment – hence the need for measures which are sensitive to the impact of development on child and adolescent experience and behaviour. There is also agreement that assessment of change in children and adolescents needs to be made from multiple vantage points. This is because change in the way the young person functions can vary across different contexts and only a multiple-perspective assessment can capture all aspects of functioning. In child mental health, Achenbach and McConaughy note that the differences which may arise when using reports from different informants about a child or adolescent 'are as instructive as agreements, because they can highlight variations in judgements of the child's functioning across situations and interaction partners' (Achenbach and McConaughy 1987: 228). A further reason for cross-informant assessment concerns the possibility of bias affecting the individual's rating. Lambert *et al.* (1986) note that therapists' ratings of a particular construct tend to show a larger degree of change than self-ratings of the same construct. Relatives' views may be biased negatively or positively by their emotional involvement with the young person. Also, adults are not necessarily aware of how anxious or depressed an adolescent is, and these states may be important factors which underlie externalizing problems such as school refusal and substance abuse (see Kolko and Kazdin 1993). The effect of bias on the picture of the young person can hopefully be controlled when there is more than one source of evaluation.

The use of repeated measures of outcome during the course of treatment, as well as measures at the beginning and end of treatment and a follow-up evaluation, is also desirable. Because there is a high rate of attrition among adolescents participating in long-term, open-ended psychotherapy, a valuable opportunity to assess the impact of treatment is lost if evaluation is limited to the beginning and end of treatment. Repeated measures also assist in assessing the relationship between the length of treatment in terms of the number of sessions and the benefit to the young person depending on the symptomatic presentation (Howard et al.1986; Howard et al. 1993; Kordy et al. 1988). This is critical in the treatment of young people because so many drop-out prematurely (Baruch et al., in press). Researchers also stress the need to follow up adolescents after treatment has terminated since a number of studies have shown that they may continue to improve many months after the end of treatment (Levitt 1957; Kolvin et al. 1988). However, this requirement is especially difficult to fulfil with an adolescent population, many of whom are bound to move address during their late teenage years and in early adulthood.

Baruch (1995) has described the careful process of introducing self-report and significant-other forms into psychotherapeutic work at the Brandon Centre. The therapists were understandably anxious that the administration of these forms would interfere with the therapeutic process. Despite these initial anxieties, they are routinely used by all therapists, including adult and child psychoanalysts, child psychotherapists, adult psychotherapists and clinical psychologists. They have found them useful as part of the assessment process at the beginning of treatment, both for the information they provide and for their use as an 'ice-breaker' with some young people who find it difficult to talk about their concerns and anxieties. However, the therapists find the forms can be an interference when they are read-ministered later in treatment since they are bound to intrude on the therapeutic process. Yet, without exception, each therapist has found a way of accommodating them into therapeutic practice by using, if necessary, the young person's response as part of that which can be interpreted both in and out of the transference.

In this chapter we shall focus on our findings after one year using patient self-report data only. As yet, we do not have sufficient significant-other and therapist data to present for this time period. We shall report on the outcome of treatment after a year, the dose–effect relationship between treatment length and the amount of change, and the factors which predict improvement or deterioration – such as diagnostic group, demographic characteristics and therapeutic factors, including method of referral and therapeutic training.

Method

Setting and treatment

The Brandon Centre specializes in the treatment of troubled adolescents and young people with once-weekly, and in a few cases twice-weekly, psychoanalytic psychotherapy. As well as referring themselves, young people are referred by family doctors, teachers, social workers and professionals working with adolescents and young people. The young person's name is put on the waiting list. When a vacancy becomes available the young person is offered an appointment by letter. The assessing psychotherapist treats the young person. Although the boundary between assessment and treatment is flexible, the first three sessions are used for assessment. Usually the psychotherapist explains to the young person that they can meet for three appointments in order to develop an idea of why the young person needs help. The therapist also explains that ongoing help is available and that the length of this can be decided and agreed upon after the third appointment. However, the line between assessment and treatment is often unclear in these early sessions because many young people – especially young people at risk from deliberate self-harm, adolescents in acute anxiety states, or adolescents at risk of being excluded from school because of disruptive behaviour or being in trouble with the police – require immediate intervention as well as assessment. After five appointments most young people have engaged in a therapeutic process and a contract of treatment has been agreed. Most often this consists of open-ended therapy with regular reviews between the therapist and the young person. There is a weekly staff meeting, at which the assessing psychotherapist reports the early encounters with the patient. Unless the patient meets specific exclusion criteria, such as having a clear psychotic illness or being at severe physical risk – for instance due to an eating disorder, drug and alcohol abuse or the threat of suicide, which require immediate psychiatric or other specialist intervention – it is assumed that the therapist will seek to work with the young person in individual treatment.

During the period of study 13 psychotherapists (11 female, two male, aged between 28 and 47 years old; median = 42) have provided treatment. Two therapists were completing training as clinical psychologists, two were completing training as counsellors, two therapists were qualified in counselling as well as having a medical qualification, two were qualified adult psychotherapists, two were qualified adult psychoanalysts and three were qualified child psychotherapists. The length of time qualified staff had worked with young people ranged from five to ten years. Based on their training, the therapeutic approach of the adult psychotherapists, counsellors and clinical psychologists involved therapeutic interventions primarily aimed at supporting the young person's ego functions; the therapeutic approach of the child psychotherapists and psychoanalysts involved therapeutic interventions primarily aimed at interpreting the unconscious conflict behind the young person's presentation. Cases have been allocated randomly except for victims of sexual abuse or rape, who have seen a female therapist, and bereaved young people between 12 and 18 years old and 12–16-year-old adolescents, who have seen one of the child psychotherapists.

Subjects

The sample is drawn from 231 adolescents and young people who used the psychotherapy service for the first time between 1 April 1993 and 31 March 1996. By the time the analysis for this chapter was carried out (November 1996) there were 57 subjects who had been assessed at intake and reassessed at three months, six months and one year, and there were 4 subjects who had been assessed at intake and one year, and either at three months or at six months.

For the total population, the mean age was 18.00 years (SD (standard deviation) = 3.5); 71 per cent were female; 30 per cent lived with a lone parent, 23 per cent lived alone or in hostel accommodation. Thirty-seven per cent were still at school, 25 per cent were in higher education or training and 18 per cent were unemployed; 30 per cent had a boyfriend or girlfriend. Mean score for Global Assessment of Functioning Scale (GAF) was 51.26 (SD = 10.93), i.e. moderate to serious psychological symptoms, or moderate to serious impairment in social, occupational or school functioning: the median score for Severity of Psycho-social Stressors scale was 4 (severe), i.e. acute events such as divorce of parents, unwanted pregnancy or arrest, or enduring circumstances such as harsh or rejecting parents, chronic life-threatening illness in a parent or multiple foster-home placements. The most common principal ICD-10 diagnosis was mood disorder (42 per cent), followed by neurotic, stress-related or somatoform disorder (25 per cent). Mean number of diagnoses was 2.28 (SD = 1.39) and the mean number of problems presented was 6.98 (SD = 4.55); 56 per cent were self-referred; 76.7 per cent lived in Camden and Islington which, based on the Jarman Index, is an area of high social and economic deprivation (Camden and Islington 1994).

Given that this report is based on a relatively small subset of a considerably larger group for whom follow-up data at one year are not yet available, we were keen to establish the representativeness of this group so that we could get a realistic picture of the generalizability of our findings. We found that membership of the reported group was predicted by higher age, self-referral, the absence of conduct disorder and a reduced likelihood of developmental problems (specifically, a significant discriminant function emerged distinguishing those analysed (N = 61) from those not (N = 170), with a Canonical R = 0.28, Wilks Lambda = 0.92, χ^2 = 19.0, $p <$ 0.001). It seemed that these differences largely reflected a broad age-trend within the sample (Roy-Bargman Step-down analysis revealed that, after controlling for age, none of the other intake variables significantly predicted group membership). The mean age of the sample presented in this chapter was 20.0 years (SD 3.5), whereas that for the group for whom data are not yet available was 18.0 (SD 3.5). The analysed group also differed significantly in the number of sessions attended. The sample presented in this chapter had attended considerably more sessions, with a mean of 34.9, compared with a mean of 8.3 for the wider group ($t(229)$ = 14.52, $p <$ 0.0001).

Measures

Young people are assessed with a number of measures by the treating psychotherapist at the beginning of treatment. These measures, including reliabilities, have been presented in detail in an earlier paper (Baruch 1995). The areas of interest assessed include the young person's demographic characteristics, method of referral, psychosocial stressors, overall level of functioning, diagnostic status and current problems. The measures and the areas of interest assessed are summarized in Table 8.1.

Outcome measures

All new patients are administered the Youth Self-report Form (YSR), which is a modified version of the Child Behaviour Checklist (CBCL) developed by Achenbach and Edelbrock (1986, 1987).[1] The

Table 8.1 Measures and areas of interest assessed at intake

Measure	Areas of interest assessed
Standard form	Subject and demographic characteristics, including place of residence, gender, age, main legal carers, family composition, parental characteristics, occupation, education attainment, partner relationship, method of referral (referred v. recommended, i.e. self-referred), ethnicity
Global Assessment of Functioning Scale (American Psychiatric Association 1994)	Overall level of functioning
Severity of Psychosocial Stressors (American Psychiatric Association 1994)	Stressors, including acute events and enduring circumstances
ICD-10 Diagnosis (World Health Organization 1990)	Diagnostic groupings describing psychological problems, principal diagnosis and number of diagnoses
Presentation of problems form	Thirty-nine items grouped into seventeen problem areas describing the young person's current situation

YSR was designed for adolescents between 11 and 18 years old. We have modified the form slightly to make it easier to fill out for young people who are not used to 'American' English, and also to make it more appropriate for older adolescents. The YSR presents the adolescent with 118 statements which are rated according to whether the statement is not true, sometimes true or very true/often true.

The great strength of the YSR is the way it allows a wide range of adolescent disorders to be assessed. Eight syndrome scales have been empirically identified, each of which is associated with a cluster of items on the questionnaire and reflects a common theme, including withdrawn, somatic complaints, anxious/depressed, social problems, thought problems, attention problems, delinquent behaviour and aggressive behaviour. Norms for each syndrome scale, which take account of age and gender, have been calculated by Achenbach and Edelbrock from a carefully chosen sample designed to reflect a cross-section of the American population. Using these norms, it is possible to assign a T-score to the raw scores of each scale, which indicates whether the young person is within the normal or clinical range on a given syndrome scale. For the scales, a T-score of 67 (the 95th percentile) is normally considered to mark the cut-off point between the normal and the clinical ranges.

The syndromes have also been banded together so that scores exist for internalizing problems (including withdrawn, somatic complaints and anxious/depressed), externalizing problems (including aggressive behaviour and delinquent behaviour) and total problems. Norms have been calculated for these scales and the cut-off between the non-clinical and clinical populations is 60.

One-week test–retest reliabilities have been calculated for the YSR syndromes and their totals. The correlation for the internalizing, externalizing and total problems scales was very high ($r = 0.91$) (Achenbach 1991a).

The CBCL has been widely praised in the literature as a highly reliable and valid means of assessing child and adolescent psychopathology, and is relatively easy to administer. Many researchers stress the difficulties, particularly in child and adolescent disorders, of assessing behaviours that are deviant only when seen in combination and when compared in severity with norms for the person's age and gender (King and Noshpitz 1991). The CBCL solves this problem by basing its entire set of results on comparisons with appropriately matched norms. The YSR is the only self-report questionnaire for adolescents which looks at a broad and meaningful range of disturbing behaviours and feelings, and organizes them into relevant disorders.

The YSR is administered by the patient's therapist. The form is administered to all new patients at the beginning of treatment (no later than the second appointment), with follow-ups at three months, six months, a year and thereafter annually. If the young person has finished or dropped out of treatment the form is sent for completion.

Three ways of measuring outcome are used in this report, which presents findings for YSR scores at one year. Outcome has been assessed by examining the change in mean YSR internalizing, externalizing, and total problems scores. The advantage of this method of assessing outcome is that it is sensitive to relative change; for instance, it notes the young person who has a very high clinical score at intake and improves substantially but does not improve enough to get into the non-clinical population.

Outcome has also been assessed by examining the change in numbers from the clinical to the non-clinical range or vice versa. The advantage of this method is that a clinically reliable and valid distinction established by Achenbach and Edelbrock and many others is used. The disadvantage of this method is its insensitivity to relative change.

Finally, outcome has been assessed by categorizing cases according to the presence of statistically reliable change in adaptation level, using the method proposed by Jacobson *et al.* (1984) and modified by Christensen and Mendoza (1986). This uses the standard deviation for each scale, together with the interjudge reliability of the measure, to indicate the size of change necessary to identify cases where change could not be due to measurement error and chance. The index of reliable change in YSR ratings is given by the formula:

$$reliable\ change = 1.96 \times \sqrt{2} \times s \times \sqrt{(1 - rxx)}$$

where rxx is the best estimate of inter-rater reliability. In our data this gives the following reliable change index:

	YSR (points)
Internalizing problems	8
Externalizing problems	7
Total problems	7

Statistical analyses

Before proceeding with the statistical analyses of these outcome data we carried out a series of procedures to check that our sample would meet the general assumptions of the statistical techniques that we anticipated using in this report. In particular, examination of the distribution of internalizing, externalizing and total problems at each of the four time points revealed no serious deviations from univariate normality. Checks were also performed for univariate outliers (cases with unusually high or low scores, SD > 3.0). No cases emerged as outliers by this criterion.

Changes across time were analysed using paired samples, *t*-tests and the Multivariate Approach to Repeated Measures Analysis of Variance in SPSS for Windows 6.0. Stepwise discriminant function analysis was used to identify predictors of positive change in YSR problems using SPSS DISCRIMINANT (SPSS for Windows 6.0). The procedure adopted for these analyses minimized the value of Wilks Lambda.

Results

The results of this one-year follow-up report are presented in two sections. The first deals with the degree of change in self-reported behaviour problems from intake to one-year follow-up as indexed by three assessments of change described above: (1) *mean change*, (2) change from *clinical to non-clinical* status and (3) *reliable change*. This section also examines the relationship between attendance rate and extent of improvement in problem behaviour. The second section describes a series of exploratory analyses aimed at identifying factors associated with positive change at one year.

Evaluating the effectiveness of therapy at one-year follow-up

Mean change

Mean scores for internalizing, externalizing and total problems all showed statistically significant levels of improvement between intake and one year (see Table 8.2). Notably, by one-year follow-up the group averages for internalizing, externalizing and total problems were within the non-clinical range, despite initial scores well within the clinical range for internalizing and total problems.

An examination of mean scores at intake, three months, six months and one year seemed to indicate broad improvement at each point, although greater gains seemed to be made early on, between intake and six months (see Figure 8.1). Unsurprisingly, there were significant differences between these four time points for internalizing, externalizing and total behaviour problems (Repeated Measures Analysis of Variance for internalizing: Wilks Lambda = 0.51, Exact F $(3, 54)$ = 17.23, $p < 0.001$; externalizing: Wilks Lambda = 0.66, Exact F $(3, 54)$ = 9.30, $p < 0.001$; total problems: Wilks Lambda = 0.45, Exact F $(3, 54)$ = 19.82, $p < 0.001$).

Confirming the impression gained from Figure 8.1, significant differences were found in internalizing and total problems between intake and three months (univariate contrasts: F $(1, 56)$ = 41.85, $p <$

Table 8.2 Mean YSR internalizing, externalizing and total problems at intake and one year (*n* = 61)

	Mean (intake)	Standard deviation	Mean (one year)	Standard deviation	t-value (n = 61)
Internalizing	68.07	9.0	59.40	11.4	6.71***
Externalizing	56.0	7.77	51.49	8.71	4.27***
Total	63.8	8.10	54.9	10.23	7.44***

Note: *** *p* < 0.001

0.001 and F (1, 56) = 57.83, *p* < 0.001, respectively), and between three- and six-month assessments (univariate contrasts: F (1, 56) = 5.34, *p* < 0.05 and F (1, 56) = 4.82, *p* < 0.05, respectively), but none between six months and one year (univariate contrasts: F (1, 56) = 0.36, NS and F(1, 56) = 0.26, NS, respectively). Only the period between intake and three months showed significant improvement in externalizing problems (univariate contrast: F(1, 56) = 26.94, *p* < 0.001).[2]

A similar series of analyses (Repeated Measures ANOVAs – analysis of variance) were carried out in order to examine the effect of attendance rate on degree of improvement. The total number of sessions attended between intake and one year were median-split into those who had attended more than twenty-eight sessions and those who had attended fewer. Contrary to expectation, there appeared to be no significant difference in the rate of improvement for those who had attended more than twenty-eight sessions compared to those who had attended fewer (no significant interaction effect between attendance and mean change in internalizing, externalizing or total problems (F(1, 59) = 2.27, *p* < 0.14; F(1, 59) = 0.59, *p* < 0.45; F(1, 59) = 0.14, *p* < 0.71, respectively).

To summarize:

- Significant and substantial improvements occurred in internalizing, externalizing and total problems between intake and one-year follow-up.
- Greater gains were made between intake and six months.

Change from clinical to non-clinical levels of YSR behaviour problems

Using a score of 60 as the cut-off point for clinical levels of problem

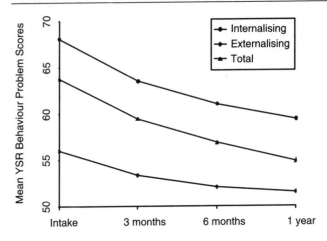

Figure 8.1 Mean change in YSR internalizing, externalizing and total problems between intake and one-year follow-up (*n* = 56)

behaviour as recommended by Achenbach and Edelbrock (1987), substantial improvements were seen between intake and one year in the proportion of subjects reporting clinical and non-clinical problems (see Table 8.3). As can be seen from Table 8.3, 39.3 per cent of this sample moved from clinical to non-clinical levels of internalizing problems by one-year follow-up and 52.5 per cent of this group showed improvement in total problems. Rather less improvement was seen by this criteria in externalizing problems, with 20 per cent of the group moving from the clinical to the non-clinical range. Nonetheless, it should be borne in mind that only one-third of the sample reported clinical levels of externalizing problems at intake, so proportionally fewer gains were to be expected.

To summarize:

- Significant and substantial movement occurred from the clinical to the non-clinical range in all problems between intake and one-year follow-up.

Reliable change

Using reliable change as the criterion for improvement in problem behaviour, similar levels of improvement were seen at one-year follow-up. Table 8.4 shows the frequency of reliable improvement and deterioration evident at one year for internalizing, externalizing

Table 8.3 Frequency of clinical and non-clinical levels of YSR internalizing, externalizing and total problems at intake and one-year follow-up (n = 61)

	Intake	One year	Number	McNemar Chi-square (df = 1)
Internalizing	clinical	non-clinical	24 (39.3%)	16.96*
	clinical	clinical	27 (42.3%)	
	non-clinical	non-clinical	8 (13.1%)	
	non-clinical	clinical	2 (5.3%)	
Externalizing	clinical	non-clinical	12 (19.7%)	** (binomial)
	clinical	clinical	7 (11.5%)	
	non-clinical	non-clinical	39 (63.9%)	
	non-clinical	clinical	3 (4.9%)	
Total	clinical	non-clinical	32 (52.5%)	27.27***
	clinical	clinical	16 (26.2%)	
	non-clinical	non-clinical	12 (19.7%)	
	non-clinical	clinical	1 (1.6%)	

Notes:
* $p < 0.01$
** $p < 0.05$
*** $p < 0.001$

and total problems. It is noteworthy that the numbers that showed statistically reliable *deterioration* were very small in this sample for internalizing, externalizing, and total problems.

Chi-square analyses revealed no significant effect of the attendance rate on reliable improvement in internalizing and total problems. However, there was a marginally significant relationship between attendance and reliable improvement in externalizing problems ($\chi^2(1) = 3.6$, $p = 0.059$).

Thus there is some evidence in these data that higher attendance rates are associated with greater levels of reliable improvement in externalizing problems.

To summarize:

- The majority of patients reliably improved for internalizing and total problems between intake and one year, and a smaller proportion improved for externalizing problems.
- The number who showed deterioration was very low.
- Improvement in externalizing problems was more likely to occur for those patients who attended more frequently.

Table 8.4 Reliable change in YSR internalizing, externalizing and total problems between intake and one-year follow-up (n = 61)

	No change n	Improvement n	Deterioration n
Internalizing	29 (47.5%)	31 (50.8%)	1 (1.7%)
Externalizing	35 (57.4%)	23 (37.7%)	3 (4.9%)
Total	21 (34.4%)	37 (60.6%)	3 (5.0%)

Identifying intake factors associated with improvement

As a way of exploring the factors associated with improvement a year after intake, a series of exploratory analyses, known as discriminant function analyses, were carried out. Discriminant function analysis allows one to predict improvement from a *composite* of several intake variables rather than examining individual intake variables one by one in a piecemeal fashion. Discriminant function analysis thus reveals *factors* associated with change that are not directly measured but are a combination of intake variables. The meaning of such factors can be understood by looking at the 'loadings' of each variable on the underlying factor, a large loading (near 1.0) indicating that the factor is strongly related to that variable. Thus discriminant function analysis can reveal more complex relationships that may not be apparent from simple univariate analyses. It is hoped that such an approach is consonant, to some extent, with the complexity of the processes involved in therapeutic outcome.

Intake variables of interest included age, gender, GAF, method of referral, presenting problems and diagnoses, and initial YSR problem scores. Of the three assessments of change discussed above, we felt that reliable change would be the best way of examining factors associated with meaningful improvement in problem behaviours.

Predictors of positive change in YSR internalizing problems

In order to explore the factors associated with positive change in internalizing problems a stepwise discriminant function analysis was carried out. This analysis indicated that those adolescents who benefit most from treatment in terms of internalizing problems are likely to have higher somatic complaints at intake (mean for improvers = 66.44, non-improvers = 59.00, $t(59) = 3.25$, $p < 0.001$), more likely to have a diagnosis of conduct disorder (improvers – 33 per cent, non-improvers – 6.7 per cent, $\chi^2(1) = 5.16$, $p < 0.05$), more likely to have parents who abuse drugs (1.3 per cent v. 3.3 per cent, $\chi^2 (1) = 4.15$, $p < 0.05$) and more likely to exhibit aggressive behaviour ($t(58) = 2.37$, $p < 0.05$). The analysis produced a factor that accounted for a substantial proportion of the variance in outcome in internalizing problems (Canonical R = 0.60, Wilks Lambda = 0.64, $\chi^2 (4) = 19.43$, $p < 0.001$). Using this discriminant function, 79.2 per cent of cases could be correctly classified as improvers or non-improvers. The factor loadings (or discriminant function coefficients, as they are sometimes known) are given below for each of the identified predictors.

	Loading of predictor on discriminant function
YSR somatic complaints at intake	0.71
Hyperkinetic or conduct disorder	0.47
Parents' misuse of drugs	0.42
YSR aggressive behaviour	0.37

Clearly the discriminating function was most strongly related to intake levels of somatic complaints. Indeed, somatic complaints emerged as the only *independent* predictor of positive change after controlling for the effects of the other predictors (Wilks Lambda = 0.80, Significance of F to Remove < 0.01). It is also notable that age, GAF and SPS were not found significantly to predict outcome.

Predictors of improvement in YSR externalizing problems

In the same way as that described above, a second analysis revealed a constellation of intake factors associated with positive change in externalizing problems. Broadly speaking, it seems that those who improve across the course of a year after intake evidence lower thought problems (mean = 56.6 v. 59.6, univariate t-test non-significant), greater levels of aggressive behaviour (mean = 58.0 v. 54.1, $t(58) = 2.37$, $p < 0.01$), are more anxious/depressed (mean = 74.7 v. 69.0, $t(59) = 1.84$, $p < 0.05$), have more family problems ($t(59) = 2.01$, $p < 0.05$) and are more likely to have an intact parental couple (50.0 per cent v. 21.6 per cent, $\chi^2(1) = 5.10$, $p < 0.05$). It was also seen previously that attendance levels tended to be higher for those who reliably improved in terms of their externalizing problems than for those who did not. The discriminant function that emerged from these analyses accounted for a significant and substantial proportion of the variance in improvement in externalizing problems between intake and one-year follow-up (Canonical R = 0.67, Wilks Lambda = 0.56, $\chi^2 = 25.26$, $p < 0.0005$) accounting for 45 per cent of the variance in outcome. The factor loading for each of the predictors on the underlying discriminating factor are presented below:

	Loading of predictor on discriminant function
YSR thought problems	0.81
YSR aggressive behaviour	0.67
YSR anxious/depressed	0.62
Intact parental couple	0.57
Attendance	0.52
Family problems	0.29

Of those variables that loaded on the discriminating factor, higher aggressive behaviour and being more anxious/depressed, fewer thought problems, a greater likelihood that parents were married and, importantly, attendance were significant *independent* predictors of positive change in externalizing problems (Wilks Lambda = 0.60, Significance of F to Remove < 0.01; Wilks Lambda = 0.65, Significance of F to Remove < 0.05; Wilks Lambda = 0.64, Significance of F to Remove < 0.05; Wilks Lambda = 0.65, Significance of F to Remove < 0.05; Wilks Lambda = 0.56, Significance of F to Remove $p < 0.05$, respectively). It is notable that this multivariate analysis revealed that fewer thought problems were strongly related to improvement in externalizing problems, whereas a simple univariate analysis did not.

Using this discriminant function 80 per cent of cases could be correctly classified in the reliable change or no-change groups.

Predictors of improvement in YSR total problems

A final analysis was performed in order to explore the factors associated with positive change in self-reported total problems. In this analysis two intake variables appeared to contribute to a factor discriminating those who improve from those who do not. Those adolescents who improved reliably over this period showed greater intake levels of externalizing problems (mean = 58.3 v. 52.3, $t(58)$ = 3.15, $p < 0.01$) and greater self-reported aggressive behaviour at intake ($t(58)$ = 2.16, $p < 0.05$). Again, the underlying factor accounted for a significant and fairly substantial proportion of the variation (23 per cent) in reliable improvement in total YSR behaviour problems (Canonical R = 0.48, Wilks Lambda = 0.77, χ^2 = 14.63, $p < 0.001$). The factor loadings of the predictors of total problems on the discriminating factor are given below:

	Loading of predictor on discriminant function
YSR externalizing problems	0.81
YSR aggressive behaviour	0.52

Each of these intake variables was a significant independent predictor of positive outcome, even after controlling for age, GAF and SPS (Wilks Lambda = 0.93, Significance of F to Remove < 0.001; Wilks Lambda = 0.84, Significance of F to Remove < 0.05, respectively).

Discussion

The follow-up sample (N = 61) includes adolescents who have completed YSR forms at intake, three months, six months and one year. These adolescents present a number of characteristics which suggest that they are more motivated regarding treatment compared to the larger unanalysed group (N = 170). They are older, are more likely to refer themselves than be referred, and are less likely to have conduct problems or developmental problems than the total population. In a recent study of attrition at the centre most of these characteristics discriminated between young people who continued in treatment for more than twenty-one sessions and another group of young people who dropped out early or late in treatment (Baruch *et al.*, in press). Of the present sample, 47 out of 61 young people were still in treatment when they were administered the YSR at one year.

At intake, young people who comprise the follow-up sample are characterized by a high level of morbidity. This suggests that they, unlike individuals with a higher starting level of adaptation, would be unlikely to benefit from psychotherapy (Luborsky *et al.* 1993). However, this was not the case. After one year of treatment a large majority of young people's scores for internalizing and total problems had significantly improved. Improvement in externalizing problems was less marked because, according to self-report assessments at intake, young people reported fewer of these problems. The question arises whether these improvements were due to non-treatment factors such as maturation and therefore represented alterations in presentation due to development. We think that this is unlikely. First, most young people in our sample are coming to the end of adolescence, which suggests that their disorders are more 'structuralized', i.e. integrated with the young person's personality (Target and Fonagy 1994), than would be the case for younger adolescents. Second, at intake they present with a multiplicity of problems and have a low level of functioning. There is a growing body of evidence which suggests that without treatment many behavioural and emotional disorders, including depressive disorders, in childhood and adolescence persist, and worsen in adulthood if left untreated (Ollendick and King 1994; Strauss *et al.* 1988; Caspi *et al.* 1996; Target and Fonagy 1996). In summary, we can be fairly confident that the improvements in young people's problems shown by the three methods of evaluating change were due to psychotherapy. Nevertheless, we cannot exclude the possibility that they were due to spontaneous remission since our study did not consist of young people randomly assigned to a treatment or control group.

We hoped that this investigation would tell us not only about the overall treatment response rate but also whether there was a dose–effect relationship between the number of sessions attended and the amount of change. On both counts there are some encouraging findings. The percentage of young people showing a reliable change in total problems after a year is comparable to Kopta *et al.*'s finding that 60–86 per cent of a sample of adult patients achieve remission of chronic distress symptoms characterized by anxiety, depressive mood and cognitive disturbance, as well as interpersonal problems, after approximately one year of therapy (Kopta *et al.* 1994). Our results are also comparable to those identified by Weisz *et al.* (1987) in their meta-analysis of outcome studies of psychotherapy with children and adolescents. For adolescents (13–18 years) there was a mean effect size of 0.58 ($p < 0.05$). However, the findings regarding the magnitude of change for internalizing problems are somewhat contradictory: the mean change score shows a substantial change, whereas the percentage of young people moving into the non-clinical range is less than we would expect based on the analysis of mean scores. This may be because their internalizing problems score was so high that a great deal of change was required in order for them to move into the non-clinical range. The finding in this study that length of treatment contributes independently of other predictors to improvement in externalizing problems is consistent with Howard *et al.*'s psychotherapy dosage model, which relates improvement to the number of sessions (Howard *et al.* 1986). In their study they found that more psychotherapy increased the probability of improvement, although the rate of improvement diminished with more sessions. However, we failed to find an effect of attendance on improvement in internalizing problems and total problems. The results show the greatest improvement occurring within the first six months of treatment, with fewer gains after this. From psychotherapy outcome studies of other adolescent (Target and Fonagy 1994) and adult populations (Howard *et al.* 1993), our findings suggest that young people initially improve symptomatically, with later gains perhaps being made in relation to entrenched personality problems and social difficulties. This picture certainly fits with clinical experience at the centre.

Unexpectedly for a population that is distinguished from the unanalysed group by a relative absence of conduct disorder, this diagnosis emerged as an important predictor of reliable improvement for internalizing problems and total problems, as did a presenting problem of violence and problems of aggression. For total problems, a high externalizing problems score at intake also emerged as an important predictor. These findings are in contrast to those of studies which have shown that the presence of violence, serious aggression and conduct disorder make young people more vulnerable to other disorders (Lewinsohn *et al.* 1991), are linked to greater severity and poor prognosis (Loeber and Keenan, in press; cited in Tolan and Henry 1996), and reduce the effect of treatment on other co-occurring disorders (Biederman *et al.* 1991). The presence of conduct disorder, aggressive behaviour and externalizing problems is a powerful predictor of dropping out of treatment, which suggests that in order to remain in and benefit from treatment the sample population is highly motivated. We speculate that for young people who are at the end of adolescence and who are about to enter adulthood the experience of this presentation and the context in which it arises may provide an important motivation to make effective use of psychoanalytic psychotherapy. From histories taken at intake we know that young people's violence and aggression is impulsive, and tends to arise in the context of close friendships or intimate relationships which are either breaking down or have repeatedly broken down. At this late stage of their adolescent development, when they would hope to be successful in these areas of functioning, young people with these difficulties may be ready to acknowledge problems of impulsive aggression and violence because they are proving so costly to crucial areas of their life. It is also possible that younger adolescents in this sample may be highly motivated to benefit from psychotherapy because they recognize the harm their behaviour is doing to their academic prospects and friendships.

A high YSR score for somatic complaints emerged as a powerful predictor of reliable improvement for internalizing problems. Somatic complaints, which are often entrenched, might be expected to hinder the use the young person can make of an insight-oriented therapy. However, we speculate that, once again, developmental considerations may be crucial in the role somatic problems play in therapy. Younger adolescents are often unaware of or resistant to acknowledging the connection between these and other problems and their internal state. Older adolescents, because of their motivation for therapy, may be much more open to recognizing this connection, especially if somatic problems such as bingeing and vomiting are adversely affecting important areas of functioning.

Parental misuse of drugs was found to predict internalizing problems. Usually this involved the use of 'hard' drugs, with much damage being done to the parent and family life. For older adolescents, this experience may provide a powerful incentive to use therapy productively since they may fear that unless they are helped they may become like the parent.

Substance abuse, fewer thought problems, being more anxious/depressed, parents being married, family problems and high attendance predicted improvement in externalizing problems for over 80 per cent of the sample. In our earlier study we found that substance abuse was a contraindication of being able to make effective use of psychoanalytic psychotherapy because many troubled young people use drugs and alcohol to ward off insight and understanding of their problems (Baruch 1995). However, we think that because of their age the young people in the present sample may recognize that their misuse of drugs and alcohol, although originally for recreational purposes, interferes with their relationships, and their educational and work prospects. It is interesting that an intact parental couple and family problems predicted improvement in externalizing problems. This suggests the possibility that despite problems in the family there may be certain strengths within the parents' marriage which may provide the young person with a useful basis for forming a therapeutic relationship with a well-functioning adult. The finding that fewer thought problems and being more anxious/depressed predict improvement in externalizing problems confirms a similar finding from Fonagy and Target's investigation into the efficacy of psychoanalysis for children and adolescents with disruptive disorders. Their study showed that '65% of disruptive children with an additional diagnosis of anxiety showed significant improvements after at least one year's treatment, as compared with 50% without' (Fonagy and Target 1994: 51).

The study has a number of limitations. The sample represents only 26 per cent of the young people who used the psychotherapy service for the first time during the period of study, and differs from the unanalysed group according to crucial demographic and diagnostic characteristics. Therefore it is difficult to generalize our findings. However, we have outcome data for larger samples at six months and at three months, which we shall report in the future. Generalizability is further weakened by the problem of attrition (Kazdin 1990; Kazdin and Mazurick 1994). Our sample at one year consists mainly of young people who have remained in treatment or, if they terminated treatment before one year, cooperated in completing and returning the YSR form routinely sent to clients at this time. There are two types of attrition which affect generalizability: first, young people who may have ended treatment consensually before one year but for a variety of reasons, including change of address, do not return the YSR form; second, young people who drop out of treatment. Predictors of outcome identified by the current study can apply only to those young people who continued in treatment for a relatively long time. The problem of attrition is a complex one and it should not be automatically assumed that dropping out is indicative of a poor outcome. For instance, young people who establish themselves in therapy but drop out of treatment before twenty-one sessions may feel satisfied with their treatment and not feel the need to continue further. Also, it is not uncommon for younger adolescents who drop out before establishing themselves in treatment to return when they are older, are more aware of their difficulties and are self-motivated to take up treatment (see Baruch *et al.*, in press).

A serious limitation concerns the use of the YSR form with young people up to 25 years old, since the form is designed for adolescents up to the age of 18. Even if the forms can be shown to be valid instruments for young people at that age, the scale-factor analyses, internalizing and externalizing groupings, and norms were all calculated for a younger sample. There are no guarantees that the YSR has equally powerful validity or reliability to a population not within its empirical base. However, the YSR appears quite robust because it has performed well in other cultures and circumstances alien to the original sample. Nevertheless, we do not know how it performs with an older sample.

A further weakness of the study is the lack of follow-up data, which is crucial in determining whether improvement has been maintained. There is contradictory evidence as to whether improvement is maintained following termination of treatment (Levitt 1957; Kolvin *et al.* 1988) or whether there is deterioration (Kazdin 1990). However, we would argue that the rate of improvement which emerged during the course of our study may substantially affect the lives of the young people at the time of undergoing treatment and should therefore not be underestimated. We think that a standard of change which is based on the adolescent being once and for all returned to psychological well-being is a much too stringent and unrealistic way of judging treatment outcome (Tramontana 1980).

A further limitation of this study concerns the potential for bias by using only self-report assessment data. We noted earlier the need for assessment from multiple vantage points because of the variability of the young person's behaviour depending on the social context. From our previous analysis, which the present study appears to confirm, we know that self-report assessment of externalizing problems underestimates them and that significant other assessment is more likely to provide reliable information on this area of functioning. In the future we shall report a comparative study of self- and significant-other assessments at six-month follow-up.

Despite these limitations, the study demonstrates the effectiveness of psychoanalytic psychotherapy for this group of older adolescents, who are also likely to be self-referred, less likely to have developmental problems or a diagnosis of conduct disorder and more likely to attend longer compared with the total population. Within this group it was possible to predict those who benefited and those who did not benefit. Longer-lasting treatment predicted improvement in externalizing problems; paradoxically, having a diagnosis of conduct disorder, presenting problems of aggression and violence, and a higher externalizing score predicted reliable improvement for total problems; and, in addition, somatic complaints and parents who abused drugs predicted reliable improvement for internalizing problems.

The study also suggests a number of other important findings: first, rigorous outcome work can be put into effect with a clinic population consisting of adolescents and young adults, who are notoriously difficult to reach; second, on the basis of their rate of improvement it would appear that therapeutic practice, although affected, is not harmed by the therapists implementing outcome assessment; third, as other studies have suggested, developmental considerations appear to influence the predictions of which young person is likely to benefit most from psychoanalytic psychotherapy (Target and Fonagy 1994; Kendall *et al.* 1984). In the future we hope that similar centres and departments running a psychoanalytic psychotherapy service for young people will be in a position to replicate our approach to outcome in order to establish the generalizability of the findings of our study.

Notes

1 Patients are also given the significant-other form (SOF), which is a slightly amended version of the teacher's report form (Achenbach 1991b). This form, like the YSR, is derived from the CBCL and is filled out by someone significant in the patient's life. The SOF is essentially similar to the YSR. The SOF is also completed by the patient's therapist (see Baruch 1995).
2 This analysis was based on a sample of 57 young people, for whom the data had been collected at intake, three months, six months and one year.

Acknowledgements

Staff at the Brandon Centre have contributed to the present work and are gratefully acknowledged as is the contribution of Dr. Mary Target and Professor Peter Fonagy.

References

Achenbach, T. M. (1991a) *Manual for the Youth Self-Report and 1991 Profile*, Burlington, VT: University of Vermont Department of Psychiatry.

—— (1991b) *Manual for the Teacher's Report Form and 1991 Profile*, Burlington, VT: University of Vermont Department of Psychiatry.

Achenbach, T. M. and Edelbrock, C. (1986) *Manual for the Teacher's Report Form and Teacher Version of the Child Behaviour Profile*, Burlington, VT: University of Vermont Department of Psychiatry.

—— (1987) *Manual for the Youth Self-Report and Profile*, Burlington, VT: University of Vermont Department of Psychiatry.

Achenbach, T. M. and McConaughy, S. H. (1987) *Empirically Based Assessment of Child and Adolescent Psychopathology: Practical Applications*, Newbury Park, CA: Sage Publications.

American Psychiatric Association (1994) *Diagnostic and Statistical Manual of Mental Disorders*, 4th edn, Washington, DC: American Psychiatric Association.

Baruch, G. (1995) 'Evaluating the outcome of a community-based psychoanalytic psychotherapy service for young people between 12 and 25 years old: work in progress', *Psychoanalytic Psychotherapy* 9: 243–67.

Baruch, G., Gerber, A. and Fearon, P. (in press) 'Adolescents who drop out of psychotherapy at a community-based psychotherapy centre: the characteristics of early drop-outs, late drop-outs and those who continue treatment', *British Journal of Medical Psychology*.

Biederman, J., Newcorn, J. and Sprich, S. (1991) 'Comorbidity of attention hyperactivity disorder with conduct, depressive, anxiety and other disorders', *American Journal of Psychiatry* 148: 564–77.

Camden and Islington (1994) *Camden & Islington Public Health Report*, London.

Caspi, A., Moffitt, T. E., Newman, D. L. and Silva, P. A. (1996) 'Behavioral observations at age 3 years predict adult psychiatric disorders', *Archives of General Psychiatry* 53: 1033–9.

Christensen, L. and Mendoza, J. L. (1986) 'A method of assessing change in a single subject: an alteration in the RC index', *Behaviour Therapy* 17: 305–8.

Fonagy, P. and Higgitt, A. (1989) 'Evaluating the performance of departments of psychotherapy', *Psychoanalytic Psychotherapy* 4: 121–53.

Fonagy, P. and Target, M. (1994) 'The efficacy of psychoanalysis for children with disruptive disorders', *Journal of the American Academy of Child and Adolescent Psychiatry* 33(1): 45–55.

Howard, K. I., Kopta, S. M., Krause, M. S. and Orlinsky, D. E. (1986) 'The dose effect relationship in psychotherapy', *American Psychologist* 41: 159–64.

Howard, K. I., Lueger, R. J., Maling, M. S. and Martinovich, Z. (1993) 'A phase model of psychotherapy outcome: causal mediation of change', *Journal of Consulting and Clinical Psychology* 61: 678–85.

Jacobson, N. S., Follette, W. C. and Revenstorf, D. (1984) 'Psychotherapy outcome research: methods of reporting variability and evaluating clinical significance', *Behaviour Therapy* 15: 336–52.

Kazdin, A. E. (1990) 'Premature termination from treatment among children referred for antisocial behaviour', *Journal of Child Psychology and Psychiatry* 31: 415–25.

Kazdin, A. E. and Mazurick, J. L. (1994) 'Dropping out of child psychotherapy: distinguishing early and late dropouts over the course of treatment', *Journal of Consulting and Clinical Psychology* 62: 1069–74.

Kendall, P. C., Lerner, R. M. and Craighead, W. E. (1984) 'Human development and intervention in childhood psychopathology', *Child Development* 55: 71–82.

King, R. A. and Noshpitz, J. D. (1991) *Pathways to Growth: Essentials of Child Psychiatry, vol. 2: Psychopathology*, New York: Wiley.

Kolko, D. J. and Kazdin, A. E. (1993) 'Emotional/behavioural problems in clinic and non-clinic children: correspondence among child, parent and teacher reports', *Journal of Child Psychology and Psychiatry* 34: 991–1006.

Kolvin, I., Nicol, A. E. and Wrate, R. M. (1988) 'Psychotherapy is effective', *Journal of the Royal Society of Medicine* 81: 261–6.

Kopta, S. M., Howard, K. I., Lowry, J. L. and Beutler, L. E. (1994) 'Patterns of symptomatic recovery in psychotherapy', *Journal of Consulting and Clinical Psychology* 62, 5, 1009–1016.

Kordy, H., von Rad, M. and Senf., W. (1988) 'Time and its relevance for a successful psychotherapy', *Psychotherapy & Psychosomatics* 49: 212–22.

Lambert, M. J., Hatch, D. R., Kingston, M. D. and Edwards, B. C. (1986) 'Zung, Beck, and Hamilton rating scales as measures of treatment outcome: a meta-analytic comparison', *Journal of Consulting and Clinical Psychology* 54: 54–9.

Levitt, E. E. (1957) 'The results of psychotherapy with children: an evaluation', *Journal of Consulting Psychology* 21: 186–9.

Lewinsohn, P. M., Rohde, P., Seeley, J. R. and Hops, H. (1991) 'Comorbidity of unipolar depression: 1. Major depression with dysthymia', *Journal of Abnormal Psychology* 100: 205–13.

Loeber, R. and Keenan, K. (in press) 'The interaction between conduct disorder and its comorbid conditions: effects of age and gender', *Clinical Psychology Review*.

Luborsky, L., Diguer, L., Luborsky, E., McLellan, A. T., Woody, G. and Alexander, L. (1993) 'Psychological health-sickness (PHS) as a predictor of outcomes in dynamic and other psychotherapies', *Journal of Consulting and Clinical Psychology* 61: 542–9.

Ollendick, T. H. and King, N. J. (1994) 'Diagnosis, assessment and treatment of internalizing problems in children: the role of longitudinal data', *Journal of Consulting and Clinical Psychology* 62: 918–27.

Roth, A. and Fonagy, P. (eds) (1996) *What Works for Whom? A Critical Review of Psychotherapy Research*, New York and London: Guilford Press.

Strauss, C. C., Last, C. G., Hersen, M. and Kazdin, A. E. (1988) 'Association between anxiety and depression in children and adolescents with anxiety disorders', *Journal of Abnormal Child Psychology* 16: 57–68.

Target, M. and Fonagy, P. (1994) 'The efficacy of psychoanalysis for children: prediction of outcome in a developmental context', *Journal of the American Academy of Child and Adolescent Psychiatry* 33: 1134–44.

—— (1996) 'The efficacy of treatments for child and adolescent psychiatric disorders', in A. Roth and P. Fonagy (eds) *What Works for Whom? A Critical Review of Psychotherapy Research*, New York and London: Guilford Press.

Tolan, P. H. and Henry, D. (1996) 'Patterns of psychopathology among urban poor children: comorbidity and aggression effects', *Journal of Consulting and Clinical Psychology* 64: 1094–9.

Tramontana, M. G. (1980) 'Critical review of research on psychotherapy outcome with adolescents: 1967–1977', *Psychological Bulletin* 88: 429–50.

Weisz, J. R., Weiss, B., Alicke, M. D. and Klotz, M. L. (1987) 'Effectiveness of psychotherapy with children and adolescents: a meta-analysis for clinicians', *Journal of Consulting and Clinical Psychology* 55: 542–9.

World Health Organization (1990) *I.C.D.-10, 1990 Draft of Chapter V, Mental and Behavioural Disorders (Including Disorders of Psychological Development)*, Geneva: World Health Organization.

Chapter 9

Clinical practice guidelines for the psychotherapies

John Cape

Introduction

Clinical practice guidelines are being put forward in the UK and the USA as a means of promoting evidence based practice and clinical effectiveness. In the UK the Department of Health has strongly endorsed the development and use of clinical guidelines, and has funded a programme of development and evaluation of national clinical guidelines led in part through the Medical Royal Colleges and professional bodies (Department of Health 1996). In the USA the Agency for Health Care Policy and Research (AHCPR), funded by the Federal Government, has organized a major national development and dissemination programme of clinical practice guidelines, including within mental health (AHCPR 1995; Field and Lohr 1990).

The potential and problems of the application of clinical practice guidelines to the psychotherapies are examined in this chapter. Although the focus is on clinical guidelines, the issues addressed are common to other methods of promoting clinical effectiveness and evidence-based practice in the psychotherapies. As there is little experience of clinical practice guidelines in the psychotherapies to date, the chapter has been written as an exploration of the implications of extending into the psychotherapies this evidence-based approach from medicine. Its main conclusion is that there are already areas where clinical practice guidelines development for the psychotherapies could be useful, but at present the knowledge base about which psychotherapists can agree is not sufficient to develop guidelines that will generally be found useful by well-trained, experienced psychoanalytic psychotherapists.

What are clinical practice guidelines?

Clinical practice guidelines (often shortened to 'clinical guidelines' in the UK) are decision-making tools to assist in clinical decisions. The standard definition from the Institute of Medicine is that clinical practice guidelines are 'systematically developed statements to assist practitioner and patient decisions about appropriate health care for specific clinical circumstances' (Field and Lohr 1990). It is important to note that they are designed for use by both practitioners and patients, and also that they are discretionary ('to assist decisions'), not mandatory. As any decision-making tool, they may be deemed useful by practitioners and adopted, or not useful and discarded. They are not management tools to define what clinicians should and should not do, or commissioning tools to define what services should be purchased. However, in a particular service it may be decided by the clinicians in the service that everyone will use a particular guideline and audit their cases against the guideline.

Any clinical circumstance can, in principle, be the subject of a guideline. Most common in medical and general mental health settings have been condition-based guidelines (e.g. assessment and management of depression in primary care – AHCPR 1993) and problem-based guidelines (e.g. management of violence in clinical settings – Royal College of Psychiatrists 1998). The guideline sets out the specific clinical *process* that will lead to optimal *outcomes* for the specific circumstances and patients under consideration.

A guideline may vary in length from a sheet of A4 to a short book. Typically, both a brief practitioner desktop version and a longer version with a summary of the evidence are produced. In general medical (family) practice, where there is a particular need for ready access to decision-making tools, computerized decision-support versions of guidelines are being explored. Where relevant, it is recommended that patient versions of the guideline are produced. Each AHCPR guideline comprises a patient version (in English and Spanish), a quick-reference guide for clinicians and a full technical report as well as the main guideline (AHCPR 1995).

The difference between clinical practice guidelines and standard literature reviews, chapters and text books is in the manner of their construction. Clinical practice guidelines use a systematic and explicit development process, usually involving a representative guideline development group, and a systematic approach to identifying, evaluating and incorporating evidence in the guideline.

Clinical guidelines may be developed both by local groups of clinicians and by national bodies or agencies. There is evidence that locally produced guidelines are more likely to be followed, although nationally produced guidelines are more likely to be valid (Grimshaw and Russell 1993a). A common recommendation is that national and local efforts should be coordinated, with local clinicians adapting national guidelines to local circumstances (Clinical Resource and Audit Group 1993).

Purpose of guidelines: effectiveness and equity

Clinical practice guidelines are primarily advocated as a means of improving the effectiveness and appropriateness of health care. In medicine, the performance of individual doctors is frequently found to be outdated and substandard compared to optimum care, when an agreed standard of optimum care is established (Ramsey *et al.* 1991; Sackett *et al.* 1997). The advice of clinical experts in text books and literature reviews is frequently inconsistent and in disagreement (Sackett *et al.* 1997), and is also at variance with systematic reviews of the evidence (Antman *et al.* 1992). It is assumed that clinical practice guidelines, through their systematic development and approach to evidence, will be a more valid guide to clinicians, and that following such guidelines will result in better health outcomes for patients. Evidence that clinical practice guidelines can have this effect has been systematically reviewed by Grimshaw and Russell (1993b).

A secondary, less commonly noted purpose of clinical practice guidelines can be to promote equity in provision of treatment. Clinicians are often in the position of controlling access to valued treatments, and their decisions may be influenced by systematic biases (especially educational level and socioeconomic status) rather than evidence-based criteria. Psychotherapy is such a valued treatment, and studies from the USA have noted the association of assessment of suitability for psychotherapy with the YAVIS factors (young, attractive, verbal, intelligent, single) and with ethnicity (Garfield 1986; Weber *et al.* 1985).

Clinical guidelines, in order to be effective, need to be acceptable to and reflect the views of patients. A well-designed guideline will ensure that the health outcomes aimed at are those that are valued by patients (Duff *et al.* 1996). At an individual level, choices available for a patient should be made explicit. For example, the Royal College of Psychiatrists monograph on clinical practice guidelines (Marriott and Lelliott 1994) suggests that where the evidence indicates that a form of psychotherapy and antidepressant medication are equally effective a clinical guideline for depression should indicate that patient preference should guide choice of treatment.

Effectiveness, evidence and guidelines

Clinical practice guidelines, in order to be valid and helpful for practitioners and patients, need to define correctly the clinical practices that lead to optimal health outcomes. This raises questions of what are appropriate outcomes for psychotherapy and how best to evaluate evidence for the effectiveness of different clinical practices in psychotherapy.

In medicine, symptom change, change in the underlying pathological disease process and quality of life may all be relevant outcomes depending on the particular circumstances. Thus clinical trials of anti-retroviral drugs in early HIV commonly assess effectiveness both on emergence of AIDS-defining symptoms and on laboratory measures of viral load (Fleming and DeMets 1996), while palliative and terminal care in AIDS focuses on symptom control and on quality of life. In psychotherapy, similar considerations apply, with brief cognitive behaviour and supportive therapies usually focusing on symptom alleviation, while longer-term psychoanalytic psychotherapies more commonly target internal psychodynamic change, a measure of the underlying pathological process, and interpersonal change (Lambert and Hill 1994; Malan 1973; Mintz 1981). In relation to clinical practice guidelines, it is consequently important to clarify the outcomes relevant to the specific clinical circumstances and interventions under consideration.

While in medicine the randomized controlled trial (RCT) is the agreed methodology for evaluating therapeutic effectiveness, particularly of drugs, the limitations of RCTs for evaluating the effectiveness of the psychotherapies are well rehearsed (Howard *et al.* 1994; Seligman 1995). Even in medicine the limitations of RCTs are increasingly being questioned (Black 1996; Charlton 1996). A number of alternative empirical research methods for evaluating the effectiveness of clinical practices in the psychotherapies are available (Miller *et al.* 1993), and the chapter by Target (Chapter 7) gives examples of such methods.

In addition to research evidence, which is not always available or adequate, the effectiveness of clinical practices may also be evaluated through consensus of clinical practitioners. Such clinicians may be either well-respected, skilled and experienced practitioners or the agreed experts in the field. Even where research evidence does exist its clinical applicability is often usefully evaluated against the opinion of experienced practitioners. A number of structured consensus methods are available to establish strength of agreement and to facilitate agreement (Linstone and Turoff 1975; Olson 1995; Scott and Black 1991; Woolf 1992). Such structured consensus methods are important given evidence about the inaccuracy of unstructured group decisions (Gigone and Hastie 1997).

The emphasis of the national clinical practice guidelines programmes in both the UK (Department of Health 1996) and the USA (AHCPR 1995; Field and Lohr 1990) is on using systematic reviews of research evidence, and in particular of RCTs, as the basis of clinical guidelines, and then moderating and supplementing the research evidence against panels of expert clinicians, and often also of patients. Thus primacy is given to research evidence, but moderated in the light of consensual evidence.

Guidance from the American Psychological Association on developing guidelines for psychological therapies and psychosocial interventions (American Psychological Association 1995; Barlow 1996) also weights research evidence ahead of consensual evidence in evaluating the efficacy of treatments for a guideline. However, it suggests that guideline developers need to give equal weight to a second axis concerning the feasibility, generalizability and clinical utility of proposed treatments. Some efficacious treatments may have limited clinical utility, for reasons of poor acceptability to patients, applicability to only small numbers of patients with the relevant condition, or high cost. Accordingly, recommendations in clinical practice guidelines need to take account of evidence on both efficacy and clinical utility.

The evidence used as the basis of clinical practice recommendations in any particular clinical practice guideline will vary according to the nature of the total evidence available. Of necessity in the psychotherapies, where there is often limited research evidence, in part because of limited historic research funding, there will be greater dependence on consensual evidence than in some other areas. What is important is that the nature and strength of the evidence for each recommendation in the clinical guideline is made explicit. This allows those using the guideline to be clear about the evidence base and reasons for each recommendation.

Clinical guidelines and clinical judgement

Clinical practice guidelines are not protocols to be followed under all circumstances. They are designed to inform and assist in decisions about what *usually* would be best practice in the specific clinical circumstances which they cover. A thorough guideline will specify exceptions and alternative courses of action under these exceptions, but it would never be possible to detail all exceptions. Clinical judgement is required to determine whether the clinical guideline is relevant to a particular patient, given that patient's clinical state, personality and preferences.

As there is understandable concern among clinicians, and perhaps especially psychotherapists, about the potential inappropriately to limit and prescribe clinical practice, we give some quotations from authoritative sources on this issue. First, David Sackett, the premier exponent of evidence based medicine, states:

> External clinical evidence can inform, but never replace, individual clinical expertise. An external guideline must be integrated with individual clinical expertise in deciding whether and how it matches the patient's clinical state, predicament and preferences and thus whether it should be applied. Clinicians who fear top-down cook-books will find the advocates of evidence based medicine joining them at the barricades.
>
> (Sackett *et al.* 1996: 72)

Second, the Department of Health document on clinical guidelines states in a brief section on clinical freedom:

> Even when endorsed by the relevant professional bodies or commended by the NHS [National Health Service] Executive, clinical guidelines can still only assist the practitioner, they cannot be used to mandate, authorise or outlaw treatment options. Regardless of the strength of evidence, it will remain the responsibility of the practising clinicians to interpret their application taking account of local circumstances and the needs and wishes of individual patients. It would be wholly inappropriate for clinical guidelines to be used as a means of

coercion of the individual clinician, by managers or senior professionals.

(Department of Health 1996: 10)

A corollary of the limitation that clinical guidelines can only inform decisions as to what would *usually* be best practice is that where it is not possible to define or agree what would *usually* be best practice it is not possible to develop a clinical guideline. For many issues in psychotherapy, in common with other areas of health care, it is not yet possible to define or agree what would be an average appropriate response. This is because of both the uniqueness of individual patients and the difficulty of reaching agreement in certain areas about appropriate practice because of divergent theoretical perspectives. Thus there will always be areas where clinical judgement alone has to be relied on.

Who might use psychotherapy guidelines?

Psychotherapy in the NHS is provided and embedded in a complex system, at a number of points of which clinical decisions can influence whether a patient receives optimum treatment. Accordingly, clinical guidelines, as decision tools, have potential relevance for various groups. The main groups involved in decisions affecting psychotherapy provision in the NHS are:

- referrers for psychotherapy (e.g. GPs, general psychiatrists);
- counsellors, clinical psychologists and others providing brief psychotherapies outside dedicated psychotherapy services;
- trainees/honoraries, who provide a major part of the therapy (as opposed to assessment) resource in many dedicated psychotherapy services;
- fully trained and experienced psychotherapists.

As the clinical practice decisions about psychotherapy and the decision-making context of each of these groups is different, different clinical guidelines would generally be required for each group. However, there would be overlap between guidelines of specific relevance to each group. Thus a clinical guideline specifically targeted at GPs regarding which patients it might be most appropriate to refer in the first instance to their practice counsellor and which to a dedicated psychotherapy service might also have some implications for a practice counsellor assessing a patient referred by the GP in deciding whether to treat the patient him- or herself or to refer on to a dedicated psychotherapy service.

Examples of psychotherapy clinical guidelines

This section gives examples of guidelines that have or might be developed for different groups of clinicians and specific clinical circumstances. Most are outlines of possible guidelines rather than actual guidelines, given the lack of experience of developing clinical guidelines in the psychotherapies to date.

Guidelines for the psychotherapies can be classified into those that relate primarily to assessment and triage decisions and those that relate primarily to treatment decisions. By assessment and triage is meant the process of deciding whether psychotherapy and what form of psychotherapy might be most appropriate for a patient and making a referral or disposal accordingly, a decision that will be made both by GPs and other primary referrers for psychotherapy and also by assessing psychological therapists of different kinds. Guidelines about treatment decisions are those that relate to decisions made by psychological therapists (both generic and specialist) once they have decided to take on a patient for treatment.

In addition, guidelines for psychotherapy may be condition/disorder specific (e.g. focusing on borderline personality disorder) or general and of relevance to all patients. The condition-specific v.

Table 9.1 A classification of psychotherapy guidelines

	General	Condition-specific
Assessment and triage	Cape et al. (1995)	AHCPR (1993b)
	BPS CORE (1997)	American Psychiatric Association (1993b)
	American Psychiatric Association (1985) Suitability for psychodynamic psychotherapy	
Treatment	Treatment focus	Panic disorder
		Borderline personality disorder
		Quality Assurance Project (1991a)

general dimension, and the assessment and triage v. treatment dimensions can be conceptualized as distinct giving a 2 × 2 matrix. Table 9.1 represents this diagrammatically and notes how the guideline examples given below fit into this scheme. Other ways of classifying guidelines of relevance for decisions about psychotherapy are possible, and the author would not wish to give any special significance to this scheme of classification.

Examples of three types of guidelines are given below:

- guidelines designed primarily for GPs and other primary referrers for psychotherapy to assist in decisions as to whether psychotherapy and what form of psychotherapy might be most appropriate for a patient;
- guidelines that might be developed for a variety of psychological therapists (psychologists, psychotherapists and counsellors) to assist in integrating treatment approaches from different theoretical orientations for specific conditions/disorders;
- guidelines that might be developed specifically for use by those working in psychoanalytic psychotherapy services.

Examples of guidelines for GPs and primary-care practitioners on matching patients to the most appropriate treatment

Two examples of clinical guidelines for GPs and primary-care practitioners on matching patients to the most appropriate treatment including psychotherapy are given. The first is the AHCPR guideline on treatment of major depressive disorder in primary care (AHCPR 1993b). The second is a local UK clinical guideline on counselling and psychological therapies developed for GPs by a working group of Camden & Islington's Medical Audit Advisory Group (Cape *et al.* 1995; Cape *et al.* 1998). In addition, mention is made of a project funded by the NHS Executive developing a national clinical guideline for the psychological therapies targeted at GPs (BPS CORE 1997).

Other relevant clinical guidelines on appropriateness for psychotherapy, targeted primarily at general psychiatrists, have been developed by both the American Psychiatric Association (1993a, 1993b) and the Royal Australian and New Zealand College of Psychiatrists (Quality Assurance Project 1982a, 1982b, 1991a, 1991b). These focus on specific conditions/disorders and include guidance to assist in decisions on whether to treat with medication, psychotherapy or a combination. A review by Persons *et al.* (1996) compared the evaluations and recommendations regarding psychotherapy in the American Psychiatric Association guideline for depression (American Psychiatric Association 1993b) and the AHCPR depression guideline (AHCPR 1993b) and concluded that the American Psychiatric Association guideline significantly understated the value of the psychotherapies compared to both the AHCPR guideline and the total evidence, and that, in addition, the American Psychiatric Association guideline made recommendations about choosing among psychotherapies that are not well supported by empirical evidence. The authors attributed this in part to the lack of the use of a multidisciplinary, representative panel in the production of the American Psychiatric Association guideline.

The AHCPR depression in primary care guideline (AHCPR 1993a, 1993b) was developed by a multi-professional panel of experts, including a consumer representative, for use by primary care practitioners such as GPs, family physicians, internists, nurse practitioners, mental health nurses and other workers in primary care settings. It focuses on major depressive disorder and comes in two volumes, one concerning detection and diagnosis (AHCPR 1993a) and the other on treatment (AHCPR 1993b), as well as a quick-reference guide for clinicians (AHCPR 1993c) and a patient guide (AHCPR 1993d).

The treatment guideline (AHCPR 1993b) considers four main treatment options: medication, psychotherapy, combination of medication and psychotherapy, and electroconvulsive therapy (ECT). The key recommendations on selection of the first three of these options for acute-phase (first-line) treatment are as follows. For medication, 'Patients with moderate to severe major depressive disorder are appropriately treated with medication, whether or not formal psychotherapy is also used' (*ibid.*: 39). For psychotherapy alone:

> Patients with mild to moderate major depression who prefer psychotherapy alone as the initial acute treatment choice may be treated with this option. Psychotherapy alone is not recommended for the acute treatment of patients with severe and/or psychotic major depressive disorders.
>
> (AHCPR 1993b: 40)

For combined medication and psychotherapy:

> Combined treatment may have an advantage for patients with

partial responses to either treatment alone (if adequately administered) and for those with a more chronic history or poor
interepisode recovery. However, combined treatment may
provide no unique advantage for patients with uncomplicated,
non-chronic major depressive disorder.

(AHCPR 1993b: 41)

In relation to selection of a form of psychotherapy (i.e. psychodynamic, cognitive behavioural, interpersonal, etc.) it states:

> In most cases, therapies that target depressive symptoms (cogni-
> tive or behavioural therapy) or specific interpersonal recurrent
> psychosocial problems related to the depression (interpersonal
> psychotherapy) are more similar than different in efficacy. Long-
> term therapies are not currently indicated as first-line acute
> phase treatments for patients with major depressive disorder.

(AHCPR 1993b: 84)

In addition to the above recommendations, the guideline also makes
recommendations about appropriate objectives for psychotherapy
for depression, frequency of sessions ('at least once-a-week visits on
regular basis' (ibid.: 85)), what to do if there is a failure to respond to
psychotherapy and other issues.

The AHCPR depression guideline treatment recommendations
were favourably reviewed by Persons et al. (1996), with the exception
that they considered the AHCPR guideline to understate the value of
psychotherapy alone in the treatment of more severely depressed
outpatients. Munoz et al. (1994) gave a less favourable review,
although their criticisms were primarily targeted at the depression
guideline Quick Reference Guide for Clinicians (AHCPR 1993c).
They concluded that the careful and balanced review in the main
guideline was not reflected in the quick-reference guide, which in
consequence misrepresents the potential significance of psychotherapy as a first-line treatment.

The Camden & Islington Medical Audit Advisory Group
(MAAG) local guideline on counselling and psychological therapies
(Cape et al. 1995; Cape et al. 1998) was produced by a multi-
professional group comprising a GP, a practice counsellor, a
consultant psychotherapist, a clinical psychologist and a lay representative (ex-director of local mental health charity MIND). It was
designed to assist GPs and other local health practitioners in

selecting adult patients for the most appropriate of three psychological treatments: brief counselling, cognitive behaviour therapy and psychodynamic psychotherapy. These three psychological treatments were selected as they were the psychological treatments most commonly provided locally and for the most part took place locally in different organizational settings – brief counselling being provided primarily by practice counsellors in GP premises, cognitive behaviour therapy in NHS psychology departments, and psychodynamic psychotherapy in NHS psychotherapy departments. Thus decisions by GPs locally about suitability for these three treatments were relevant in decisions on referral pathways.

The guideline comprises a 22 page document with three separate easy reference guideline summaries. It defines pragmatically the three treatments, restricting counselling to brief (6–12-session) counselling, cognitive behaviour therapy to simple cognitive behaviour therapy (CBT) (excluding complex approaches targeted at personality disorders) and psychodynamic psychotherapy to longer-term (over six months) psychodynamic psychotherapy. Its recommendations relate to the impact of four characteristics of patients' problems (nature of major problem/disorder, chronicity, severity, complexity) and three other characteristics of patients (treatment preference, interest in self exploration, capacity to tolerate frustration and psychic pain) on decisions about suitability of the three treatments. Examples of two of the guideline's recommendations are given in Tables 9.2 and 9.3, and an example of one of the guideline summaries is given in Table 9.4.

As part of the NHS Executive funded clinical guidelines development programme in the UK, a project has been funded to develop a clinical guideline for the psychotherapies targeted at GPs and other primary referrers for psychotherapy (BPS CORE 1997). The project is a collaboration of the British Psychological Society (BPS) Centre for Clinical Outcomes Research and Effectiveness, the Royal College of General Practitioners (RCGP) Clinical Practice Guidelines programme, the Royal College of Psychiatrists Clinical Practice Guidelines programme, the Royal College of Psychiatrists Psychotherapy Section, the British Association for Counselling and the Eli Lilly National Clinical Audit Centre. The guideline, which is projected for dissemination in mid-1999, will focus on indications for referral for psychotherapies, indications for referral for brief therapies versus longer-term therapies, and indications for specific psychological therapies.

Table 9.2 Patient preference

Patient preference	Treatment
Preference for a short treatment	Counselling or cognitive behaviour therapy more likely
Preference for a structured treatment focused on symptom change	Cognitive behaviour therapy more likely
Preference for a longer, explorative treatment	Psychodynamic psychotherapy more likely

Source: Cape et al. (1995).

Table 9.3 Problem complexity

Complexity	Treatment
Less complex – no comorbid problems, no history of prior unsuccessful treatment, no involvement of other agencies	Counselling may be appropriate
More complex – comorbid problems or personality difficulties, history of prior unsuccessful treatment and/or involvement of other agencies	Psychodynamic psychotherapy or cognitive behaviour therapy are likely to be indicated

Source: Cape et al. (1995).

Table 9.4 Summary of indications for each treatment

Choice of treatment needs to be guided by the individual case, including patients' views as to their goals and preferences for treatment.

The table below summarizes general indications for each treatment in the absence of other determining factors for the individual case.

COUNSELLING

Treatment focused on helping people cope with crises, understand feelings, identify issues, explore/make choices and ease distress, usually short term (maximum of 6–12 sessions), carried out by practice counsellors and some voluntary organizations

Problems

- adjustment to life events, illnesses and losses (including bereavement)
- situational anxiety/stress
- low mood, subclinical depression

Table 9.4 continued

- marital and relationship problems
- interpersonal problems (assertion, self-confidence, problems of intimacy)

Severity
- low to moderate

Chronicity
- recent onset (less than a year), except for interpersonal and relationship problems, which may be more chronic

Patient factors
- preference for brief treatment

COGNITIVE BEHAVIOUR THERAPY

Structured treatment focused on symptomatic change or other concrete/practical objectives agreed with patients, carried out primarily in NHS psychology departments

Problems
- marked symptomatic anxiety (panic attacks, phobias, post-traumatic stress disorder, generalized anxiety disorder, obsessions and compulsions)
- depression, especially associated with negative thinking about self or others
- behaviour problems (eating disorders, sleep problems, impulse/anger control, habit disorders)

Severity
- moderate to severe

Chronicity
- 6 months +

Patient factors
- preference for symptom change or other concrete/practical targets, rather than self exploration

PSYCHODYNAMIC PSYCHOTHERAPY

Treatment focused on understanding of self and problems, and on fostering internal change, usually longer term (more than 6 months), either individual or on a group basis (group therapy), carried out in NHS psychotherapy departments and some voluntary organizations

Problems
- personality problems and severe interpersonal difficulties

Table 9.4 continued

- any symptomatic presentation where the problem can be understood in terms of the patient's life circumstances or way of viewing the world

Severity
- moderate to severe

Chronicity
- 1 year +

Patient factors
- interest in self-exploration
- adequate capacity to tolerate frustration and psychic pain

Source: Cape et al. (1995).

Examples of integrative treatment guidelines for specific conditions

Many psychological therapy practitioners in both the USA (Jensen *et al.* 1990) and the UK (Department of Health 1996) draw on more than one psychotherapeutic treatment orientation in their treatment of patients. In the UK this is the norm for clinical psychologists and is increasingly common for counsellors and counselling psychologists; in addition, there is an emerging trend for dedicated psychotherapy departments to offer a range of specialist psychotherapies rather than only psychodynamic psychotherapy. Integrative treatment guidelines would aim to inform such clinical practitioners in their treatment decisions.

At time of writing, no such integrative treatment guidelines exist. Roth *et al.* (1996) give clinical examples of evidence-based practice in the psychotherapeutic treatment of post traumatic stress disorder to demonstrate how appropriate treatment needs to vary according to a number aspects of patients' presentation and history. These clinical examples and others could be used to construct an appropriate integrative clinical guideline for post traumatic stress disorder. Panic disorder is used below as another example of where a possible condition-specific integrative treatment guideline could be constructed.

Cognitive behaviour therapy is often considered the psychotherapeutic treatment of choice for panic disorder based on the research evidence (Mattick *et al.* 1990; Roth and Fonagy 1996). However, the specific cognitive and behavioural treatment strategies that are effective may depend on the patients' presentation (Roth and Fonagy 1996), and for other patients and presentations it is likely that there would be clinical consensus that simple cognitive and behavioural treatments would be inappropriate and ineffective. An integrative clinical guideline for panic disorder might therefore include the following kinds of recommendations:

- For patients whose panic symptoms involve catastrophic interpretation of bodily symptoms as indications of illness, madness or similar, use a cognitive approach (Clark 1986; Clark *et al.* 1994; Salkovskis and Clark 1991).
- For patients with panic disorder accompanied by moderate or severe agoraphobia that has lasted longer than six months, use exposure therapy (Mathews *et al.* 1981; Trull *et al.* 1988).
- For patients whose panic disorder has been precipitated by and is associated with re-evocation of disturbing childhood memories (e.g. an early maternal death), use a psychodynamic approach.
- For patients whose panic disorder is part of a complex presentation of comorbid problems, including personality disorder, consider alternative formulations of the patient's problems and their relationship with each other. Select a treatment approach based on these formulations that is most likely to optimize treatment goals that are considered important by both patient and therapist within the pragmatic (time) constraints of the specific therapeutic context of the treating psychological therapist and patient.

The above recommendations are intended as speculative (as no review or research evidence or clinical consensus has been undertaken) and are also incomplete; they are intended solely as an example of how such an integrative guideline might be developed.

Examples of guidelines for dedicated psychoanalytic psychotherapy services

Guidelines for dedicated psychoanalytic psychotherapy services would be those designed specifically for use by services and practitioners where psychoanalytic psychotherapy is the only psychotherapeutic treatment provided. Such is the case for many UK NHS psychotherapy departments and individual practitioners in both public and private practice. Three examples of possible guidelines are considered:

- An assessment guideline to assist assessing psychotherapists in decisions as to suitability for psychoanalytic psychotherapy (including suitability for brief psychodynamic psychotherapy v. longer treatment and suitability for treatment by a novice/trainee v. an experienced psychoanalytic psychotherapist).
- A treatment guideline to assist in identification of the most appropriate psychodynamic formulation and in focusing interpretations on patients' core conflicts.
- A psychodynamic psychotherapy treatment guideline for borderline personality disorder.

Criteria for appropriateness for intensive psychoanalytic psychotherapy have been developed by the American Psychoanalytic Association as part of the American Psychiatric Association *Manual of Psychiatric Peer Review* (American Psychiatric Association 1985). Criteria include chronicity of symptoms, failure or likely failure to respond to other forms of treatment, capacity to form and maintain a therapeutic relationship and adequate dynamic formulation of the case. Although not presented as a clinical guideline, these criteria are of a kind that might be incorporated into an assessment guideline for suitability for psychoanalytic psychotherapy after appropriate review of the evidence and representative structured consensus process. The American Psychiatric Association criteria are of two kinds: those that relate to severity and complexity defining cases suitable for third-party and public-sector treatment, and criteria related to likelihood to benefit from treatment. Other sources on assessment criteria for suitability for psychoanalytic psychotherapy are those by Bachrach and Leaff (1978), Coltart (1988), Garelick (1994) and Malan (1979).

An attempt to develop a local clinical practice guideline for assessment and review of suitability for psychoanalytic psychotherapy incorporating the American Psychiatric Association (1985) criteria has being reported by Gray (1996). This includes recommendations on assessment for combined treatment with psychoanalytic psychotherapy and antidepressant medication. While the guideline is reported to have been found useful locally in Baltimore and Washington, DC, where it was developed, it is likely to have limited generalizability for reasons argued by Cohen (1997), including idiosyncratic interpretation of the American Psychiatric Association (1985) criteria and narrow focus on medically qualified psychoanalytic psychotherapists and on use of medication. These limitations are likely a result of the fact that Gray (1996) did not use any representative or structured development process in formulating the guideline (see also the section below on 'What makes a good guideline?').

In many psychoanalytic psychotherapy departments, assessing psychotherapists need to make decisions not only as to whether patients are suitable for psychotherapy, but also as to whether they are treatable in short-term psychotherapy and/or by trainee, novice and inexperienced therapists. The resource constraints of many UK NHS psychotherapy departments result in a dependence on trainee and inexperienced practitioners and in limitations on the number of longer term treatment vacancies that can be offered. Assessment guidelines for suitability for short-term psychodynamic psychotherapy and for treatment by trainees and inexperienced practitioners could be designed for such circumstances. The former might, for example, include Malan's (1976) four criteria for planned brief psychotherapy: identification of a problem/focus for therapy; response by the patient in the assessment interview to interpretations concerning the focus; patient motivation to work with this focus; and a lack of foreseeable unavoidable dangers to brief therapy. A guideline for cases suitable for trainee and inexperienced practitioners might include criteria drawn from Baker (1980).

A number of empirical research measures have been developed to assess reliably psychodynamic formulation in brief and medium-term psychodynamic psychotherapy (Barber and Crits-Christoph 1993; Henry et al. 1994; Perry et al. 1989). Research using these measures gives empirical support to the psychoanalytic assumption that accuracy of transference interpretation, including relation to core conflicts and themes, is important in effective psychotherapy (Crits-Christoph et al. 1988; Norville et al. 1996; Piper et al. 1993). In effect, this research relates to the accuracy of psychodynamic formulation and the ability to stick through the vagaries of the transference and countertransference to key psychodynamic issues for the patient. A treatment guideline to assist psychotherapists in appropriate psychodynamic formulation and implementation of a consistent dynamic focus could build on this work, and on clinical expertise and consensus, to construct peer-based methods for agreeing psychodynamic focus and self-monitoring methods to monitor focus of interpretations in treatment.

The Australian and New Zealand Royal College of Psychiatrists treatment outlines programme has included a guideline on treatment for borderline, narcissistic and histrionic personality disorders (Quality Assurance Project 1991a). This is essentially a psychodynamic psychotherapy guideline for these personality disorders drawing heavily on the consensus of three experts, and has been criticized for this limitation (Burvill 1991). The three experts were selected through a modified Delphi procedure, whereby nominations for potential experts to serve on the panel were circulated and voted on by a larger reference group. The expert panel reviewed the literature and made recommendations on the classification and dynamic understanding of borderline, narcissistic and histrionic personality disorders. The recommendations of the panel about treatment focus exclusively on borderline personality disorder. They include:

- the particular importance of supervision when working with this patient group;
- the need for a more active engagement with the patient;
- empathy as central to the psychotherapist's engagement with these patients;
- maintaining awareness of and acting as a link to the patient's external world, as well as focusing the patient's attention on his or her internal world.

These recommendations are extracted from the narrative treatment outline (Quality Assurance Project 1991a). In the outline the recommendations are not sufficiently distinct or related to evidence to comprise a useful clinical practice guideline, but they do give an indication of what might be included in a clinical guideline for borderline personality disorder.

What makes a good guideline?

Desirable attributes of clinical practice guidelines have been suggested by the Institute of Medicine (Field and Lohr 1992), the McMaster group (Hayward and Laupacis 1993) and in the UK Effective Health Care Bulletin on Clinical Guidelines (Effective Health Care 1994). The latter are usefully summarized in the Department of Health clinical guidelines document (Department of

Health 1996). Key attributes of a good guideline are that the guideline:

- *covers a significant topic*: topics for clinical guidelines, as topics for clinical audit, should address areas where clinical decisions are likely to have a significant impact on health care. This may be because they are common, resource-intensive or have a significant impact on morbidity, or because there is evidence of wide variation in practice (Department of Health 1996).
- *includes a clear definition of the clinical circumstances covered by the guideline*: the patient populations and specific clinical circumstances covered by the guideline need to be unambiguously defined so that those using the guideline can be clear as to when and with which patients to use it.
- *is based on a systematic and representative development process*: the guideline should be developed by a representative multi-professional group, including patient representatives where appropriate, and be developed through a systematic structured development process. Ideally the methods of development should be described in the guideline document to allow others to understand how the recommendations in the guideline were derived.
- *is soundly evidence-based*: whether the recommendations are based on research evidence or on structured consensus, the specific evidence base and strength of evidence for each recommendation should be clearly specified.
- *is user-friendly*: clear, unambiguous language, understandable to practitioners and – where appropriate – patients, should be used, along with easy-to-follow formats.

Several instruments incorporating desirable guideline attributes into specific standards have been developed to evaluate clinical guidelines formally (Field and Lohr 1992; Cluzeau *et al.* 1997; Sutton 1996). A system of evaluating through an externally commissioned body and then endorsing appropriately evaluated clinical guidelines for the UK NHS is being planned by the Clinical Outcomes Group (Department of Health 1996).

Implementation of guidelines

There is little purpose in developing guidelines if they are not used. Guidelines may not be used because the recommendations in the guidelines are not accepted by practitioners, because they are not sufficiently understood, or because there is some memory or other impediment to using the guideline when appropriate. Different strategies are needed in each of these circumstances.

Grimshaw and Russell (1994) have summarized evidence on strategies that facilitate the use of guidelines by clinicians. Ownership, and hence use, of guidelines may be facilitated by clinicians being involved themselves in the development of a guideline, or in adaptation of an existing guideline to local circumstances, or in derivation of local audit criteria for an existing guideline. Education about a guideline and its use appears to be helpful. Systems to remind clinicians when a guideline might be relevant (e.g. tagging the files of patients for whom the guideline might be appropriate) also appear to have some effect. There is also evidence that feedback to clinicians from clinical audit of criteria derived from a clinical guideline can be helpful.

Audit of guidelines

Clinical guidelines are not designed to be directly audited, but the recommendations of a guideline should be capable, where possible. of translation into explicit audit criteria (AHCPR 1995; Department of Health 1996; Field and Lohr 1992). The purpose of guidelines, to assist practitioners and patients in clinical decisions, is different from the audit function of providing feedback on whether practice has met agreed standards, but there is evidently an overlap, with guidelines being prospective (guiding practice) and audit retrospective (providing feedback on practice). It is helpful as a practitioner when using a guideline to have the ability to get feedback on how you use the guideline.

The examples of existing psychotherapy guidelines given earlier have generally not been translated into auditable criteria. In addition, for some, the guideline recommendations are not sufficiently precise to be capable of translation into explicit objective audit criteria. The one exception is the American Psychoanalytic Association criteria for appropriateness for intensive psychoanalytic psychotherapy (American Psychiatric Association 1985), which were designed in the first instance as audit criteria. Although the author is not aware of any published examples of audit criteria for the AHCPR depression guideline (AHCPR 1993b), the AHCPR guideline recommendations lend themselves easily to derivation of audit criteria. A UK audit proforma for treatment of depression in primary care focused on antidepressant medication and cognitive therapy, based on the UK Effective Health Care Bulletin on treatment of depression in primary care (Effective Health Care 1993), has been produced by the Eli Lilly National Clinical Audit Centre (1996).

Since, as indicated in the section above on clinical guidelines and clinical judgement, it is unlikely that a clinical guideline will be able to specify all exceptions to its applicability, 100 per cent conformance to audit criteria derived from a guideline should not be expected (AHCPR 1995). Both overly slavish and overly lax conformance to audit criteria from guidelines should be cause for concern.

Issues for the development of psychotherapy guidelines

Agreement on what is best clinical practice is necessary in order to establish a clinical practice guideline. Agreement may be based on research evidence or on clinical consensus. Both are problematic for the psychotherapies.

In medicine, research evidence of clinical efficacy is the main yardstick for establishing agreement for recommendations in clinical guidelines. In the psychotherapies there is a relative lack of large-scale primary empirical research compared to many areas of clinical medicine, which benefit both from commercial research funding from drug companies and from funding from specialist research charities. The empirical research on psychotherapy that is conducted is heavily concentrated on brief and structured forms of psychotherapy (Bergin and Garfield 1994; Roth and Fonagy 1996). Thus there is both an overall lack of major empirical research in the psychotherapies and specific lacunae in empirical research on particular kinds of – especially longer – psychotherapies. In addition, there is disagreement among psychotherapists regarding appropriate research methodologies and even on whether empirical research on psychotherapy is valid at all (Morrow-Bradley and Elliott 1986; Chapter 7, this volume). With the lack of primary research and the lack of agreement as to what kind of research would be appropriate, using research as a basis for agreement on appropriate practice for construction of a clinical guideline in the psychotherapies is potentially problematic.

Establishing consensus between psychotherapists on appropriate clinical practice is not easy either. The history of psychotherapy has been marked more by theoretical divisions and divergence than by consensus, although some commentators perceive a recent trend towards convergence (Garfield and Bergin 1994; Norcross and Goldfried 1992). The tradition of autonomy in psychotherapy, with its strong individual private practice base and lack of dependence on third-party or public reimbursement schemes, contains no particular incentive for agreeing common methods of practice. The valuable and special focus of psychotherapists on the uniqueness of the individual patient inevitably draws attention to differences between patients rather than to the commonalities of patients and treatment processes, which are the necessary basis of agreement about practice. Together, these factors of theoretical divergence, tradition of autonomy of practice and focus on uniqueness of the individual patient contribute to a climate where it is inevitable that there will be areas where consensus is difficult.

In the first instance, agreement about messages from research and at a clinical level will generally be more common the broader the nature of the recommendation. Thus, for psychotherapy, a recommendation that the more complex the patient (operationalized in research terms by comorbidity), the more complex the treatment and the less optimistic the outcome would be likely to attract broad agreement, while a recommendation about the specific kind of treatment required for specific kinds of complex presentations would be less likely to achieve agreement. Such broad recommendations are especially useful for non-specialist clinicians who deal less frequently with decisions about psychotherapy (e.g. GPs) and for those in training and who are inexperienced, and many of the examples of psychotherapy guidelines given earlier were of this kind. Such rules of thumb, even if appropriate in only 50 per cent of cases, may well be an improvement if without them relevant practitioners make appropriate decisions in only 25 per cent of cases. Experienced psychotherapy practitioners will have internalized such rules of thumb, and will be more aware of the exceptions to them and of the theoretical foundations on which such rules of thumb are based. It is much more likely to be difficult to agree an appropriate general practice response to the clinical issues and decisions which consciously engage experienced psychotherapy practitioners, and accordingly to develop an appropriate clinical practice guideline around them. However, this is not to say that the more broad clinical practice guidelines and audit of criteria derived from such guidelines may not be useful also for more experienced psychotherapy practitioners. The possibility of seeing special exceptions when the general rule of thumb in fact applies is a real one, and for experienced psycho-analytic psychotherapists self-monitoring prospectively against guide-lines and retrospectively in audit can, in principle, be a tool to add to the internal self-monitoring fostered by their own analytic experi-ence.

Acknowledgements

With thanks to Dr Phil Richardson, Dr Sarah Marriott and to colleagues on both the Camden & Islington MAAG counselling and psychological therapies guideline development group and on the national steering group for clinical guidelines for counselling and psychological therapies, for their contributions to the development of ideas on the application of clinical practice guidelines to the psychotherapies.

References

AHCPR (1993a) *Depression in Primary Care: Detection and Diagnosis*, Clin-ical Practice Guideline No. 5, Washington, DC: US Department of Health & Human Services.

—— (1993b) *Depression in Primary Care: Treatment of Major Depression*, Clinical Practice Guideline No. 5, Washington, DC: US Department of Health & Human Services.

—— (1993c) *Depression in Primary Care: Detection, Diagnosis, and Treat-ment. Quick Reference Guide for Clinicians*, Washington, DC: US Department of Health & Human Services.

—— (1993d) *Depression is a Treatable Illness: A Patients' Guide*, Wash-ington, DC: US Department of Health & Human Services.

—— (1995) *Using Clinical Practice Guidelines to Evaluate Quality of Care*, Washington, DC: US Department of Health & Human Services.

American Psychiatric Association (1985) *Manual of Psychiatric Peer Review*, 3rd edn, Washington, DC: American Psychiatric Association.

—— (1993a) 'Practice guideline for eating disorders', *American Journal of Psychiatry* 150: 207–28.

—— (1993b) 'Practice guideline for major depressive disorder in adults', *American Journal of Psychiatry* 150(4), supplement.

American Psychological Association (1995) *Template for Developing Guide-lines: Interventions for Mental Disorders and Psychosocial Aspects of Physical Disorders*, Washington, DC: American Psychological Associ-ation.

Antman, E. M., Lau, J., Kupelnick, B., Mosteller, F. and Chalmers, T. C. (1992) 'A comparison of results of meta-analyses of randomised control trials and recommendations of clinical experts', *Journal of the American Medical Association* 268: 240–8.

Bachrach, H. and Leaff, L. (1978) 'Analysability: a systematic review of the clinical and quantitative literature', *Journal of the American Psychoanalytic Association* 26: 881–920.

Baker, R. (1980) 'The finding "not suitable" in the selection of supervised cases', *International Review of Psycho-Analysis* 7: 353–64.

Barber, J. P. and Crits-Christoph, P. (1993) 'Advances in measures of psychodynamic formulations', *Journal of Consulting and Clinical Psychology* 61: 574–85.

Barlow, D. H. (1996) 'Health care policy, psychotherapy research, and the future of psychotherapy', *American Psychologist* 51: 1050–8.

Bergin, A. E. and Garfield, S. L. (eds) (1994) *Handbook of Psychotherapy and Behaviour Change*, 4th edn, New York: Wiley.

Black, N. (1996) 'Why we need observational studies to evaluate the effectiveness of health care', *British Medical Journal* 312: 1215–18.

BPS CORE (1997) *Development of a Clinical Guideline for the Psychological Therapies*, London: BPS Centre for Clinical Outcomes Research and Effectiveness.

Burvill, P. W. (1991) 'Quality Assurance Project reports on the treatment of personality disorders', *Australian and New Zealand Journal of Psychiatry* 25: 311–13.

Cape, J., Durrant, K., Graham, J., Patrick, M., Rouse, A. and Hartley, J. (1996) *Counselling and psychological therapies guideline*, London: Camden & Islington MAAG.

Cape, J., Hartley, J., Durrant, K., Patrick, M. and Graham, J. (1998) 'Development of local practice guidelines to assist G.P.s, counsellors and psychological therapists in matching patients to the most appropriate psychological treatment', *Journal of Clinical Effectiveness*, (in press).

Charlton, B. G. (1996) 'Megatrials are based in a methodological mistake', *British Journal of General Practice* 46: 429–31.

Clark, D. M. (1986) 'A cognitive approach to panic', *Behaviour Research and Therapy* 24: 461–70.

Clark, D. M., Salkovskis, P. M., Hackmann, A., Middleton, H., Anastasiades, P. and Gelder, M. (1994) 'A comparison of cognitive therapy, applied relaxation and imipramine in the treatment of panic disorder', *British Journal of Psychiatry* 164: 759–69.

Clinical Resource and Audit Group (1993) *Clinical Guidelines: A Report by a Working Group*, Edinburgh: Scottish Office.

Cluzeau, F., Littlejohns, P., Grimshaw, J. and Feder, G. (1997) *Appraisal instrument for clinical guidelines*, London: St Georges Hospital Medical School.

Cohen, M. (1997) 'Response to "Developing practice guidelines for psychoanalysis," by S. H. Gray', *Journal of Psychotherapy Practice and Research* 6: 81–7.

Coltart, N. (1988) 'Diagnosis and assessment for suitability for psychoanalytic psychotherapy', *British Journal of Psychotherapy* 4: 127–34.

Crits-Christoph, P., Cooper, A. and Luborsky, L. (1988) 'The accuracy of therapists' interpretations and the outcome of dynamic psychotherapy', *Journal of Consulting and Clinical Psychology* 56: 490–5.

Department of Health (1996) *Clinical Guidelines: Using Clinical Guidelines to Improve Patient Care Within the NHS*, Leeds: NHS Executive.

Duff, L. A., Kelson, M., Marriott, S., McIntosh, A., Brown, S., Cape, J., Marcus, M. and Traynor, M. (1996) 'Clinical guidelines: involving patients and users of services', *Journal of Clinical Effectiveness* 1: 104–12.

Effective Health Care (1993) *The Treatment of Depression in Primary Care*, Bulletin No. 5, Leeds: University of Leeds.

—— (1994) *Implementing Clinical Practice Guidelines*, Bulletin No. 8, Leeds: University of Leeds.

Eli Lilly National Clinical Audit Centre (1996) *Management of Depression in General Practice*, Audit Protocol CT11, Leicester: Eli Lilly Centre.

Field, M. J. and Lohr, K. N. (eds) (1990) *Clinical Practice Guidelines: Directions for a New Program*, Washington, DC: National Academy Press.

Field, M. J. and Lohr, K. N. (eds) (1992) *Guidelines for Clinical Practice: From Development to Use*, Washington, DC: National Academy Press.

Fleming, T. R. and DeMets, D. L. (1996) 'Surrogate end points in clinical trials: are we being misled?', *Annals of Internal Medicine* 125: 605–13.

Garelick, A. (1994) 'Psychotherapy assessment: theory and practice', *Psychoanalytic Psychotherapy* 8: 101–16.

Garfield, S. L. (1986) 'Research on client variables in psychotherapy', in S. L. Garfield and A. E. Bergin (eds) *Handbook of Psychotherapy and Behaviour Change*, 3rd edn, New York: Wiley.

Garfield, S. L. and Bergin, A. E. (1994) 'Introduction and historical overview', in A. E. Bergin and S. L. Garfield (eds) *Handbook of Psychotherapy and Behaviour Change*, 4th edn, New York: Wiley.

Gigone, D. and Hastie, R. (1997) 'Proper analysis of the accuracy of group judgements', *Psychological Bulletin* 121: 149–67.

Gray, S. H. (1996) 'Developing practice guidelines for psychoanalysis', *Journal of Psychotherapy Practice and Research* 5: 213–27.

Grimshaw, J. M. and Russell, I. T. (1993a) 'Achieving health gain through clinical guidelines I: developing scientifically valid guidelines', *Quality in Health Care* 2: 243–8.

—— (1993b) 'Effects of clinical guidelines on medical practice: a systematic review of rigorous evaluations', *Lancet* 342: 1317–22.

—— (1994) 'Achieving health gain through clinical guidelines II: ensuring guidelines change medical practice', *Quality in Health Care* 3: 45–52.

Hayward, R. S. A. and Laupacis, A. (1993) 'Initiating, conducting and maintaining guidelines development programs', *Canadian Medical Association Journal* 148: 507–12.

Henry, W. P., Strupp, H. H., Schacht, T. E. and Gaston, L. (1994) 'Psychodynamic approaches', in A. E. Bergin and S. L. Garfield (eds) *Handbook of Psychotherapy and Behaviour Change*, 4th edn, New York: Wiley.

Howard, K., Orlinsky, D. and Lueger, R. (1994) 'Clinically relevant outcome research in individual psychotherapy', *British Journal of Psychiatry* 165: 4–8.

Jensen, J. P., Bergin, A. E. and Greaves, D. W. (1990) 'The meaning of eclectism: new survey and analysis of components', *Professional Psychology: Research and Practice* 21: 124–30.

Lambert, M. J. and Hill, C. E. (1994) 'Assessing psychotherapy outcomes and processes', in A. E. Bergin and S. L. Garfield (eds) *Handbook of Psychotherapy and Behaviour Change*, 4th edn, New York: Wiley.

Linstone, H. A. and Turoff, M. (1975) *The Delphi Method, Techniques and Applications*, Reading, MA: Addison-Wesley.

Malan, D. H. (1973) 'The outcome problem in psychotherapy research: a historical review', *Archives of General Psychiatry* 29: 719–29.

—— (1976) *The Frontier of Brief Psychotherapy*, New York: Plenum Press.

—— (1979) *Individual Psychotherapy and the Science of Psychodynamics*, London: Butterworths.

Marriott, S. and Lelliott, P. (1994) *Clinical Practice Guidelines*, College Report CR34, London: Royal College of Psychiatrists.

Mathews, A. M., Gelder, M. G. and Johnston, D. W. (1981) *Agoraphobia: Nature and Treatment*, New York: Guilford.

Mattick, R. P., Andrews, G., Hadzi-Pavlovic, D. and Christensen, H. (1990) 'Treatment of panic and agoraphobia: an integrative review', *Journal of Nervous and Mental Disease* 178: 567–76.

Miller, N. E., Luborsky, L., Barber, J. P. and Docherty, J. P. (eds) (1993) *Psychodynamic Treatment Research: A Handbook for Clinical Practice*, New York: Basic Books.

Mintz, J. (1981) 'Measuring outcome in psychodynamic psychotherapy: psychodynamic vs symptomatic assessment', *Archives of General Psychiatry* 38: 503–6.

Morrow-Bradley, C. and Elliott, R. (1986) 'Utilization of psychotherapy research by practicing psychotherapists', *American Psychologist* 41: 188–97.

Munoz, R. F., Hollon, S. D., McGrath, E., Rehm, L. P. and VandenBos, G. R. (1994) 'On the AHCPR depression in primary care guidelines: further considerations for practitioners', *American Psychologist* 49: 42–61.

Norcross, J. C. and Goldfried, M. R. (eds) (1992) *Handbook of Psychotherapy Integration*, New York: Basic Books.

Norville, R., Sampson, H. and Weiss, J. (1996) 'Accurate interpretations and brief psychotherapy outcome', *Psychotherapy Research* 6: 16–29.

Olson, C. M. (1995) 'Consensus statement: applying structure', *Journal of the American Medical Association* 273: 72–3.

Perry, J. C., Luborsky, L., Silberschatz, G. and Popp, C. (1989) 'An examination of three methods of psychodynamic formulation based on the same videotaped interview', *Psychiatry* 52: 302–23.

Persons, J. B., Thase, M. E. and Crits-Christoph, P. (1996) 'The role of psychotherapy in the treatment of depression: review of two practice guidelines', *Archives of General Psychiatry* 53: 283–90.

Piper, W. E., Joyce, A. S., McCallum, M. and Azim, H. F. (1993) 'Concentration and correspondence of transference interpretations in short term psychotherapy', *Journal of Consulting and Clinical Psychology* 61: 586–95.

Quality Assurance Project (1982a) 'A treatment outline for agoraphobia', *Australian and New Zealand Journal of Psychiatry* 16: 25–33.

—— (1982b) 'A treatment outline for depressive disorders', *Australian and New Zealand Journal of Psychiatry* 17: 129–48.

—— (1991a) 'Treatment outlines for borderline, narcissistic and histrionic personality disorders', *Australian and New Zealand Journal of Psychiatry* 25: 392–403.

—— (1991b) 'Treatment outlines for antisocial personality disorders', *Australian and New Zealand Journal of Psychiatry* 25: 541–7.

Ramsey, P. G., Carline, J. D., Inui, T. S., Larson, E. B., LoGerfo, J. P., Norcini, J. J. and Wenrich, M. D. (1991) 'Changes over time in the knowledge base of practicing internists', *Journal of the American Medical Association* 266: 103–7.

Roth, A. and Fonagy, P. (1996) *What Works for Whom? A Critical Review of Psychotherapy Research*, New York: Guilford Press.

Roth, A., Fonagy, P. and Parry, G. (1996) 'Psychotherapy research, funding, and evidence-based practice', in A. Roth, and P. Fonagy, *What Works for Whom? A Critical Review of Psychotherapy Research*, New York: Guilford Press.

Royal College of Psychiatrists (1998) *The management of imminent violence: clinical practice guidelines to support mental health services*, London: Royal College of Psychiatrists.

Sackett, D. L., Richardson, W. S., Rosenberg, W. and Haynes, R. B. (1997) *Evidence-based Medicine: How to Practice and Teach EBM*, New York: Churchill Livingstone.

Sackett, D. L., Rosenberg, W. M. C., Gray, J. A. M., Haynes, R. B. and Richardson, W. S. (1996) 'Evidence based medicine: what it is and what it isn't', *British Medical Journal* 312: 71–2.

Salkovskis, P. M. and Clark, D. (1991) 'Cognitive therapy for panic attacks', *Journal of Cognitive Psychotherapy* 5: 215–26.

Scott, E. A. and Black, N. (1991) 'When does consensus exist in expert panels?', *Journal of Public Health Medicine* 30: 35–9.

Seligman, M. E. P. (1995) 'The effectiveness of psychotherapy: the Consumer Reports study', *American Psychologist* 12: 965–74.

Sutton, P. A. (1996) *Clinical Guidelines Evaluation: Final Report of Department of Health Guidelines Evaluation Project*, Hull: University of Hull.

Trull, T. J., Nietzel, M. T. and Main, A. (1988) 'The use of meta-analysis to assess the clinical significance of behavior therapy for agoraphobia', *Behavior Therapy* 19: 527–38.

Weber, J. J., Solomon, M. and Bachrach, H. M. (1985) 'Characteristics of psychoanalytic clinic patients: report of the Columbia Psychoanalytic Centre Research Project (I)', *International Review of Psychoanalysis* 12: 13–26.

Woolf, S. H. (1992) 'Practice guidelines, a new reality in medicine II: methods of developing guidelines', *Archives of Internal Medicine* 152: 946–52.

Index